God and the Human Condition
VOLUME ONE: GOD AND THE HUMAN MIND

F. J. SHEED

God and the Human Condition

VOLUME ONE: *God and the Human Mind*

SHEED AND WARD: NEW YORK

Nihil obstat:
   Thomas J. Beary
   Censor Librorum

Imprimatur:
   † *Robert F. Joyce*
   Bishop of Burlington
   May 23, 1966

The Nihil Obstat and Imprimatur are official declarations that a book or pamphlet is considered to be free of doctrinal or moral error. No implication is therein contained that those who have granted the Nihil Obstat and Imprimatur agree with the contents, opinions or statements expressed.

Contents

Contents

Introduction

I had planned to put what I have to say of God and Man into one volume, under the title *God and the Human Condition*. It has seemed to be better to bring out two volumes with that as over-all title. The present volume is *God and the Human Mind*. The second will be *God and the Human Race*.

The whole represents my attempt at aggiornamento—which does not mean presenting as much of the Church's teachings as men today can accept. It means (1) presenting it *as it now is*, at the point of its—and our own—present development; (2) stating it with such an understanding of today's difficulties, today's ways of thinking, speaking, asking, that today's man may know what we are saying, and may see what the same truths might mean for him too.

My concern in this first Volume is with what the human mind can know of God—with God's revelation of himself; with Theology, which is Revelation explored by men with God's aid; with how each can make all this his own, not verbally only, not even mentally only, but vitally.

Not verbally only, I say. But words are a large part of the matter. We must examine them closely, it is not sufficient to use them as consecrated formulas. They are telling us something about God, we must find out what it is. We must see why we use one set of words, avoid another, reject another. We must draw light from them to the limit of our present knowledge, without envy of our children to whom they may yield more light.

The aim of the present study is practical and at three depths. For the intelligent living of life nothing can be more practical than to know How we (or anything) came to be here, and Where we are supposed to be going: only God can tell us.

There is a second depth of practicality: what we learn of God can nourish, develop, vitalize the selves which have to live the life.

And a third: God is not a problem to be solved, not even a solution to be admired, but a reality to be possessed, contemplated, conversed with, loved, enjoyed: this is fullness of living.

With God One and Three, with Creation, Incarnation, Redemption, with every matter treated in either Volume, the effort will be made to see how life is richer for our knowing it. The reader new to this kind of thinking will find it helpful at every point to pose himself the question—What difference does the doctrine make to me? If it had never been revealed, would I have lost anything? To this last question he should constantly return.

At the moment Christians find themselves in what looks to them like a crisis of theology. They get the feeling that age-old certainties are being called into question and that it might be wiser to leave Theology alone until the storm has blown over. Storm there is, but running for cover is not a good way to live through it, and no way at all to grow surer and stronger in it.

The air is filled with such a swirl of questionings as we have never known at one time, but there are levels of seriousness, largely because anybody feels that he can say his say. There is some pretty wild talk. But even at saner levels, I seem to be coming all the time upon "new" questions which in fact I had been hearing, "new" doctrinal ideas which in fact I had been teaching, these past forty years. Some of our more revolutionary thinkers seem to me to have led pretty sheltered lives.

None of this applies to the Rahners, the Schillebeeckxes, the Durrwells, the Benoits. For there are serious developments under discussion, their possibility rooted in the very nature of human utterance. No statement either as given in Revelation, or as developed by the Church's living with it and by it, can be more than a beginning. Even if finite words could contain the infinite, finite minds could not extract the infinite from them. But the great definitions proclaimed by the Church as contained in Revelation or issuing from it are light-bearing; possessing them, we are in the light. In that light we can grow, not by extinguishing and substituting, but by growing in capacity to receive and respond.

God who gave the light has continued to guard men's growth in it. There are moments when the sense of God looms so immense that the phrases of Revelation and Doctrine seem to mock us with their shallowness: they are shallower than God certainly, but they are not shallower than we, and by them we can move out of our shallows. We shall move deeper all the more surely by knowing the depth at which we now stand. Organizing, surveying, living fully in the territory already won is the best preliminary for conquering new areas for light.

For growth in the light everything serves—Scripture of course, but philosophy and mysticism too, and all the ways by which men advance in knowledge of the created universe. No one mind could cope with all of these, all do not serve equally, all have something to give. But Scripture, above all.

"From the study of Scripture," says Pius XII, "all branches of theology can be rejuvenated." In our century we have seen this notably illustrated in the emergence from obscurity of the doctrine of the Church as Christ's Body, and the new awareness of all that is bound up in Christ's Resurrection. Our own day is clarifying the relation between the Word of God in the Church and the Word of God in Scripture. The study of each can rejuvenate the other, too often they have been used solely to drown each other's voice. The distortion of Scriptural texts to prove dogma is vanishing, as the Concordism has already vanished which tried to make Genesis say what the newest scientist was saying. Scripture is no more a manual of theology than of science.

Using texts old style, whether to prove the Church's teaching *or* to disprove it—each was a way of treating Scripture as what it was not. Church teaching and Scripture are different ways of approach under the direction of one same Word, to one same Reality. The appearance of disharmony is not a challenge to reject one or the other, but a call to re-study both in all confidence.

In our study of Scripture we have the Biblical specialists to help us, the linguists, the archeologists, the exegetes. The student of Theology cannot do without them; but unless he knows how to keep his balance, he may find that he cannot easily do with them either. Balance? I mean between their learning, which is myriad and dazzling and far beyond the mere theologian's testing, and their theological or philosophical systems, which any intelligent man can judge for himself and which can vary from brilliant to very dim indeed. Rudolf Bultmann, Oscar Cullmann and C. H. Dodd may be surprised to find themselves grouped as "Egyptians," but I have certainly "spoiled" them—and among the spoils I count not only things they have given me from their own special learning and their own deeper insights, but a better understanding of Catholic teaching at points where their refusal of it forced me to look closer at it.

Philosophy not only can but must serve Theology. Theology is the literacy of Religion, and there is no field in which Philosophy cannot aid literacy. But here too there is need of balance. Aristotle's Pure Act is one of the human mind's most splendid achievements; it has been used for Theology's deepening, but for its desiccation as well. Unless we balance it with Scripture, the Infinite of the philosophers can be used almost as a way of telling God to keep his distance. The more active of today's philosophers by-pass God, and this must concern us. What concerns us more is that so much of today's religion (not as lived perhaps but as preached and written) by-passes God too—does not reject him but does not very much advert to him, has no strong idea of him, does not emphasize contact or communication with him. In this kind of religion, God is a lightless cloud at Reality's center, hardly distinguishable from sheer blankness.

Why we exist, what follows death, cannot be known if there is no God or no revelation from God. To keep God and refuse his Revelation leaves the questions unanswered. By too many the questions are not even asked, all concentration being on love of neighbor in the fragment of life between conception and death, studied without reference to how life came to be and where it is leading, or any awareness that these might have a bearing.

Some of today's ablest religious writers, poles apart in everything else, yet are one in removing God from life as men must live it here below—this in the name of his Transcendence, or his Difference, or his Un-Necessity, or his Irrelevance to our problems. The exclusion of God—I mean by believers in him—has been a long process. The Trinity was dropped, or lingered on as a picturesque survival of an older thought-pattern. In the Twenties I heard speakers at a Religious Week refer to God as the Nobler Hypothesis, the Wider Experience, That Transcendent Other. In our own day we have him as Depth. One way or another, God was being purged of function and even of meaning.

The next steps cried out to be taken. Taken they were. Pastor Bonhoeffer cut the cord of man's dependance on God —his reaction, one imagines, to the agony of concentration camps and gas chambers and a God who let them happen.

Now we have ministers of religion who deny God's existence altogether. Yet they hold on to religion.

If this moves us to mockery, we have not understood the situation. To those who have remained steadfast in their faith, a smile sometimes comes too easily. When Dr. Bultmann demythologized the New Testament, with only the kerygma left standing, the certainty was inescapable that de-kerygmatization must come next. And it has come. But like the clinging to religion without God, it is a reaction to an Ultimate Mystery which can be neither grasped nor wholly unfelt. There is no place for mockery of men who find the unutterable beyond utterance and make what synthesis they can of as much as they can utter. There might be more depth in this than in any amount of unreflective swallowing. But there is pathos in what can seem to us only an effort to make some sort of "Establishment" out of questions unasked, needs not felt, hungers that do not torment, thirsts that do not parch.

COMING TO KNOW GOD

ONE
Theology and Vitality

1. Mental Equivalents

Learning theology does not mean simply memorizing words shaped into a pattern of orthodoxy. It means making the truths our own, a living part of our being.

The trouble is that it has to come to us in words. It is in a clothing of words that the truths of theology enter the intellect. The teacher's intellect frames them, our intellect receives them. And words have a strange power of setting up in business on their own, independently of the ideas they exist to express: it is rather like the Hans Andersen story of the man whose shadow left him, and went about its own affairs. Cardinal Manning said of Herbert Spencer that he had no mental equivalent for his terms; and one can get along so well and so effortlessly with the terms, while not adverting to their

mental equivalents, that one can lose touch with these altogether.

One has heard discussions of human rights, or the arrangement of human society, in which the word "man" has figured
as hardly more than a noise made by the mouth, accompanied
by a mental picture of a biped to give it authority—which
gives the two legs disproportionate importance and omits the
decisive element in the discussion, namely what a man is. It
is even easier to talk like that, for hours at a time, about God,
the word carrying no real meaning but setting up certain mild
vibrations in the emotions.

A third example: Faced with the question how our Lord,
if he possessed the Beatific Vision, could have suffered sorrow
almost unto death in the Garden of Gethsemani, one has
heard learned men answer that of course he was still *in statu
viae*, not *statu termini*, and proceed to the next question as
though that one at least had been satisfactorily answered.
Here there is no examination in depth such as Karl Rahner
has given the matter in his *Theological Investigations:* simply
the technical terms are being used without mental equivalents.
For the reason why the Beatific Vision would seem to exclude sorrow lies in what it is, not in where it is received; it
applies therefore equally whether the soul has reached the
end of the journey or not. We have, in fact, an example of
one of the commonest of all fallacies—reliance on a difference
that makes no difference, a difference that has no bearing.

And this is possible when one is using the terms only. For
the man who wants to take theology seriously, the intellect
must go to work, pierce through the words to the meaning,
and enrich the words with the meaning—that they may be
real words. And it must build the reality they utter into its

own substance. This is the essence of learning, whether theology or anything else. Unfortunately examinations do not always test it.

When the intellect has made the reality its own, then the whole man takes over—will, emotions, imagination. This is essential, but there is danger in it, since these may wrench the truth away from intellect after all. The trouble is that intellect works with effort and anguish, and the others easily. Imagination, the power to make mental pictures of things we have experienced through the senses, works most easily of all and is always ready to offer its aid. Its aid too often takes the form of doing the whole job for the intellect. The results are always fatal.

To take a rough example. One of the great problems for philosopher and theologian alike is how the will can be free, if God knows in advance what we are going to do. The intellect may well blench. Imagination does not blench at all, it accepts the challenge with delight. It produces a picture of a winding river, and a man on the bank who cannot see what happens round the next bend. Take the man up in an aeroplane, and he can see the whole winding of the river at once. Substitute God for the man in the aeroplane, and where is your problem?

Where indeed is your problem? It has not been solved, it has not been partly solved, not the faintest gleam of light has been shed upon it, it has not been touched. The next bend of the river already exists, the man has simply got rid of an obstacle which prevented his seeing it; but when something hasn't happened yet, doesn't exist yet, what is there to see? What is there for even God to see? To make it worse, the aeroplane analogy is based upon a misunderstanding of the nature of God's knowledge. Its only advantage is that the problem no longer bothers the intellect: imagination seducing, the intellect has by-passed the problem, and goes on its way with an error about God built into it. If it had waved imagination aside and coped with its own job itself—as we shall try to cope in a later chapter—it would have gained a certain amount of light upon the problem, it would have added to its understanding of God and eternity and time; though it would not have seen the whole answer, it would have discovered why it could not, and this too is a valuable piece of knowledge.

It is not only intellect that is the loser by letting imagination do its work for it, imagination is the loser too. For it is meant to be stimulated by truth to its own proper exercise, which is not a substitute for intellect's. Once the mind has the truth, imagination can range all over the universe finding correspondences and interrelations and interlinkings, at every level from lowest to highest, family likenesses which show one mind at work throughout.

Imagination cannot give the meaning. But it can give new resonance and immediacy to the meaning once intellect has arrived at it; and in so doing it is most splendidly itself and brings powerful aid to intellect. For the new resonance and immediacy at once stimulate the intellect to plunge deeper, and are themselves facts for the intellect to take note of. In the same way will and emotion can help. Where will, emotion, imagination, do not enter, but intellect goes it alone, what we have is not Theology, which is the most concrete of all the ways of uttering reality. What we have is Theometry, which is only a kind of geometry of God, with all God and man formulated, labelled and indexed—even mystery only one item in the list, not the felt darkness wrapping everything.

It has been observed that the great proofs for the existence of God are unanswerable, but seldom move an unbeliever to accept: we do not lose arguments with atheists, but we do not often persuade them that God exists—by the use of the proofs, that is. People feel that they are a little thin, and indeed they are—conclusive but thin. The reason is that in them intellect does go it alone, the appeal is purely to reason. Will is sternly excluded, imagination and emotion are not even tempted to intervene. But intellect without will and the rest *is* thin; just as will and the rest without intellect are thick—thick-headed, so to speak. It is in the taking possession of truth by the whole man that the whole man lives.

I have already spoken of the necessity to move from the terms to their mental equivalents, but even there we cannot stay: we must go forward to their vital equivalents, getting down to the depths where something within ourselves stirs to life in response. An example may make this clearer. If we take the truth which most of us learned in our catechisms that God made us of nothing, and examine those who rest in the terms and go no further, we shall find, I think, one of two results. They either attach no meaning at all to the words, do not dwell on them longer than it takes to say them, use them, when they use them at all, as a kind of litany or tuneless chant; or, if they go one stage further, they see "nothing" as a kind of material that God used in the making of things, as though there were a vast reservoir of nothing on which he was able to draw.

But if the terms are given mental equivalents, we have a doctrine superbly coherent: that whereas all other makers use some material, it goes with God's omnipotence that he made without material.

There *was* nothing: there *is* something.

And this something owes the whole of its being to the creative act of God, is produced in its totality by the act of the divine will, and therefore needs the continuing act of that same will to hold it in existence from moment to moment. So that the formula for every being from electron to archangel is nothingness made into something by God, given existence by the will of God, and by him held continuously in existence.

To this statement, nothing is contributed by will or emotion or imagination. But once it exists it can and should have the most profound effect upon all of them. *Emotion,* to begin with, feels shattered by it, knows real panic at the realization that no material has gone to our making, that we are made of nothing, that we have therefore no hold of our own upon existence. *Imagination* is stimulated to produce pictures of analogous instances of dependence in the created universe, and though none of these instances can be total, they do develop our awareness of what dependence can mean, and this reflects back on the intellect's understanding. The *will* can accept the truth, try to live by it, come to love it, come to better control of itself in the awareness that some of its own movements are the effect in us of a kind of nostalgia for our original nothingness. Then *feeling* can enter again. We come to feel more secure when thus totally dependent on God. At a different angle, we find ourselves feeling fools when we sin, because sin is an effort to gain something against the will of God—that will which alone stands between us and annihilation!

This is what I mean by having a vital equivalent for our terms, this is studying theology. We may think of the terms as one-dimensional, of the mental equivalents as two-dimensional, only of the vital equivalents as three-dimensional. There is what may be a fourth dimension, the mystical, which will be looked at later: of it I have no personal experience. I can only give my own testimony that three are wonderful. Wonderful but not easy to enter into. All ease is in the terms. Knowledge maketh a bloody entry, says the proverb. But words come in bloodlessly. They are so easy to handle and so compact, they sound as if they had a beginning and an end. Compared with them, thoughts are sprawling, messy, not ending when they end but always opening out onto some further reality: when you have thought a thought you have not thought it, so to speak, you have only started something. Once terms acquire mental and vital equivalents, we have no longer the old luxury of shutting off the mind and letting the pen coast.

All the immediate advantages are with words reduced to mere counters. But of course we must pay a price for them. And one way in which the mass of us humans pay is that it is almost impossible not to feel that what cannot be put into words cannot *be:* worse still that words are the measure of meaning, the measure of importance. Thus we find it hard to believe that what can be said briefly can possibly be of cosmic importance. When we come upon a discussion of whether God is the efficient cause or the formal cause or the quasi-formal cause of grace in the soul, we feel at once that the question really matters. But the importance of a truth is measured not by length but by meaning, and not by intellectual meaning only. Take two truths about Our Blessed

Lady. *She was the Virgin Mother of Christ.* The length is
under a line. How long is the meaning? Three words—Christ,
mother, virgin—each by itself a deep well of meaning, the
three thus combined more than the mind of man has been able
to exhaust in twenty centuries. *She shared Christ's suffering,
she had suffering of her own.* A whole line there, if length is
our main concern! But Christ is the glory of mankind: suffering is the anguish of mankind: these are not little words, shallow words, easily lapped up by the hurrying mind.

The word *is* is the meagrest-sounding word in the English
language; but *He is* is the name of God, the whole truth of
God, and in all eternity we shall not have unpacked all it
contains.

2. Vital Equivalents

What I have called "vital equivalents" means an intimacy
deeper than the words or the concepts. Normally, once we
have attained it, it lives in the soul, pouring its energy—I had
almost said automatically, serenely anyhow—into the soul's
whole relation with reality. But there are moments, not long
moments usually or frequent, when it floods up into the consciousness, and the greatest theologian or the rawest beginner,
uttering some truth long held in all serenity, can find himself
shaken to the roots of his being by it.

Nor is this the mystical experience, properly so called. It
is a perfectly normal operation of the mind—the God-aided
mind as we shall see—doing its own proper work. One who
does not know this can never have experienced the dynamic
quality of truth really possessed, the excitement of it, the
luxury.

Work, indeed, it is. The intellect must not rest in the terms or idle in the images. There is sweating labor for it, because it has no habituation in its muscles for this kind of effort, indeed it has almost no muscles and must somehow grow them. The truths of religion are so through-and-through spiritual that our minds, coming new to them, simply have not the muscles to cope with them. No other subject that we study calls for these particular muscles in anything like the same degree. So far we have been considering the kind of initial effort needed to master the meaning of the truths, and the kind of continuing effort needed to keep them alive and alert. But, when we have done all this, it still remains that the realities we are dealing with seem thin compared with the material world.

The thinness may make itself felt poignantly. We may, as an example, see someone suffering agonies in a disease that is incurable. The agonies are so very evident, the spiritual realities—God's goodness, the joy of heaven—seem so remote in comparison. It is not only that we feel it would be a mockery to remind the sufferer of them; *in our own minds* we feel them inadequate—not actually irrelevant, perhaps, but too pale. This is a special case; we are not continuously in that sort of crisis; the patient dies, and our own trouble of spirit grows dimmer and passes away.

But there is a profounder difficulty, not bound up with a special experience like this, but contained in the daily routine of life. It lies in the apparent thinness of spiritual realities compared with the things the mind usually deals with. The trouble about the great mysteries is not to believe them true, but to see them as real; the mind finds it hard to get a grip on them, they seem to give it no hold, to slip through its fingers, so to speak. Once we have grasped what Trinity and

Eucharist, Infinity and Eternity mean, there is no earthly reason for rejecting them; but there are moments when they seem remote and lacking in substance; as I have said, it is difficult not so much to believe that they are true, as that they are there at all. They do not contradict themselves, or one another, or our reason: but they still do not seem to be quite there: when we turn the mind's gaze upon them, they seem to vanish. They are intellectually coherent, but they are like a coherent dream.

It is easier to see the reason for this than the remedy. The whole problem can be put in one phrase—we want the same comfortable, effortless, unquestioning awareness of the spiritual world as we have of the material world, and we find ourselves trying to apply the norms of certitude and the feeling of certainty which suit the one kind of reality to the other. On two counts what we are feeling for is impossible.

The first is that upon the material world we are using our senses and our imagination all the time; we do not need to make a choice about it, there is no effort, it does itself; senses and imagination get plenty of practice. But our intellect we use sparingly, we would rather not use it at all, we have not only to force it into action but to force ourselves to force it into action. Certainly we do not use it continuously enough to acquire any facility in it; even when we do use it, for the most part we confine it to matters on which senses and imagination can help. Even in religion we use intellect sparingly, all our effort goes into the mastering—one can hardly call it the cultivation—of the will.

The second is that we cannot have the same possession of something greater than ourselves as we have of something less. The material universe is a smaller thing than the mind of man;

whatever is positive in it, the mind of man can cope with. But God is not only greater, he is infinitely greater: we cannot take him, embrace him wholly, make him our own in the same way. One way or another we can see that it would be folly to expect the same easy familiarity with the spiritual world as with the material, folly to expect the same kind of easy certitude—the certitude flowing from the effortless contact of the senses with the lower grades of reality.

What kind of certainty can we expect in purely spiritual matters, even with the support of God's grace, and how can we test our certainty? By our willingness to direct our lives in accordance with them even when it costs us felt hardship which may reach the point of agony, and by our willingness to die rather than deny them. We note that Our Lord gave as the high point of love not any sort of mystical ecstasy but willingness to die—"Greater love has no man than this, that a man lay down his life for his friend" (John 15. 13). We do not always live by the truths we accept, we may not feel very confident that we would die for them; but in the very depths of our being we wish we could live by them and we hope we should die for them. Surprisingly often men have done both; and to our so easy and comfortable and unquestioning certainties about the material world, there is in us no comparable testimony.

So we tell ourselves, and rightly. But spiritual reality may still feel thin! We set our minds to work upon it, develop the needed muscles, understand it better, but we sometimes find that this only strengthens the coherence without removing the sense of dream. This sense of dream is not at all the same thing as doubt, though it could grow into doubt, and it is uncomforting to live with. If we have studied God only in the textbooks, it could fret the mind powerfully. If, as we should, we have accompanied our study of the Church's teaching upon the divine mysteries by close reading of Scripture, meeting God in his action upon men and seeing men react so variously, the pressure is eased, perhaps.

But the one sure remedy is to grow in intimacy with Christ Our Lord. In a way he focusses the infinite and the eternal. He makes the solid framework of the material reality to which our minds are habituated seem less absolute. He puts it on the defensive, by so obviously transcending it: spiritual reality becomes more real since he is real, it becomes real with his reality. This operates in two ways. First he is so evidently too large for the material universe, the mere fact of him means that there must be a real universe adequate to himself. And second, the spiritual things we find so difficult to take hold of are so real to him that his conviction tends to become ours: we take him and them together in the impossibility of taking him without them.

What we must do then is to go back and forth between theological thinking and Gospel reading, thus making ourselves at home and coming to *feel* at home in what truly is the real world. Established in reality, we use the doctrines we know to be true; using them we find them taking on their own proper kind of rightness, find ourselves less and less troubled by the difference between their reality and matter's.

The conscious, willed effort to bring the great realities into our vision of lesser things becomes in a way automatic after a while, so that when we see anything at all, we see *them*, indeed we should find it impossible not to see them. The feeling of unreality can still return, but transiently, very much as there are moments when the material world itself seems an illusion.

3. The Necessity of Faith

I have been discussing throughout this chapter the intellectual operation upon the doctrines by which we grow in comprehension. This must not be confused with the virtue of Faith by which we accept them and hold them, to the extent in which we possess, and are possessed by, God himself. Faith may exist with the very minimum of knowledge; whereas the mightiest mental effort would be almost valueless without it. There *is* a psychological activity and it is of vast importance. Yet it would be a bad error to see it as primary. The grace of Faith must be there, to give our thinking the initial impulse and to support it throughout. Those who obey the commands, says Our Lord—that is those who live the life—shall know of the doctrine "Whether it is from God or whether I am speaking on my own authority" (John 7.17).

Because Catholic theology can be set down in words, a man might study it without faith, entirely from outside. He could learn the words and be able to state the main ideas accurately; but it would be rather like learning the recipes in a cookery book without eating the food—the reality would elude him, he would not know the thing he was discussing, he would only know about it.

This applies in a measure to any vital experience—marriage, for example. But to the Christian revelation it applies totally. God is not there at our mercy, to be taken or left at our choice, to be taken as much or as little as our fancy wills. He cannot be taken by storm, no matter what the natural power or vehemence of the mind, he must give himself or we cannot have him. "No one can come to me unless the Father who sent me draws him" (John 6.44). Faith is a gift of God; growth in faith is more important than growth in conscious awareness, for it is needed to support the awareness, support it in being, support it in growing.

We shall be discussing the virtue of Faith and the gift of Understanding later. Here it is enough to remind ourselves that prayer and the sacraments are essential; without them, study is breathing in a vacuum. Yet they are not the same thing as study, and it too is necessary. In the *Imitation of Christ* we read that it is better to please the Trinity than to be able to discuss the Trinity. So it is. But it is best to do both. As the author of the *Imitation* did.

No doctrine is merely academic; that anybody should think it is suggests that he must have been taught it very badly. One of our leading Catholic scholars has said: "If our presentation of Catholic doctrine is to be vital . . . it must be something more than the presentation of an abstract dogmatic code and an exacting moral ethic." And another: "We lose the whole flavor of the word of God if we want to have its teaching parcelled out in neat, clearly labelled compartments." And a third: "Faith is a special kind of knowledge, eminently con-crete, not the coldly rational acceptance of an intellectual position regarding certain truths." *Abstract dogmatic code, neat clearly-labelled compartments, coldly rational acceptance,* the phrases shed a bleak light on so many teachers, so much teaching: one feels that the writers are venting their spleen on some long-dead professor. And indeed the purely academic mind has a habit of syphoning the blood out of truth before presenting it to the pupil: which means, to come back to our starting point, that the pupil is not really getting the doctrine but only the terms.

For there is a proper interaction between knowledge and love. Knowledge serves love, each new truth learnt is a new reason for loving God. Love craves knowledge, craves to know: it would be strange to love God and not want to know more and more about him.

Love craves not only to know but to be known. That surely is why Christ revealed to us the inmost secret of the divine life, which is the doctrine of the Blessed Trinity. As man, he gave what he himself had called the greatest proof of love, he laid his life down for us; as God, he laid his life open to us. It is strange enough that so many Christians should ignore this proof of his love, leaving the Trinity to others as a burden too heavy for themselves: it is surely incredible that they should do so in the name of love—as if they were trying to keep their love of God untarnished by that knowledge of himself which in his love he offers to us.

The study of theology is not easy, but love calls us to it. In the *Vision of Piers Plowman,* the medieval poet William Langland combines the two elements in the beginner's experience with almost clinical precision:

> I have threatened Theology a thousand times over,
> The more I muse on it the mistier I think it;
> And the deeper I dive the darker I find it.
> I should think it idleness if love were not in it.
> But because it holds love best I love it the better.
> Where love is the leader, grace is never lacking.

TWO

Mystery

Apart from the labor involved in the mastery of individual doctrines, there are two keys to the understanding of every doctrine, and into familiarity with these and their handling we must be continually growing. They are spirit, which enters into the constitution of every reality theology treats, and mystery, which is the atmosphere in which all must be seen. Let us think first about mystery.

1. Difficulties for the Finite Mind

Every truth revealed by God plunges deeper than finite mind can follow it. As we concentrate the mind in the effort to understand what is being said, we find two levels of difficulty.

There is the difficulty of seeing at all; we hear the words, but they do not seem to be saying anything. Of words like infinite and eternal, the sounds reach us, but we have no present experience in ourselves of being infinite or eternal, no possibility indeed of ever becoming either; and we have no equipment in the mind to supply for the experience we lack. We can decide to learn the words as counters to be used in a complicated game called Theology; we can solve problems in which they occur; provided we can spell them, we can even pass examinations and be licensed to teach them to other people. But reality is not primarily a problem to be solved but a richness to be entered into and made our own. In every doctrine the light is wonderful; but the darkness so soon closes in.

This first level— the difficulty of seeing—does not bother most of us as much as the second—the appearance of contradiction in what we do see. We can be philosophical about darkness unpierced, as we cannot about flat contradiction. For that is what it sounds like to be told, for instance, that there are Three each of whom is God, yet only one God. Or that all the acts by which Our Lord redeemed us were the actions of a divine Person, yet that there was a human responsibility in his acceptance of suffering and death. Or that after Consecration, the taste of bread remains but no bread to taste like that, the intoxicating power of wine remains but no wine to account for the intoxication.

Catholics accept the mysteries. But there is a way of accepting them which does not help. There are those who swallow them without a blink. They do not think about them enough to find the meaning in them. Where there is no meaning, there is no problem; but there is no nourishment for the mind either. This unreflective swallowing of whatever the Church puts into our mouth should not be equated with the act of Faith. Acceptance means more than not denying. Christians in their thousands have died for refusal to deny doctrines to which they had given very little thought. They were dying for love of God and his Christ, of course, and no doctrinal competence is a substitute for that. But the mysteries have it in them to nourish love, if we make the effort to extract the reality from them and build it into our own substance.

A first condition for this is to think about mystery—what it is, why it must be. Mystery is not darkness, it is light; but light ringed by darkness. God, revealing mysteries to us, was not revealing darkness; unless there is light, nothing is revealed. So we do all that is in us to make our own what God, through Christ and the Church and the Scriptures, is actually saying to us.

Studying a particular doctrine, we try to get at the meaning of the words—what they mean in themselves, what they meant when the Church said them: and that may involve studying what error she was answering—it is all too easy to misunderstand an answer if we happen not to have heard the question. Then we try to see our doctrine in the totality of revealed truth. Individual truths cast light upon each other— as, for example, to study Our Lady's Assumption into heaven, we must look long and closely at her Son's Resurrection.

All the truths are linked one to another organically. You cannot damage one without damaging all, yet the links may be hidden from our gaze. Theologians are continually throwing a stone in one direction and breaking a window in another. Men who refused to call Our Lady Mother of God did not see how inevitably their sons would move on to the denial of *her* Son's divinity. These three elements—the meaning of the words, the context in which they were uttered, the place in the totality of revelation—will occupy us as we come to each mystery in turn. But behind them all lies the question why the light must be ringed with darkness.

It must, of course. We cannot know God as well as he knows himself. Given that God exists, darkness there must be for us. Even within the order of our own finitude, we make contact with minds greater than ours, and both in their processes and in their findings they outrange us. The disproportion between our mind and God's is immeasurably vaster, vaster beyond our conceiving. We must dwell on the concept of infinity, not simply filing away a definition but mentally living with it, looking at it, praying in awareness of it.

So we grow into a new habit—the habit of accepting the disproportion as a living fact—a sort of intimacy with infinity. We can still not say in words what we have learnt, but it is true learning. We feel around for analogies, knowing them for no more than that, but finding a certain contentment in them. The divine mind is an infinite ocean of light. Only flashes and sparkles of that light reach us, with darkness between. Or again infinite love has exploded into our universe; theology is an effort to diagram the explosion. The diagram is indispensable, but it is not the reality and it must not obsess us. What matters is the love, and that cannot be diagrammed.

One way or another we come to see how inevitable is the darkness. Indeed as we begin to realize the disproportion between infinite and finite, it is no longer the darkness but the light that is the problem—how can the finite have *any* light upon the infinite? The word disproportion is not strong enough, there is no proportion at all. Whatever concept we use is drawn from finite experience: it is obvious that it must be inadequate: it cannot tell us everything: but can it tell us anything?

We might speculate upon this metaphysically, without ever convincing ourselves that we had arrived at a certain answer. For the Christian fortunately the question has been answered and the doubt removed. For God has given us a revelation of himself, using the words of human language to utter it. We still know that the words cannot tell us the whole reality, that even if finite words could contain the infinite, finite minds could not extract the infinite from them. But we know that they are light-bearing, and that possessing them we are in the light. We must grow in the light.

There are three stages in spiritual growing:
We begin from a condition of destitution,
pass from that into a second stage of true ownership,
and from that into a third, which *seems* to be a return to the first, but no longer destitute.

Thus in speaking of God, or to God, we begin with silence because we have nothing to say, progress from that into speech, and from that into silence again, not a silence we lapse into but a silence we rise into, not the absence of speech but the presence of the action of not speaking—because words cannot utter even as much as we see. Silence has no grammar, no solecisms. It has no tenses, which gives it a sort of cousin-ship with the eternal. Perhaps in heaven we shall find an utterance on the other side of silence, containing all the excellences of silence.

Everything we say—to others, to ourselves—about the mysteries should carry its silences with it: the teacher from whom we hear only words and not silences will not help us greatly. Thinking in the light, loving the light, we must feel the darkness—knowing it as light too strong for us, praying for growth in strength.

Because of all this, theology cannot develop simply by the way of logic. We need the Holy Spirit. That is why the theologian, as distinct from the theometrician, is not readily argumentative. He does not talk for victory, to force others to admit that he is right. He would rather lay open his mind as clearly and richly as lies in him, and leave the rest to his listeners and the Holy Spirit. And this not only because talking for victory carries with it the moral danger that sooner or later we will cheat—the history of polemic is stained with cheating. What matters more profoundly is that the great realities are not best handled thus. It is not that the laws of thought are not valid in this high field, but that too much is beyond our gaze which is yet relevant to the things we do see.

"It is as absurd," says Newman, "to argue men, as to torture them, into believing." Like all epigrams, this oversimplifies; but there really is an analogy between torture, which breaks down the body's resistance, and argument, which breaks down the mind's. The theologian, even the greatest, must walk warily, continually aware of other dimensions not within his range of vision. For he is dealing with the infinite—either with the infinite itself or with truths whose depths vanish away and are lost to sight in it; and there is no map of the infinite.

There is danger in arguing that this or that cannot be, be-

cause. . . . . If the doctrine of the Trinity had not been revealed by God and a new sect arose teaching it, how easily
we should have proved that it could not be; if the Real Presence had not been revealed, the very perfection of the
philosophical doctrine of substance and accidents would have
been regarded as excluding it; if Christ Our Lord had not
agonized in Gethsemani, then we should have been certain
that with the Beatific Vision there could be no agony. Before
the Immaculate Conception was defined, there were great
theologians who proved it impossible—because. . . .

So the theologian must walk warily. Which does not mean
that he must not walk at all. Growth in the light depends for
all of us upon his walking. He ponders the diagram as far as
Theology has been able to draw it, sees gaps in it, strains to
see what may lie between them. But always with the awareness of the great mass of reality his eyes cannot reach at all,
with the certainty therefore that his conclusions cannot be
certain—until the Church has spoken.

That is why theologians can accept, once it is infallibly
defined, a doctrine that they may have spent their lives con-
testing, and the evidence for which they still cannot see. They
have avoided the folly of treating conclusions based upon
partial vision as if they had been based upon total. It is the
theologians who have forgotten the limitation of their vision
of reality whose bones lie whitening where the track ends.

But you and I are not great creative theologians, working
on the frontiers of revelation, trying to extend a little the
area of light. We are students of theology, doing our best to
enter into and make our own the truths which the Word in
his Church has already given us. How much of reality have
we got from what has been formulated for us? There is

enough occupation here to last for our lifetime, and enough light for our intellects to grow into continually and not exhaust. Yet even for us there is a temptation not unlike that which can assail the great masters of theology.

Looking at the apparent contradictions in what we do see, we too can forget the great mass of relevant reality that our eyes cannot pierce. In what God has taught us through his Church, we find not only elements at which our *intellects* cry a challenge, but certain others which stir our *feelings* to something like revolt. We see the doctrine of human freedom as impossible to reconcile with God's omniscience. We find the doctrine of eternal separation from God, the evident facts of child suffering and animal suffering, so painful that we cannot reconcile them with a loving God.

If we are weak in faith, we may decide to reject what mind or emotions cannot cope with. If we are intellectually incurious we may memorize formulas without thought for the meanings, repeating the words as a kind of incantation. Either way, faith suffers. But, avoiding both, we may slide into a position which seems to us orthodox, and even reverent, but is not fully either. We may tell God that since he has taught these things and we are sure he knows best, we accept them, but we will not pretend that we see them or like them.

We feel we are acting very properly, rather like St. Peter— "Thou hast the words of eternal life." Perhaps we are, but not necessarily. That we must not pretend anything to God is, of course, certain. But there is a way of telling God these truths about ourself, a kind of frank man-to-man downrightness, which altogether loses the disproportion or non-proportion between us and God. We must not heckle God, or lapse into a tone which seems to call upon him to justify himself to us—not because it is irreverent to do either, but because it is ridiculous. There must be no merely verbal tribute to God's superior knowledge. There must be the most absolute confidence that what God does and God reveals is supreme truth and supreme love.

In that total confidence, we can pray God for light to see how it is truth or love—not to remove our doubt, for doubt we need not feel, only to bring a gleam of light into our darkness. Our trust should not be diminished if our prayer for that extra gleam of light remains ungranted. We must not fret because we are not omniscient. No one must—not St. Peter, nor Our Lady, certainly not we.

2. Special Difficulties for Today

So far we have been looking at the difficulties which the mysteries present to the human mind because it is finite. These would be much the same in any age, in any place. But there are difficulties special to here and now, and these also must be considered. We are not thinking of God in a vacuum but in a world. The world has a mind of its own, and this mind must largely be ours. Its discoveries and its interpretation of them, its concepts and interests and values, its assumptions, its vocabulary—these make the atmosphere which you and I breathe. Some of it is good, some of it is bad, some serves our understanding of the mysteries, some deflects our minds from them so that they seem irrelevant, some casts their truth into question. It is always acting upon us, it leaves nothing in us untouched, precisely because (to return to our atmosphere metaphor) we are breathing it all the time.

So it is important that we should know what we are breathing. We cannot just go on happily breathing it. We must analyze it, sorting out the good and the bad, making all use of the one, taking necessary action against the other, not surrendering our mind's freedom to its pervasiveness.

We sometimes talk of the contemporary mind as though it were a disease. It is not. Along with its genuine splendors there are diseased elements, certainly. But even for the use of religion, there is much that is very good. It was God who created the universe which science is so brilliantly exploring today; we know God better in knowing his creation better, we serve God better by developing its possibilities. No one of us has yet heard all that the material universe has to tell us of God. Every advance in our knowledge of created being enriches our knowledge of uncreated—if only we let it. What the historians and the anthropologists and the psychologists discover about man can serve us in the same way. Their discoveries may need sifting, but the sifting is immeasurably worthwhile: we shall neglect it to our great loss. The same is true of the philosophers—not one of them but has light in him, some of the darkest-seeming may have most precious light.

Upon this the Church's mind works, using her theologians and philosophers as instruments—assimilating, nourishing itself with all that it finds true. Truth is always nourishing, nothing else is; if a particular truth does not nourish us, we are sick, we need healing. There are moments when the "instruments" work more surely, moments when they seem blunt and ineffective. But the assimilation goes on, and the nourishing. We remember what St. Augustine made of Plato, what St. Thomas found in Aristotle. If we are impatient, we remind ourselves that seven hundred years lay between Plato and Augustine, that Aristotle had been sixteen centuries dead before Thomas conscripted him into the apostolate. If we feel (wrongly, as I think) that today's philosophers have not much to offer, who knows where we may strike gold again? The Greek miracle may not be the last—the mysteries may one day be formulated in terms as yet unheard, to the enchantment of Augustine and Thomas.

Meanwhile it is for us to study what the Church gives us —Scripture and dogma and Sacrament—with minds enriched by what the world gives us. But not all that the world gives us enriches; some of it is very bad. I am not thinking now of individual truths denied or errors asserted—we have usually been warned against these. Nor am I thinking of the world's assumption that the Church had her chance, failed, and has nothing to offer. I mean the whole atmosphere and attitude of the time in relation to the supernatural.

Hardly any of us realize how much we are creatures of our time. Its assumptions tend to be ours, without even a question stirring in us. And there is a continuous seeping in from it which makes for a kind of damping and discoloration even of values we hold sacred. We have been taught to make examinations of conscience; we should build the habit of examining our intellects too, for any assumptions, any seepage which may be in them unnoticed.

A first step is to take a good look at the religious atmosphere of our time and place, and isolate what is characteristic in it. One thing surely must emerge, the curious state of belief in God—not dead certainly, but not very vividly alive either.

And this is true not only of the mass of people who practise no religion at all. In varying degrees it is true of great numbers of Christian groups for whom Christianity almost wholly expresses itself as social service, philanthropy, kindness to one another—with God reverenced but no longer the decisive consideration, or indeed much adverted to. The first commandment—in which Our Lord told men to love God with every element of energy in them—is still recited. But for too many the concentration, the emphasis, is upon the second, love of neighbor.

This view of religion is not without its own sort of excellence, and has shown that it can work for the reduction of cruelty and injustice with a vigor that can leave ourselves embarrassed at our own less impressive efforts. But it eliminates what through all the history of mankind has been the essentially *religious* thing, the sense that in embracing a religion man is being initiated into divine mysteries: there are no divine mysteries in the religion of social service, but Christ Our Lord's teaching is glowing with them—now brilliantly, now somberly—all the time. Nor is a religion mainly of social service, of philanthropy, of kindness to one another, soil in which adoration can flourish; and throughout the ages adoration has been the supreme religious act.

There has been an extraordinary vanishing of the sense of the sacred. Where God is adverted to at all, the gulf that divides us from God is reduced to a respectful difference of degree. You will find this—as clear, and in its own grotesque way as beautiful, as a medieval illumination—in Kipling's *Dedication* to *The Barrack Room Ballads*. He takes the kind of men he most admires in this world, and pictures them in the next world—still living daringly, still the selves who had always fascinated him. When God came in to them

They rose to their feet, gentlemen unafraid.

That they rose to their feet is something, after all they were gentlemen. But unafraid? The poem is respectful to God, it really is a religious poem. Yet the whole thing is a monument of unawareness, unawareness of the infinite being of God, the infinite majesty of God, the infinity of his power and his mercy, of the first fact of our being—that he made us of nothing and by his will keeps us from falling back into our native nothingness. The poor fellows were gentlemen, English gentlemen at that, so they could not fall upon their faces. Neither could Kipling, who had turned his poetic vision so searchingly upon gentlemen and so much less searchingly upon God. One remembers Keats' comparison of himself, reading Homer for the first time, with the Spanish leader as he

> Gazed at the Pacific and all his men
> Stared at each other with a wild surmise
> Silent upon a peak in Darien.

The wild surmise, the silence, with which the Spaniards looked at the new ocean and Keats read Homer (in translation!)—these things are human and right. A man is less than a man who can gaze upon great scenery, or hear great music, or contemplate human heroism without any catching of the breath, any faintest beginning of a shudder of awe. But God is a vast ocean of being in which a man might feel he could drown, a vastness of truth and beauty which the mind cannot contemplate without reeling under it, a holiness the very thought of which means anguish at our own meagerness. A polite standing to attention is no adequate reaction to the thought of God. No one on earth can stay continuously in the silence of adoration, the human organism would break under it; but never to have had any racing of the pulse at all, any missed heart-beat in the sudden realization of God, means never to have felt a very life-pulse of religion.

So far we have been considering people who have maintained some sort of conscious connection with religion. For a great mass of people there is no such connection. Yet they have not rejected God. To me the militant atheists are a kind of nightmare, working so industriously to rob men of hope. They are kindly men, sure of themselves. They know it all, all but how fractional their all is. They offer man a present of himself, or rather of his surface, for it is always depth they mock at—never more so than when they make "depth" their key word. With all that unwearying zeal in their chilly cause they have not destroyed belief in God; convinced atheists are still a rarity.

If we take as reference points the four great realities—God, and the soul, and the world to come, and Christ Our Lord—I think it would be true to say that most people have not rejected any, yet they have no living awareness of any, no living contact. They have no idea of what the God is whose existence they are not prepared to deny, or what difference it makes whether he exists or not. The light and love he would share with them are as unregarded as the will he would communicate to them. Similarly they could not say anything very clear about the spiritual element by which they differ from their dog, or anything at all about what follows death. They believe that there is something in Christ that is not in other men, though they do not know what it is and have heard that Socrates was rather remarkable too.

In other words they hold these beliefs in a state of suspended animation, and animation cannot be counted on to

stay suspended forever. The atheist attack continues, making
the great realities seem distasteful, insipid anyhow, effectively
destroying any appetite for them. The effect upon many is
like that of those drugs which render alcohol nauseating, but
leave untouched the psychological anguish which drove men
to alcohol in the first place. For you do not get rid of depth
by mocking at it or translating it into something else; it is still
there and all its needs with it.

The beliefs somehow hang on. Meanwhile those in
whom they abide thus semi-animate get almost nothing from
them. They gain something, indeed, merely by having God in
their minds unrejected. He does something for them merely
by not being denied. But all the time their vitality is being
eroded by the needs in them that a God so vaguely apprehended does not meet. Undernourishment is not a strong
enough word. There is real starvation. I do not mean that
they are hungry for God, only that they are hungry for lack
of God. They do not know what they are hungry for; they
do not even know that they are hungry; they have come to
regard hunger as normal, they know no other state. In them
we can study the spiritual physiology of starvation.

3. The Mysteries as Necessaries of Life

Some of the needs that only God can meet lie so obviously
on the surface that it is hard to miss them. For the man who is
livingly aware of God—as creator and conserver in being of
all things, as revealer of truths necessary to be known which
without him cannot be known—the universe is a universe,
not a mere aggregation of items but an ordered whole. He

sees each thing related to God, and only so to each other thing.

But if God is either not seen at all, or (as by so many a churchgoer, by ministers of religion even) not seen as functioning, not heard as revealing, there is no universe. There is no shaped totality, but only myriads upon myriads of individual things, meaningless because no mind presided at their origin, purposeless because no mind intended them, a drift of things drifting where they happen to be drifting, and ourselves elements in the drift; nothing can be known in its context, for a multifold shapelessness is not a context; no integration is possible, for there is no integer.

Even if a man be not given to scanning horizons, not worried therefore by the absence of totality and total meaning, he still finds that without any revelation from God he does not know what he is himself or where he is going, his own personal life is so meaningless for want of a known goal that he finds himself going on living only for lack of any particular reason for dying, or because living has become a habit that he is vaguely attached to, like an old hat. All this, which for masses of men is normal, is a very far cry from that *seeing what is* which is sanity. To have part only of oneself, living in part only of reality, is a most miserable impoverishment.

So far we have been considering only the most obvious of the human needs which cannot be met without God. But to the very depths of his being man has needs as real. Because the purpose for which we exist is to come to total union with him, God has built into the very texture of every man's being powers to take hold of him, and a need for him which urges those powers to act. Of love we need hardly speak. But there is adoration too. The power to adore and the need to adore are part of our essential structure as man. We have already observed the vanishing of adoration; and this is not only a denial of something owed to God, but the removal of the true object which alone rightly meets man's inbuilt need to adore; in its absence, he seeks for substitute objects which never in fact meet the need, or else he despairs of meeting it and lets an essential element in himself wither away.

There are other needs as deep-lying—the need for reassurance in the loneliness and lostness of the creature; a vague but troubling sense of guilt arising from the defacement in himself of the image of God which every man is created to be, a need for vitalization when contact with the source of life is snapped; something to hope in, above all—a sure confidence that a man's own personal life is leading somewhere and not nowhere.

There are those in our world who believe wholly, but they are a minority; they do not affect the atmosphere, only breathe it. There are militant atheists, they too a minority, but they do affect the atmosphere. For they strengthen its dominant characteristic—namely to conduct life without reference to God. Moral, social, political decisions, like personal decisions, are made *as if* God did not exist. It is a kind of practical godlessness, God in a cloud not of his own too much light, but of man's too small interest.

There is no deliberate exclusion; it simply does not occur to the mass of people that God's will could have any bearing on the public well-being; and the needs within a man that only God can meet are no longer felt as needs, but as an undiagnosed malaise, discomfort, unsatisfaction, which they do not connect with the absence of God. All the affairs of the world they see as to be settled within the boundaries of the world, either because there is no other; or because the other *is* other, a world to be lived in separately by such as choose, the two worlds not impinging, only this one really mattering.

Seeing the time we live in analyzed like that, we are not likely at first to realize how much we are immersed in it. Yet it is a miracle if we are wholly untouched by it, even in our deepest certainties. We do not accept its denials or its doubts; but we are almost certainly affected by its emphases—unconsciously, for the most part. We believe in the mysteries totally; we know that all holiness is in them, that death would be better than the denial of any syllable of them. Yet. . . .

Let us look again at that word "totally." We feel the glory of having the mysteries, certainly. But have we any equal feeling of the destitution that goes with not having them? We are surrounded by millions who, lacking the mysteries, are starved of food that Christ Our Lord meant them to have. Are we in anguish at their starvation? Do we even see it as starvation? "Anguish" is perhaps asking too much of us. But do we feel anything at all? Regret, perhaps. But no very active regret, no call to relieve it, nothing to disturb our tranquillity. Not what we should feel if their starvation was bodily; for we do know the value of the bread that perishes. The world thinks that bodily starvation really matters and spiritual does not. It looks frighteningly as though we thought so too.

If we do not see God's revelation as mattering *to everybody*, then we have not grasped its reality, we believe it but not totally. That this is not a fanciful inference from our behavior is shown by the phrase we too often use to dismiss their destitution—and our own inaction: they do not know that God has revealed our doctrines and our sacraments, we tell ourselves, therefore they are not sinning by not receiving them. Their starvation need not be relieved because it is not

sinful—a strange reaction to starvation. There *is* such a thing
as invincible ignorance, though there may be some responsibility in those whose refusal to teach insures its invincibility.
People will not be lost eternally for what they honorably
do not know. But what of the richness, light, nourishment
they might be having here upon earth?

The mysteries, then, are not a luxury for the spiritually-
minded (like us!); they are necessaries of life for everyone.
Not to see them so is a key example of the damping and discoloration I have talked of. As against it we should look once
more at the mysteries, asking ourselves what difference they
actually make to ourselves, what should we really have lost if
Trinity or Incarnation, for instance, had not been revealed?
In accepting them, are we simply obeying a command, with
all virtues merged and lost in the single virtue of obedience,
all the soul's muscles left flabby from un-use save the muscle
we swallow with?

We really live in the mysteries if we realize, first, what
they mean to us, so that we should be desolate without them,
second what they mean in themselves, so that we should find
it intolerable that others should be without them. Desolate?
Intolerable? We must not fool ourselves. We may not yet
have reached the fullness of possession expressed by either
word. But that fullness is what is meant by having a vital
equivalent for our terms.

4. Sanity and Society

Insanity is all about us. I do not mean that men individually
are madmen, but they add up to a society which is not truly
sane. Sanity means seeing what's there and planning life ac-

cordingly. And *as a society* ours does not see the major part of reality at all, therefore does not see aright the minor part that it *is* aware of, shapes its activities as though the mis-seen fraction of reality were the whole of it. Secular Ethic means deciding our actions as though there were no God, while not settling the question whether there is or not. I do not mean that men of this mind are acting evilly: they may act nobly (as believers may act appallingly). But they would add a fuller rationality to their nobility if they knew the true order of reality.

To act without full vision is a formula for chaos. And in a chaos we live, exhibited to us by every newspaper we read, yet disguised from us by the care and intelligence and good will expended upon the understanding and ordering of the fraction; disguised again by the mental muscularity, the almost blinding scientific and technological brilliance, with which the seen part of reality is analyzed, is formulated and systematized, packaged, and offered for acceptance. The chaos is amiable so far; but chaos cannot be relied on to stay amiable, there are parts of the world in which it has not.

Even short of some such catastrophe befalling our own part of the world, it is not good to be the sane minority in a society that has lost contact with God. We hold our own mental health precariously when sanity so partial and defective is accepted as the norm. Insanity is catching: we grow uncertain of the cadences of normal speech when all around us men are gibbering, and gibbering so learnedly and so gravely and so confidently. Our world at its best has all the airs and graces, the rationalizations and courtesies and card indexes of sanity, so that the notion that it might not be sane may not occur to us. The card indexes especially, so tidy, so efficient, so inclu-

sive: only a fanatic would question the rationality of the mind
that produces them.

"Fanatic" is the word. We can frighten ourselves with it. I
have talked of assumptions and seepage that we are unaware
of. But there is something else: the Catholic can be *consciously*
embarrassed at his difference. There are those who feel out of
step, self-conscious because out of step, self-questioning because out of step. If they have not made the mysteries of
revelation truly their own, they may see life fluid and free,
theology all bones. There is great psychological value in a
strong affirmation, said Hilaire Belloc. No affirmation was
ever stronger than our world makes of its own rightness.

The temptation is to try to get into step with everybody
else, while somehow hanging on to the truths. Short of denying them, there is a kind of scaling down and shading off, a
resolute switching of the mind away from doctrines at which
the world would raise an eyebrow. At all costs, one must not
be a fanatic. St. Paul had met this attitude, right at our beginnings: "Be not conformed to this world, but be re-formed
in the newness of your mind" (Rom. 12.2).

It is not only Faith that demands this, but sheerest common
sense. One remembers a stock joke of the last fifty years—the
old lady watching a line of soldiers on parade and saying
proudly, "They're all out of step except my George." We all
smile, we all assume without the shadow of a second thought,
that it *is* George who is out of step. But if everybody else in
the battalion happened to be deaf, then George might well be
the only one marching in time to the music of the band.

The parallel is exact. The follower of Christ does hear a
music which does not reach the ears of other men: he is
bound to be out of step with them, for they are out of step

with it. But in our world we must listen to that music with unflagging attention: partly that it may not be drowned out of our own ears by all the tomtoms of chaos, partly that others may begin to catch from us first some hint of the rhythm, then some hint of the tune. Unflagging attention, I say. Few of us can give it that. We catch strains of the music tossed on the winds of the spirit; but how fitfully that wind can blow for us, how fitfully we listen for it.

THREE

Spirit

There are two keys, we have noted, to the understanding of Revelation. We have lingered over Mystery. There remains Spirit.

Spirit enters into everything that theology treats. If Mystery is the atmosphere we must learn to breathe, Spirit is stuff we are working in all the time and must learn to handle. We must study it as a sculptor studies stone, growing in intimacy and mastery. But also, we must first study it rather as a geologist studies stone. We must examine it in action—what it does, how it acts and reacts, what can be done with it—all the time trying to come closer to what it is in itself.

Unless we do this, we shall simply not know what the Church is saying when she applies the word spirit to God, to angels, to the human soul, to sanctifying grace. The desire to know what the Church is saying is not idle curiosity, as one has heard it called; nor is it only the natural activity of a healthy intellect, searching out meaning because knowledge is its proper business. It is deeper than either. Unless we find what the Church means, she might as well not have spoken, Christ might as well not have promised to be with her in her teaching.

"God is a spirit," said Our Lord to the Samaritan woman (John 4.24), "and they that worship him must worship him in spirit and in truth." The God we worship is spirit; our own spirit (which is spirit embodied) is what we worship with. Unless we know what spirit is, we do not know the God we worship, or ourselves who worship him, or the worship which is our approach to him: our worship can be only the approach of our scarcely-known selves to a vaguely-realized God. Without a study of spirit in depth, men must miss so much of what God's self-revelation contains.

1. Spirit in the Old Testament

"So much," notice, not all. With what seems to us an extraordinary lack of inquiry into the nature of God, the Chosen People yet made a most wonderful advance in personal relation with him. But wonderful as it was, it was insufficient. They would have died rather than contradict God's teaching, yet they so often stopped before reaching the essence of it. All their mind was concentrated upon learning his will, but they appear to have given hardly a thought to his very self. They could speak of him, they could *feel* him, as everlasting, and almighty, as possessing all knowledge. But they had no real notion, vital and vitalizing, of what eternity is, or omnipotence, or omniscience. And, at least in the greater part of the Old Testament, we find in them no concern or curiosity about these vast realities.

They could have no real notion because they had not given their minds to a serious examination of a word constantly on their lips, the word "spirit." A necessary step in the examination would have been to distinguish spirit from matter. It is a fact worth weighing that the word "matter," in the sense of non-spiritual reality, is not in the Bible: we find it in neither Testament: which seems to mean that one of the mightiest contrasts of all did not hold, or apparently even catch, their attention. They were aware of spirit, and knew it as special. They used the word for the highest things. The soul of man, the active power of God, God himself. But they got no further in their exploration of the reality the word utters than to think of it as unseen, and as powerful. Thus limited, they could not even begin to approach the notion of Trinity.

In that limitation was rooted their refusal of Christ. Without a clear idea of spirit they could only find Trinity meaningless, so that Christ's claim to Godhead had to mean a second God. Not only that, even the God whose oneness they asserted against the world could not be seen as wholly immaterial: they had no word for "invisible," God was unseen not because that was his nature but because he chose to be. Angels too had some sort of bodiliness, though it was not of the solid earthiness of ours, closer to fluidity perhaps—good angels were radiant with light, bad angels opaque. But this was towards the end of the Old Testament period. The idea lingers on in the early Church.

Their word for spirit was *ruah* which, like the Greek *pneuma* and the Latin *spiritus*, means "breath." Even the least philosophical of men see one special distinction between liv-

ing beings and dead—the living breathe: when breathing
stops, life stops. So Genesis phrases it (2.7), God took clay
and breathed upon it, and man was alive. "God," we read in
the book of Job, "has but to turn his thoughts towards men,
reclaiming the spirit he once breathed into them, and life
would fail everywhere; mankind would return to its dust"
(34.14). The same breathing and withdrawal of breathing
means life and death for animals too (Ps. 103.29–30).

As their notions of life grew deeper, they still found no
need to go beyond *ruah*, breath—God breathing, something in
men and animals responding to God's breath, men responding
more richly than animals. They knew "breath" for a figure of
speech, but they made slow progress into the understanding
of the reality it figured. Not being half-witted, they knew
that men have something which animals lack, as shown by
what each can do and even more by what it is permissible to
do to them; but they seem to have felt no call to analyze.

Even as late as Ecclesiastes—perhaps towards 200 B.C.—we
find: "Who knows whether the breath of the sons of men
goes upward and the breath of the beasts goes downward to
the earth?" (3.21). What is the author saying: Human life,
animal life, it is all one God breathing into his creatures: there
are those who say that there is a continuance for men after
death, as there is not for beasts, but who actually knows this?
—certainly in their life on earth men act sufficiently like
beasts.

Later in the book (12.7) the author seems to make his own
the phrase he has just questioned: "Dust goes back to its par-
ent earth and the spirit returns to God who gave it." But this
may be the word of a different author intervening; nor is it in
any event clear beyond question that the spirit—the *ruah*—

which returns to God is seen as a constituent element in man himself resultant from God's breathing: it may be simply God's breath drawn back again into God.

They did not, until the very end of the Old Testament period when Greek thought was having its effect on them, think of man as a union or fusion of spirit and body, he was simply man. Man and man's body—they felt no call to distinguish. "My spirit," "my soul," "my flesh"—any of these meant simply "I." Isaiah's "My soul shall be joyful in my God" (61.10) no more excludes the body than the Psalmist's "My flesh shall rest in hope" (16.9) excludes the soul. In the command to love the Lord God with their whole heart and their whole soul, they saw a distinction of man's powers, not a distinction within his being. And he had the powers because God had breathed life into him. That breathing meant everything, yet as we have noted they did not analyze it beyond considering what it enabled them to do. "Man's spirit is a lamp the Lord gives, to search out the hidden corners of his being" (Prov. 20.27)—the breathing here operates in man as conscience.

They had substantive words—body and flesh, soul and spirit: they saw men acting and reacting in ways which it was natural to state in terms of one or other of these, yet without seeing the action as issuing from distinct elements in man himself. Soul was the life-principle in the body: its relation with spirit, the breath of God in living beings, was assumed but not worked out. They were not yet ready for the later rabbinical distinction of body and soul, which goes too far in the other direction—with the body as a scabbard sheathing the soul, or as a micropolis, a small city, in which the soul dwells. Only at the very end do we come upon the notion, taken apparently from the Greeks, of a disembodied soul.

To return to the genuinely Jewish view, it distinguished the higher operations of intellect and the like, but the tendency was to see these—repentance too—as functions not of the mind or spirit but of the heart—"Rend your hearts and not your garments," says Joel (2.13): Deuteronomy has the same idea—"Circumcise the foreskin of your heart" (10.16). "Heart" is far more frequent in the Old Testament than "spirit." Both words are in both Testaments; but, by a mere count of numbers, "heart" belongs to the Old as decisively as "spirit" to the New. There is delight in the phrase of Proverbs (4.23)—"Keep your heart with all vigilance, for from it flow the springs of life."

But spirit was the only one of these words which was applied to God too. We have to await Our Lord's meeting with the Samaritan woman for the direct statement "God is a spirit." But the words God and spirit go naturally together. "The spirit of God" is the normal phrase for the divine energy, the operation of the divine power. And God could speak of "My spirit" as he could not of "My soul" or "My heart." In spirit lies the link between God and man, so that the writer can apply the word to both in one text—"the Spirit lifted me up and put me away, and I went in bitterness in the heat of my spirit" (Ezek. 3.14).

If, for the greater part of the Old Testament period, the Jews did not realize that man was a union of distinct elements, we are in danger of splitting soul and body too wide apart, not seeing man as spirit embodied, or body enspirited. We do not, as Hindus do and old-style Protestants tended to do, omit the body from religion; but at least we can feel it as an extra, not involved in our highest activities here upon earth, as a barrier between ourselves and full union with God, perhaps as an intruder into the more refined life of heaven when at the Judgment we shall be once more embodied! The Jewish insistence that the body belongs to the fullness of manhood, so that man is not man without it, is a corrective of all this, a reminder that salvation for man demands the resurrection of his body.

The failure to see and think about spirit as a true constituent element in man had as one result that it was difficult for the men of the Old Testament to grasp the next life. They saw men's bodies rotting in the tomb, what was there to survive? And what sort of life could it have? Whatever Ecclesiastes meant, in the line just quoted, by the return of the spirit to God, Christians can use the phrase with joy. Yet the joy is slightly tempered by uncertainty as to what the author himself was actually saying. In the Book of Wisdom, written perhaps a little later, we find a clear statement about which we have no such tempering doubt: "The souls of the just are in the hands of God, and no torment in death itself has power to reach them." But by then Moses is over a thousand years behind us.

Breath is air in movement. It was normal, therefore, to use the analogy of a great wind blowing to express God's activity in creation. For the one thing those spiritual kinsmen of ours knew instinctively about spirit was that in some way it differed from body and was superior to it—"Egypt is man and not God, and their horses flesh and not spirit" (Is. 31.3). The wind cannot be seen, the wind is powerful, it is the least material of material things, the least earthy of the things that affect earth, its home is the sky. God aiding us, we have learned much about God that they did not know; but we still use their word spirit, which is breath. Dr. Dodd's judgment stands unanswerable—"Judaism was failing because it had no adequate philosophy behind its faith and practice" (*The Fourth Gospel*).[1] Yet, to repeat, we can marvel at the height they attained, their living awareness of God's majesty and holiness, their conviction—reached by none before them, and by none since save men of their own tradition—of God's personality and God's nearness.

They really experienced God in his love, in his wrath, in his mercy. When we have gone as deep as our capacity enables us to go into all that God has revealed of himself, through Christ and in his church, it is still enriching, electrifying to read great parts of the Old Testament. Thus equipped with insight into God's very being, we can draw more from the long Jewish experience of God than could the men who lived it.

2. What Spirit Can Do

So we must study spirit. We begin with our own spirit, both as a specimen of that which is to be studied, and as that in ourselves with which we make the study. To return to our sculpture analogy, we must study spirit not only as the sculptor studies stone, but as he studies the mind he brings to his art, his hands and arms, and the very hammer and chisel that he uses—for the concept-forming, concept-handling power is the mind's tool in the study of Theology.

We study our spirit with our spirit, our spirit sees itself

[1] New York, Cambridge University Press, 1953.

being a spirit, sees itself *operating* as a spirit. This total self-seeing involves a total turning back upon self for which matter has no parallel, indeed could have no parallel. A given material object may be flexible, so that one part of it can act upon another part, but not the whole of it upon the whole of it. In its totality a material thing cannot be both that which acts and that which is acted upon. A spirit can. Our soul does precisely that.

We begin with our own spirit then. It is the one we know best, the only one directly available. But it is not ideal for our purpose all the same, because of its union with matter, a union so close that in us they form one single being, each element affecting the other continuously. Just as our body, enspirited, is not the best beginning for a study of the animal order, so our spirit, embodied, is not the best beginning for a study of the spiritual. It is a matter-wed spirit that we are studying, with a matter-wed spirit that we are making the study. We must train ourselves, as far as we can, to make allowance for the materiality at both ends, above all for the way time and space, which belong to the body, have so imposed themselves upon the mind that they could hardly grip it tighter if they properly belonged to it.

Spirit is the element in us by which we know and love, by which therefore we make our decisions. It is obvious that the body not only knows nothing, but loves nothing—even our most carnal delights are enjoyed by the mind. Rather more reflection may be needed to show us that thinking and loving are both of them spiritual operations. A thought has no dimensions, weight, color; in itself it is unbodily. It may be accompanied by changes in the bodily organism—grooves or scratches, electrical discharges in the brain. These may be necessary conditions, without which we could not have the thought or maintain it. But they are not the thought. We are not conscious of them at all. Until recently we did not know we had them, our ancestors had never heard of them. When we examine the truth of a thought we give no heed to the scratches. When we say that loyalty is nobler than treachery, we are not bringing together for comparison the electrical discharges occasioned by the thought "loyalty," those occasioned by the thought "treachery," those occasioned by the thought "nobility," and finding that the third lot harmonize with the first and not with the second. No one of us ever had any conscious experience of those discharges. We take the word of scientists that they happen.

It is much the same with love. There is the same absence of dimensions, weight, color. Its accompaniments in the bodily organ are more obvious, needing no microscopes, but love is *not* those; indeed love can involve bodily renunciation, and such bodily reaction as there is may be away from love, not to it. But for the moment let us concentrate upon our thoughts and the process by which we produce them.

The outer world comes in through our bodily sense-organs —eyes, ears, and the rest; this we have all experienced. The sensations are conveyed to the brain—we do not actually catch them at it, but those who have studied our nervous system seem to be unanimous about it. Then something happens which escapes observation altogether. As a result of it, we find ourselves *thinking*, building up a whole structure of thought somehow based on what came through our senses. Unfortunately, the point is dark to us in which what the senses receive and the brain records passes into what the mind thinks. It is happening all the time, but we seem unable to observe the process. What is quite certain is that thoughts, which are the end-product of the process, have none of the specifying qualities we associate with the body. They are untouchable, no microscope can make them visible, no audiometer can register them. And the gulf between thought and matter is even wider when we consider so much of what our thought contains, general ideas, ideals, philosophical systems, moral certainties.

Yet our body is in at their birth all the same, in at their very conception. This or that element of the external universe reaches our brain by way of the senses: there it makes contact with the mind, and a concept is the result of the union. By the concept, *the thing is present to our mind as what it is:* relating our concepts to one another we form judgments: these we analyze, arrange and rearrange in new relations. So thinking goes on, soaring far beyond matter's level into the inmost life of God. But at its beginning is the concept, which results from the mind's being fertilized by the objects we encounter.

We may think of a never-ending series of affairs between the mind and things, with the mind left holding the concept. And the concept is the image of its father, so to speak, but of the very stuff of its mother. The essence of the thing, what it is, is present in the concept, but spiritually. For spirit is what the mind is, spirit is all it can be, spirit is the only kind of offspring it can produce. There is no passion in the affair usually, though there may be; in great art, indeed, we get the feeling that reality has raped the artist's mind. Yet the passion is only in the conceiving mind—the universe does not know that it is fathering a concept, and naturally does not care.

None of this involves any particular difficulty or any vast research. But spirit has power too, reaching out beyond itself.

The atom, for instance, is split: it is the mind of man that split it—the atom cannot split the mind of man, cannot even split itself. Here our imagination intervenes rebelliously. Almost from the dawn of history men have known about the planets, have humbled themselves before the planets, have found all sorts of ingenious ways of asserting the night sky's mastery over the human insect. Recent discoveries have convinced men in general that astrology is illusion; but the tendency to minimize man in relation to the stars has been strengthened a thousandfold.

We have found not only more and more planets, but more and more solar systems; we have learned about the light years with which we must measure the vastness of space. Imagination is having a carnival. Man is only a speck upon a speck; he is supposed even to be humble before the spaces, to bow down before emptiness simply because there is so much of it. But the speck—the smaller speck, I mean, which is man—is the superior all the same. He knows the stars and the spaces, not they him; he calculates the light years and knows of the deaths of stars. He loves them, not they him: the beauty of the moon is for spirit not for matter.

Indeed he uses the stars, if only to steer his ships and measure his earth. But he is planning beyond that, planning to extend the range of his own movement, to go out among them: for mind has the instinct of dominion, and only mind has it. There are greater minds than man's—revelation tells us of angels—and greater power; before these man must bow, but not before mindless, impotent masses and the spaces that lie between. My body is, conveniently, smaller than the planet Jupiter; but my mind is not. Mindlessness does not become greater than mind simply by being multiplied.

Splitting the atom, calculating the light years, mind uses the body. There is no question which uses which, which is the user and which the instrument. Is the instrument indispensable? In our present situation—or perhaps I should say in the present state of our knowledge of the present situation—it seems so. Mind acts upon matter through the body, mind communicates with other minds through its own body and theirs. So it always has been, and our temptation is to regard the invariable as the necessary.

But the philosopher, examining the nature of mind and matter, sees no ultimate reason why the mind should be unable to operate outside itself except with matter as instrument. And even the non-philosopher has at every waking moment evidence in his own experience of mind acting upon matter directly: we will to raise our arm, for instance, and up goes the arm. We are carrying through a complicated anatomical activity of whose detail we may have only the faintest idea: but the will has decided, and the thing happens.

The power of the soul over its own body is the last point we need note here in this rapid glance at what the spirit we know best can do. The spirit radiates energies by which the body lives and functions, so long as the body is not damaged to such an extent that it can no longer receive or respond to them. Alone of the spirits known to us, the human spirit is a soul—that is to say the life principle of a body—just as we know of no soul but man's which is a spirit. It is only by this unique union in his own essence of spirit and matter that man has his justification for existing at all. Without him, there would be a world of spirit and a world of matter, two worlds. Man, belonging to both, locks them into one universe.

3. *What Spirit Is*

So far we have been running over in our mind the operations of spirit, its knowledge, its love, its power. But for that
understanding of reality which is theology's object, we must
not stay with what spirit *does*, we must see if we can come
closer to what spirit is.

Spirit is the being which has no parts. Whenever the
Church uses the word spirit—of human soul, angels, God
himself—this is what she is saying. A part is any element in a
being that is not the whole of it. In a spirit there is no such
element. There is no division of parts as in matter, and therefore no dispersion of powers, but total concentration of being
and powers in one single act of being. Our body has parts—
heart, liver, kidneys, arms, legs; and each has its own function,
which the others cannot perform for it. But all the things the
soul does are done by the whole soul, for there is nothing in
the soul which is not the whole of it. It has no parts among
which to distribute its activities. It knows, loves, decides, ani-
mates a body. And one single soul, I almost said one sole soul,
does *each* of these things with *the whole of itself.*

Theology is rich in words which mean something quite
different in everyday speech. I remember a movie review
which used two of the key words of the Christian faith to
describe the heroine—she was the very incarnation of grace:
she was an adulteress, as it happened. Simplicity is such a
word. We wrestle with the concept of a being that has no
parts, labor and sweat over it. It is a little startling to hear this
called simplicity. In ordinary speech, a person without much
mind is called simple, like Simple Simon. Now we must learn
to call our soul and the angels and God himself simple (at

differing richnesses of simplicity). But when at last we have made the concept our own, we see how precisely right the word is. Matter has parts, in admirable arrangement, it is complex. Spirit has no parts, nothing that calls for arrangement, it is simplex.

Why the wrestling, the labor, the sweat? Because imagination not only will not help, it is in violent opposition. If we understand this opposition, we shall already have advanced a little way into an understanding of the concept of simplicity. The absence of parts means that the being does not occupy space; but space is imagination's realm, outside which it cannot function at all. The spaceless cannot be pictured, and picture-making is the one thing that imagination can manage.

We concentrate on the statement that a partless being does not occupy space. There is no way of saying this more clearly. We must just keep looking at it, until we find ourselves seeing it. Think of anything, anything at all, that occupies space. It could not do so unless there were elements in it which are not the whole of it and not each other: this end is not that end, the upper side is not the lower, the outside is not the inside. Occupation of space means "spread": no parts, no spread. A spirit is above the need for space, has no way of subjecting itself to space.

Therefore a spiritual being is strictly unimaginable: and in everyday speech unimaginable means impossible. But observe that there are two levels of unimaginability, one that is too high for imagination to reach, one that is too low. It was a jibe, invented in the eighteenth century, that medieval Catholic philosophers wasted their time on idiotic questions like how many angels could stand on the point of a needle. There is no trace of this question in the Middle Ages, yet we spare it a glance ourselves, because it contains what I have called the two levels of unimaginability. Angels are spirits, therefore not in space. But a point has its own sort of negative relation to space too. It has position, say the geometricians, but no magnitude: which is a way of saying that it is in space, but does not occupy space—there is not enough of it. So angel and point have this in common, that both baffle imagination—each represents a different way of not having any "spread"! But whereas the angel, like every spirit, has its own higher existence and operation, a point has neither.

That distinction intellect can see. Yet imagination has so strong a hold upon most of us, until we have finger by finger broken its grip, that to say that a thing is not in space seems exactly the same as to say that it is not at all. We find it so much easier to be sure of the reality of what can be pictured; the picture makes it identifiable, seems not merely to verify, but to constitute, identity. So we almost automatically grow to feel that to exist *means* to occupy space. To this feeling our intellect, which is quite capable of seeing that to exist means to be in the real order, has contributed nothing: we are simply victims of imagination's unceasing propaganda.

For what is space, that we should feel existence unthinkable without it? Forcing ourselves to face this question, we sympathize with St. Augustine, who knew what time was provided you did not ask him. Of course we know what space is, everybody knows what space is. But now we have been asked to *say* what it is, and asked by ourselves. We begin by some such phrase as "sort of," and supplement this with embracing movements of our hands, faintly frantic movements. But "sort of" has no place in a definition, nor have gestures. The plain truth is that space is emptiness. Why should emptiness be

essential to existence? Space is indeed essential if there are
parts to be spread, but is division into parts essential for existence?

This is, after all, the bedrock question. We find it hard to
cope with the notion of a being which contains no element
that is not the whole of it. We can say the words, but nothing
seems to happen in the mind. A being without parts seems as
incapable of *doing* anything as we ourselves would be, if our
arms were somehow fused in with our body, so that they
could not get loose. It is the hardest thing to cure, this sense
that a being with no parts is all wrapped up, incapable of doing anything at all.

Our intellect struggles on to take hold of the idea of simplicity—struggling both against its sheer difficulty as an idea
and against the feeling that it is repugnant to common sense.
Here, as so often, common sense is simply imagination's alias.
We remind ourselves that imagination had been bowed out
before we reach this stage of the discussion. Parts, after all,
only mean dividedness, and why should dividedness be indispensable either for existence or operation? With that question,
intellect has decided the matter. Imagination, calling itself
common sense, may continue the battle. But it is a rearguard
action. Intellect has only to cling on and it must win.

4. Spirit in the New Testament

All this is philosophy. How far is it theology? The Old
Testament may fit with it but certainly does not utter it. Is it
in the New Testament? And how far has the Church made it
her own?

We still have body and flesh, soul and spirit in the New

Testament, but the proportions have changed and the distinctions emerge more clearly. The word "soul" surprises by its rarity, it is not a New Testament key word. We have perhaps been deceived by its use in two of the best known of all texts —Our Lady's "My soul magnifies the Lord, and my spirit rejoices in God my Saviour," and her Son's "My soul is sorrowful even unto death." In the second we do indeed have "soul," *psyche;* but in the Magnificat we haven't: the word is "spirit," *pneuma,* both times. It is the Latin translation which uses "soul" the first time (*anima* linked with another Greek word for wind, *anemos*).

In the Gospel we find the distinction between soul and body—"Do not fear those who can kill the body but cannot kill the soul. Rather fear him that can destroy both soul and body in hell" (Matt. 10.28). We find it also in James: "Whoever brings back a sinner from the error of his ways will save his soul from death" (5.20), and (with a difference) in 1 Peter: "The passions of the flesh wage war against your soul."

But it is not so easy to find it in Paul. He uses the word "soul" barely a dozen times, with no special emphasis: whereas "body" he talks of constantly, close on eighty times, and with very considerable emphasis. He sees it as dangerous if it gets out of control—"I chastise my body and subdue it lest after preaching to others I should myself be disqualified" (1 Cor. 9.27). But not only has he no Platonic contempt for it, he gives it a place in man's approach to God far beyond anything we find in the Old Testament—"Your *bodies* belong to the *body* of Christ," he tells the Colossians (6.15), and a few verses later "Your *bodies* are the temples of the Holy Spirit who dwells in you." A profitable occupation for the student would be the writing out of all Paul's references to the body.

Evidently he accepts the soul in its Old Testament sense of the life-principle of the body. And he takes for granted the separation of soul from body at death and the soul's continuance: "We know that if the earthly tent we live in is destroyed, we have a building from God, a house not made with hands, eternal in the heavens . . . we would rather be away from the body and at home with the Lord" (2 Cor. 5.1,8). But the separation is not final—there will be resurrection.

For Paul, the structure of the human being is not of first interest. To him the division that really matters is not between body and soul, but between flesh and spirit. The word *sarx*, flesh, occurs in his Epistles some ninety times. Unless the context makes it clear that he is talking of flesh in the ordinary sense, he means human nature—either humanity at large, "all flesh," or human nature as men find it in themselves with divine grace wholly necessary to it, even more as it is defiled by sin. Against flesh he places not soul but spirit—which may set us wondering whether we have rightly interpreted Our Lord's word in the Garden of Agony, "The spirit is willing but the flesh is weak." Whether indeed we have given enough thought to "The Word was made flesh."

Spirit is *the* New Testament word. We did not need to wait for computers to work out for us that it occurs nearly four hundred times in the New Testament, that Paul uses it just on one hundred and fifty times. Given that Our Lord had said: "God is spirit, and those who worship him must worship in spirit and truth" (John 4.24), neither Paul nor any other Christian teacher could fail to make spirit central. All Paul does with it we must discuss later. Here we note that his uses of the word fall into three main groups.

First, spirit is the principle of man's higher activities, thinking especially: Paul uses it too for the mind's reactions—the spirit of the world, the spirit of fear, the spirit of stupefaction. *Second* the word is used for the activity in man of the Third Person of the Trinity—"You are eager for spiritual gifts" (1 Cor. 14.12); and two verses later: "If I pray in a tongue my spirit prays, but my mind is unfruitful." (When we come to a fuller discussion, we shall have to consider the great new word *charis*, grace.) *Third*, and supremely, spirit is the Holy Spirit himself, who with Father and Son is God.

Paul does not analyze or define spirit, any more than his Master did, or the other inspired writers of either Testament. Are we entitled to say that it has for them the meaning I have written out in the present chapter? This meaning was already in the air of the New Testament world. The brilliant Jew Philo, studying Plato, had already expressed the nature of spirit in its main lines. And the rabbinical writers would soon be saying that as God is in every part of the universe, the spirit is in every part of the body. As the centuries passed, Augustine and Aquinas were in their turn to develop it. The Church has steadily used it. And Pius X, while he did not define it, gave it official currency when in 1914 he issued a list of "approved" Theses in Thomistic Philosophy.

But *was* this what the New Testament writers meant by "spirit"? Upon the general line, it seems to me that it must have been. It not only fits everything they say: it fits richly, sparklingly. And it is hard to think of any other meaning of spirit which would fit at all.

On one point only the question remains—whether Paul thought *psyche* and *pneuma* two principles or one. We have a single text which sounds as if he made man a triplicity— "May your spirit and soul and body be kept sound and

blameless" (1 Thess. 5.23). For one who accepts the position
I have outlined, it is no more than a way of saying soul and
body, while emphasizing the twofold reality of the human
soul as spirit and as life-principle. Which does not prove that
Paul saw it so—or even regarded the problem in those terms.

5. Making the Concept Our Own

In our effort to make the concept of spirit wholly our own
we must be very leisurely. We must keep on looking at the
relation between having parts and occupying space, until we
find ourselves quite effortlessly seeing that a partless being is
outside space. We must keep on looking at the meaning of
being and the meaning of part till, again quite effortlessly, we
see that such a being must by its concentration be superior in
essence and in operation—that is, in what it is and what it can
do—to those others whose being and operation are dispersed.

Continue to gaze, and we see that it must have a permanent
hold upon what it is, cannot be changed into anything else,
cannot by any natural process be destroyed. And this is the
deepest truth about spirit. Material beings *can* be destroyed
precisely because they have constituent parts: in every piece
of matter there are elements which are not the whole of it:
some of these can be broken away and linked up with parts
similarly broken away from some other piece of matter: and
so endlessly. But to a partless being none of this applies.
Nothing can be taken from it because there is nothing in it
but its whole self. Could not the whole self be taken out of
existence? This would be annihilation. But just as only God
can create from nothing—by willing a being to exist: so only
God can reduce a being to nothing—by willing it to exist no

longer; and for the human soul God has told us that there is everlasting joy or everlasting failure, but no suggestion of annihilation.

A spiritual being, therefore, cannot lose its identity. It can gain new knowledge, or lose what it has, it can transfer its love from this object to that; if it is a human soul, it can develop its power over matter, or the body it has been animating can cease to respond to its animating power with bodily death resulting: but all such changes leave it its identity. It remains itself, conscious of itself, permanent in the flux of things, indeed by memory dominating the flux and bringing the parts under tribute, casting its hold forward over the future.

I have said that intellect has only to cling on and it must win. But the battle is not soon won, perhaps never totally here below. Imagination is tireless. What, after all, is there to tire it? Space comes creeping back. We must be rigorous in exorcising it, keeping it to where it belongs. And we shall not get much co-operation. Everybody finds it so much easier to denature spiritual reality by reducing it to spatial terms. In our reading of theology, for instance, we shall meet the phrase "stain of original sin." The phrase is poetry, and one who already knows the doctrine of original sin will know exactly why it was used. But in our effort to understand, which involves freeing the understanding from imagination's usurping tendency, we cannot be trusted with poetry just yet. A stain is a discoloration, a color which happens to be the wrong color in that particular place; but color means place, means space, means "spread," and the soul, not occupying space, is no suitable ground for discoloration.

By positive effort we shall come to realize that our "need" for space is a trick that imagination has worked upon us.

Imagination needs space, because it makes pictures, and pictures need space. But intellect does not. Indeed once intellect gets into its own stride, it finds that space does not help but baffles. The philosopher, asking questions, finds space too empty of meaning to be coped with satisfactorily; quite literally it is harder to *understand* than spacelessness. The reason why imagination can take it so easily is that it asks no questions, but only makes pictures.

Once a man sees this, he has crossed one of the great divides. He has passed from the world of habit and routine into the world of the philosopher. He is in that world, if only barely and as yet precariously. To make himself at home in it, to move at ease in it, skills have to be acquired; from the use of the skills new mental habits are formed, almost a new mind. While these truths about spirit exist only as a set of teachings seen as valid by the intellect, they can drift into the back of the mind and be ultimately lost. But once they are so built in that the intellect sees by them and operates by them, lives with them so profoundly that the universe would be unthinkable without them, it arrives at an intimacy with the idea of spirit deeper than words or even concepts can express. In moments of inattention or fatigue, space can still occasionally break in where it does not belong, but it cannot maintain its position, the mind's habits have become too strong for it.

Spirit has then become an essential element in our mental world. We not only accept it but rejoice in it. There is an exhilaration, for instance, in the realization of Einstein's mind —a kind of monster machine, producing thoughts which change the world, yet still a spirit, partless, spaceless, one single act of being: it has no inside or outside, yet worlds of activity are happening within it—*whatever* "within" may mean of a spirit. And one of these partless, spaceless machines each one of us has, however reluctant or flabby and ineffective our use of it. And our being and operation can no more be explained without spirit than can Einstein's. Or God's.

FOUR

Theology and Revelation

Theology is the revelation of God
      explored by men
      with God's aid.

Revelation—the word means drawing back the veil—is God's communication of Himself to men. He is the Mystery: before the Mystery stand men, impotent to penetrate It: but with a God-given capacity to be drawn by Him within It.

How does God draw back the veil? By what he does, by what he says. "The economy of revelation is brought about by deeds and words," says the Second Vatican Council, "which are intrinsically related in such a way that the works (performed by God in the history of salvation) show forth and support the teaching and the reality signified by the words; the words, however, proclaim the works and throw light upon the mystery proclaimed in them." (*De Revelatione*, Ch. 1.)

As it happens, we do not find the Old Testament speaking of God's "works" as revealing; but in them he does in fact show himself. Yet without his "words" to "throw light upon the Mystery proclaimed in the works" there could be vast difference of opinion as to what is being proclaimed; without the "words" we could not know with certainty what the "works" are telling us. But the "works" give depth to the "words" and a sense of personal contact with God.

God reveals, draws back the veil, because he wants men to know the truth—about himself primarily, about themselves and the meaning of life consequently. For precisely the same reason, God watches over its exploration. To reveal, and then leave men with nothing but their best guess as to all that is contained in his communication, would frustrate his purpose in revealing. The inability of human language to settle once for all, to exclude all possibility of misunderstanding, means that just as we cannot know revelation save with God's aid, we cannot explore its meaning, settle definitively what God is showing us, save with his aid.

To take a couple of immediate examples out of thousands—the words "when Adam had lived 130 years, he became the father of a son in his own likeness" (Gen. 5.3) were taken by many to mean that he had previously begotten beings *not* in his own likeness, of a different nature, un-men. Again, the second-century heretic Marcion, who wanted to exclude the Old Testament, commented on the words of the voice from the cloud when Moses and Elias conversed with Christ on the Mount of Transfiguration, "This is my beloved Son . . . hear ye him": he insisted that the word *him* was emphasized, and that the whole point was to warn against listening to Moses and Elias.

God's desire to be known by us has at all times to cope with the marvellous ingenuity of the questing, discovering, uttering mind of man.

1. Doctrine and Impact

"Going teach all nations . . . teaching them to observe whatever I have commanded you, and I am with you always to the end of the world" (Matt. 28.19–20). The words read lucidly, but they have not shed the same light for all. There are those, more numerous perhaps a few years ago, who think that Christ did not say them, that they are the product of the Early Church's reflection upon Christ, and upon itself as heir in possession. Christians of other communions have generally seen the words as addressed uniquely to the Apostles. A very able statement of the case against seeing the Apostles as the first holders of an office that was to be continuous has recently been made by Oscar Cullmann in *Peter Disciple, Apostle, Martyr;* Otto Karrer replied in *Peter and the Church*—these two small books are a model of ecumenical conversation. Our own discussion of the problem must await Volume Two. At this stage my concern is to show the Catholic view of the Teaching Church as answering the question how Christ's revelation is to be preserved and explored and spread among men.

In this view Christ did not found a religion only, he founded a Church: and not only a worshipping Church, but a body of men through which he himself could carry on his own work —praying, suffering, offering, with teaching as basic, since without the teaching we should not know to whom we were praying and offering or what was the point of our suffering.

To teach does not mean simply to report the deeds and repeat the words accurately, though indeed there is a sort of vitality in the very words in which revealed truth has come to us, a vitality unlike any other, a power as of dynamite. To teach means to help men to see deeper into their meaning and unpack the reality concentrated in them. The words themselves are only a first step in a continuous process of unveiling. Phrases like "I am" with which God named himself to Moses; like "God is a spirit" with which Our Lord answered the Samaritan Woman at the well; like "God is love" and "God is light"—twin phrases in which John utters the ultimate truth of Godhead—these and a score of others are rich in uttered reality, yet they do not instantly communicate any considerable portion of the reality that is in them.

If the Church is to teach such things, she must herself see what is being said, which means that she must grow in understanding. This growing involves, primarily, that her members should live them—Our Lord has said: "He that keeps the commandments shall know of the doctrine whether it is from God or I am speaking on my own authority" (John 7.17). She must relate them to one another, one truth casting light upon another's darkness. She must relate them to the human situation—as civilization grows, the truths find new applications, which cast new light upon their own meanings: we see deeper into anything when we can watch it in operation. And she must relate what God has said in words—through Prophets, and the Word Incarnate, and Apostles—to what God has shown of himself in his *works*. The "words" she is handling are not the fruit of human thinking and praying, they are given by God.

What the Church sees of the meanings and applications of what was originally given, she must utter so that men may gain more and more of the light that is in it. She knows that God has uttered unutterable realities. Yet uttered them he has; and utterance, which brought them to birth, continues to operate in their growth. What the Church has come to see with God's aid she must try to cast into statements, because that is the normal way of communicating among men. Because of what human nature is, saying is necessary, and trying to say an ineradicable instinct. It is a truth-bearing instinct too, for words are not meant to be dead wrappings, they have light in themselves, and energies.

Yet we are capable of a kind of impatience with statement and proposition, God seems so much more than words can convey or even contain. What really matters, we find ourselves telling ourselves, is the impact revelation makes upon us, not mere accuracy in phrases necessarily inadequate.

Let us pause upon "impact." Some such experience is essential, of course. If there is no impact, nothing has happened; but if there is only impact, we do not know what has hit us. God communicates with the whole man—man as knowing; man as loving or hating, as deciding for or against; man as picturing; man as feeling. That God's purpose in revealing may be achieved, every element in man must in some way respond. And underlying these special responses there is an effect upon the whole self which is more than the sum of the separate effects; it is a reaction not only to God revealing but to God himself, a reaction in fact of man simply being, to God simply being.

Properly speaking, each separate element should receive

impact, as revelation produces the response appropriate to the element affected. The impact on man as knowing is light— seeing which flows into utterance which flows into further seeing. . . . The end intended by God for all men is the Beatific Vision, the direct seeing of himself which gives bliss. Naturally the activity which is to be the foundation of all our life hereafter begins here, since the life of heaven is a continuation of the life of earth, a flowering towards which here on earth we are growing. As Scripture reminds us, we must walk in the light, not simply stumble along in the dark knowing that we shall one day see.

Seeing, which for our spirit means knowing, is conditioned by two gaps. The first is between feeling, sensing, half-intuiting, glimpsing—and actually seeing. So that there is always more in our reaction to reality than we can see, our judgments, choices, decisions are affected by factors in ourselves we are not aware of. And then comes a more continually irritating gap, that between what we see and what we can say. God we see as in a glass darkly (1 Cor. 13.12): and we *say* more darkly still. And these limitations apply to all our seeing and saying, not only of God but of things and men—ourselves as darkly as any. Yet we must try to see and try to say —God wants it, something in ourselves, the selves God made us to be, wants it.

Yet how preferable mere impact *seems*. As the word is used, impact can mean feeling good, or feeling religious; better, it can mean feeling the goodness of goodness, feeling how good it would be to be good. Even at these levels, which are by no means the highest it can attain, it is excellent. At its highest it is overwhelming but still only an element. Yet it has certain immediate advantages.

There is a luxury in simply sensing, vibrating: thinking and uttering call for so much effort. And utterance does bind us, limiting our freedom to speculate as mere impact does not. Not only that. Once it is put into words, a doctrine exposes its limitations as it does not when merely vibrated to: impact almost *feels* infinite, it does not cry out its inadequacy as utterance does. Compared with the infinite and the absolute, the phrases we arrive at seem so slight that we are tempted to think that we serve religion, serve our own union with God, by avoiding statement and proposition altogether. Teaching seems shallow in such moods. But Christ Our Lord did say Go and teach.

As I have already noted, the propositions are shallower than God, but they are not shallower than we, and by them we can move out of our shallows. As Newman says in his *University Sermons*, "Nothing would indicate a more shallow philosophy than to say that faith ought carefully to be distinguished from dogmatic and argumentative statements." The motto he chose *Cor ad cor loquitur*, Heart speaks to heart, meant more than conversation by heart-beats: "loquitur" was not the word to choose for the exclusion of words.

Allied to this recoil from words is a strange misuse of language by which whatever has not effects direct and obvious in the material order is called "abstract," and with that word dismissed! One finds writers, I mean writers who know better, applying the word to the Trinity—which is as though the image found the original abstract; to "pure contemplation"—which, if it is anything, is direct contact with Supreme Reality; to the Divinity of Christ ("a metaphysical abstract"); to a pure spirit. Recently I jotted down the phrase "not abstract to be thought but vital to be lived"; one sees what is meant, but how strange a phrasing: it recalls the fatuous

"Deeds not words": as if words could not be deeds, as if vital living excluded thought. I think it was Goethe who deified mindlessness with his rewriting of the opening words of the Fourth Gospel—"In the beginning was the deed." Which reminds us that "the word of God" is all over the Old Testament; and the use of "word" is not for nothing. We cannot interpret it as meaning everything *but* word: whatever else the phrase means, it cannot mean that words have not an essential place in our approach to God, and his to us. I remember my unholy joy when I came upon the text of Amos —"They abhor him who *speaks* the truth"(5.10). Amos, of course, put the accent on "truth," not "speaks." The attack upon verbal utterance was perhaps not so intense or continuous in his day.

"We must be ready always to give an account of the hope that is in us to any man that asks" (1 Peter 3.15). It would be pleasanter, perhaps, just to share our vibrations with a questioner. But there is no great gain in it. Teaching involves communicating our knowledge of reality. That must be left to produce its own vibrations in the learner. "I thank God that I speak in tongues more than you all; nevertheless in church I would rather speak five words with my mind in order to instruct others than ten thousand words in a tongue" (1 Cor. 14.18–19).

2. The Relation Between Scripture and the Teaching Church

Into the Church at its beginning the Apostles brought what Christ had given them. There is something mysterious in one thing he said to them about this: "I have still much to say to you, but it is beyond your reach as yet. It will be for him, the truth-giving Spirit, when he comes, to guide you into all truth." (John 16.12) Did the phrase "I have still much to say to you" mean only that he would teach the rest through the Holy Spirit? Or had he in mind the teaching he would give after his Resurrection? Unlike the earlier teaching, not much of this has come down to us; but it must have been more important, since the Apostles would have brought the experience of Calvary and Easter into their listening, and they would have built it into the structure of the Church's mind.

The combination of things taught them, things still to be taught them, and things still dark which the Holy Spirit would lead them to see, constitutes the body of truth committed to them for the instruction of the world. They were taught it, and trained others to teach it, and the Church founded upon them has taught it ever since. The First Vatican Council distinguished between them and all the Church's later teachers: "The Holy Spirit was promised to the successors of Peter not that by His revelations they should lay open any new doctrine, but that by His assistance they should hold sacred and faithfully expound the revelation given into their hands (*traditum*) by the Apostles, which is the Deposit of Faith."

Can we, now, lay hands on this "Deposit"—the mass of truths committed to the Apostles, the "whatsoever I have commanded you"? Can we isolate it, look at it as they possessed it? To answer this question we must look more closely at what the New Testament is, as part of the larger problem of what Scripture is. Given that so much depends for us upon what Scripture contains, we must bring the whole force of our mind to bear upon what Scripture *is* and why it has such *authority*. Merely to accept Scripture, however wholeheartedly—because it is there, or because Christians always have, or because it would seem irreverent to expose our acceptance of God's word to question—or because we ourselves have gained so much from reading so much of it—means that whatever we may build upon it has an insecure foundation. The foundation must be as secure in our own minds as it is in Scripture itself. Otherwise we shall fall into two errors—either making it bear more weight than it was built to bear, or seeing it crumble under weights it could bear perfectly well. On this last point one remembers the shock given to many a devout believer by Mark Twain's ferocious attack on the God of Scripture in *Letters From the Earth*.

So we look at Scripture.

When scientific discoveries are made which revolutionize our mental picture of the universe and leave almost nothing standing of the picture that was in the mind of the men who wrote Scripture, scholars of all faiths remind us that Scripture is not a manual of science. We need constantly to remind ourselves that it is not a manual of theology either—not the Old Testament obviously, not even the New Testament. Both are concerned with the dealings of God with men and with men's varied responses. But not one of the writers sets out to give an ordered statement of any single area of revelation—God, or human life, or redemption, or sin, or the world to come. Newman reminds us, in *Discussions and Arguments*, that we shall not find the doctrine of the Blessed Trinity, for instance, "brought out in form upon the surface of Scripture." And this is so, in a general way anyhow, of all the great truths of revelation.

Where, in the New Testament, should we look for any full and formal statement of the totality of Christ's teaching?

Not in the Gospels, if we consider what they are—four accounts of the Redeemer, all four building up to the climax of the redeeming act, Passion and Death and Resurrection. (Roughly one third of the total is devoted to a single week, from Palm Sunday to Easter.) That is the Good News. That is their topic. What I have called the building up treats (apart from two swift glances at Christ's conception and infancy) of the couple of years of the public ministry, a handful of things done by Christ and things said, chosen by each evangelist for their aptness to the purpose he had in writing. They give a certain amount of his teaching—Mark less than the others.

Pause upon Mark. He sees Christ as Teacher and wants us to see him so. He records close on a dozen occasions on which he was addressed as Teacher; and he tells of the astonishment his teaching caused, without giving a word of the teaching which so astonished them. The other three give more than Mark; but such teachings as they record are, quantitatively at least, moral more than doctrinal. If we were to group together all the doctrinal teaching recorded in the Gospels as given by Christ, it could be written out in very few pages.

Matthew tells us "Jesus went about all Galilee teaching in their synagogues" (4.23), but we are not given the content of these teachings. We remember, of course, what happened in the synagogue of his own Nazareth, when he drove his hearers to such fury that they wanted to kill him—"they brought him to the brow of the hill on which their city was built, that they might cast him down headlong" (Luke 4.29). We are told what it was that so infuriated them—he talked of miracles worked by Elias and Eliseus for Gentiles: but we are not told what explanation he may have given for this new and revolutionary emphasis upon Gentiles.

There is, as we have just noted, the same silence about the teaching—decisive of the whole content and shape of the teaching his Church was to take to the ends of the earth and to the end of the ages—which Christ gave in the forty days between his Resurrection and his Ascension. Luke tells us at the beginning of Acts that "throughout the course of forty days he had been appearing to them and telling them about the kingdom of God"; but there is no detail given of what he told them on these appearances or of the questions they must have asked (apart from the question of when!), and the answers he must have given. In the last chapter of his Gospel Luke tells how Christ rebuked the two disciples on the road to Emmaus for their "slowness of heart," their failure to find in the prophets that "it was necessary that Christ should suffer these things and enter into his glory" (Luke 24.25–6). If only Luke had told us in what way Christ established it as "necessary." To this day men wrestle with the problem *how* Christ's death could redeem the human race—what the connection is between his suffering and our salvation.

Of the apparent meagerness of the space allotted in the Gospels to doctrines which were to change the world, the explanation is obvious enough—the Gospels were not written as a first introduction to Christianity, a beginners' course. In the opening of his Gospel, Luke tells Theophilus of his purpose in writing—"that you may understand *the instruction you have already received* in all its certainty" (Knox); "that you may know the truth concerning *the things of which you have been informed*" (Revised Standard Version).

The italicized phrases vary according to whether or not the

translator sees Theophilus as already received into the Church. The Jerusalem Bible takes the first reading, allowing for the other possibility in a footnote. But all accept that what Luke was to write had some link with prior knowledge in the reader, whether Theophilus was an actual person or the devout reader in general.

Certainly, all the new Christians had received a basic instruction in the truths of the Faith they had embraced, just as all proselytes to the Jewish religion received one (Père Prat notes that it included the story of Creation and the Fall). And the instructions continued. Not only the Evangelists, but all the New Testament writers assume that their readers had already been instructed. Paul, who had himself checked his teaching with James and Cephas and John (Gal. 2.2, 9)— "lest somehow I should be running or had run in vain"— could say to the Galatians: "If any one is preaching to you a gospel contrary to that which you received, let him be anathema." He reminds the Corinthians of teachings he had given them on Christ's Resurrection and on the Eucharist when he was with them (1 Cor. 11.23; 15.3). He urges Timothy to "keep to the pattern of sound doctrine you have heard *from my lips*" and the Thessalonians to "stand firm and hold to the traditions which you were taught by us, either *by word of mouth* or by letter." Jude reminds his readers of "what the apostles of our Lord Jesus Christ said to you" (verse 17).

That there was a basic instruction—Père Benoit calls it a "primitive catechesis" (*Exégèse et Théologie*, pp. 39–40)— the Epistles take for granted; and how considerable it was we can see if we try to reconstruct what the catechesis must have been which would make Paul, for instance, feel that he could assume so much doctrinal knowledge in his readers.

But of that basic instruction we have no formal record—it would be wonderful if Luke had given us an account of Paul checking his teaching with James and Cephas and John. The nearest one gets to a "syllabus" is a half-dozen headings of the "First Lessons in Christ" given at the beginning of Hebrews as already received—penance from dead works, faith towards God, baptisms, laying on of hands, the resurrection of the dead, eternal judgment. It is a splendid list, but it does not tell us what was taught under each heading, and it does not pretend to completeness—Christ himself is not listed!

That there was a unifying force at the center of the new Church is clear, and obviously it was not only a negative force, a censorship: it guarded the truths committed, and it watched over the development in their understanding. That it was powerful and immensely effective we can tell, if only from the fact that Paul could write to Churches he had never visited, Rome most notably, with the certainty that what he wrote would be in harmony with what they had been taught.

The Apostles continued to govern the Church and to carry on their teaching mission: they had been trained by Our Lord for that. But there is no record of their meeting, save for the settling of two problems—the election of a man to fill the place left vacant by Judas, and the decision how far the Mosaic law was binding upon Gentile converts. We not only have no record of the ordinary meetings of the Twelve (still the Twelve, even after Judas left them—Matthias was not elected to no purpose at all); we have no record even of a meeting between any two of the Twelve to discuss the teachings which had been entrusted to them, as to no other men, for the nourishing and healing of the whole world.

We have what has come to be called the *Kerygma*,[1] the announcement of the good news of salvation, in brief summaries of sermons preached by Peter at the very beginning to men not yet Christian, most of them never to be Christian; but in the whole New Testament there is no reporting of what any Apostle preached to believers. An outline of the sermon Paul preached to the women of Philippi would be priceless, to say nothing of the sermon at Troas which went on so long that Eutychus fell asleep—it may well have contained more words than all Paul's Epistles put together. Even if we had these sermons, we should still not have all that Christ committed to his Church: they, like all that he wrote and all that the Evangelists wrote, would have assumed that as already known.

It may be worth while to state a principle which will seem obvious as one states it, but which is frequently ignored in practice. *What a writer assumes that his readers know is a constituent part of his book.* He does not put it into words, but everything he does put into words draws meaning from it. To the extent that we do not know the content of the instruction given to the new Christian, we are hampered in our understanding of what the New Testament writers are telling him. To ignore it altogether, and proceed as though what is actually written is the whole message, would be great folly. The Evangelists are concerned with developing and enriching the understanding of what their readers already know.

[1] Read Acts 2.14–36, 3.12–16, 4.8–12, 5.29–32, 10.34–43. Note also Paul's sermon at Antioch of Pisidia, 13.16–44.

It is much the same with St. Paul. As the *Bible de Jéru-salem* says (p. 1483), we must never forget that the Epistles Paul has left us are "occasional writings, not theological trea-tises but responses to concrete situations." He writes of ele-ments in the doctrine which had been misunderstood or even denied in this place or that; he writes of elements on which he has either clarifications to offer, because he has wrestled in anguish with them, or new richness to offer, because he has been caught up in ecstasy over them. But there is no synthesis stated, no general framework—these he assumes, just as John does, and Peter, and the rest: they were not writing to be read apart from the synthesis, outside the framework.

Nor is there any effort to include everything. Had it been Paul's first Letter to the Corinthians which was lost, instead of a later one to the same Church, scholars would be affirm-ing that he knew nothing of the Real Presence. We may be grateful to these, our ancestors in the Faith, whose misbe-havior at Mass caused him to write so splendidly on the mystery they were profaning (1 Cor. 11.17–33).

Books written to meet actual situations are bound to be more "vibrant," to have more flavor, more tang of reality, than the more orderly statement of doctrine in its totality: just as studies of individual patients make livelier reading than medical text books. But for the guidance of life, medically or religiously, we need the formal statement, we need the syn-thesis.

The abiding question for us is whether the Catholic syn-thesis is in fact the one that was present in the mind of the New Testament writers, the one they were assuming as pres-ent in the mind of those first Christians for whom they were writing, without which much of what they wrote could not

convey their message. We have already considered this matter in relation to Spirit, we shall consider it more in depth in
relation to the Trinity, and we shall see how it applies to
other doctrines as we come to them.

The immediate question is how much of what Christ committed to the Apostles emerges above the surface of the New
Testament. There is no *a priori* reason why any particular
element should—only if someone was being wrong about it,
or the writer's mind had just caught fire from it. We may feel
within ourselves a certainty that all God wants us to know is
to be found there, if some of it only implicitly. Scripture does
not say this, nor does the Church. Yet so much does emerge,
that at least we can feel that God, as well as inspiring each
individual writer, was in some way making himself respon-
sible for the whole—I mean for the wholeness of the whole.

In the light of all this, there are two reasons why we do not
appeal to Scripture to prove Catholic doctrines true. The first
is that that is not Scripture's way with doctrine. The writers
were not (save occasionally) trying to prove the doctrine or
even to state it, but only clarifying and developing and drawing consequences from truths already known and accepted
by their readers. What we *can* do is find out how far such
statements as they do find cause to make are in harmony with
Catholic teaching as a totality.

The second reason is that Christ has already guaranteed
what in his name and in his power his Church teaches. We are
thus under no pressure to force Scripture to support any given
doctrine: our sole purpose is to find out what Scripture is
saying: only if Scripture says something that we cannot see
how to reconcile with our doctrine are we aware of challenge.
We read Scripture to give the doctrine a special kind of life

in us, for the great shafts of light it casts for us, above all for the sense it gives of God close to us.

The men who knew Our Lord, and the men who knew them have a unique quality in their writing. We feel him in them as nowhere else. The work of clarification and deepening of the mind's vision has gone on through the centuries; but theirs is the unique and irreplaceable foundation. It would be folly to read only the Gospel, ignoring the Acts and the Epistles as less immediate, the kind of folly of the Sadducees who would accept nothing but the Books of Moses. But it would be folly also to read only Scripture, ignoring all that has flowed into and from the mind of the Church in all the years since—as though no mind had ever worked fruitfully on God and his revelation once the Apostles were gone, as though the Holy Spirit had worked in no mind from then till now, as though the same Word which gave the revelation to begin with has not continued to guard its interpretation by his Church but has simply let it take its chance.

3. *Why We Accept Scripture*

There is but one source of revelation, God. His revelation flows to us through various channels, Prophets and the God-man, Apostles and Evangelists. We have the phrase two *fontes* of revelation, Tradition and Scripture, which is occasionally taken to mean two *sources:* but though *fons* can mean a source, it can also mean a fountain, springing from a source. We have been considering Scripture. Let us concentrate upon the New Testament.

There are twenty-seven books in it, bearing the names of five of the twelve Apostles, Matthew, John, Peter, James the

Lesser, Jude—as written by them or at least in some sense
originating in them; also the name of Paul, as his or from him;
and of Mark and Luke who had close intimacy, one with
Peter, one with Paul.

Evidently the five knew more than is written here. When
Paul and John met, they had more to say to each other than
Paul could write to the Corinthians or John to the Lady
Electa. And they must have taught more than is written here.
Paul surely wrote more than the dozen letters we have in the
twenty years of his Christian life (we actually know of one
or two now lost) and there was his preaching. Then there
are the seven whose voice has not reached us. It would be
strange if nothing had poured into the Church from them. It
has, of course. They helped to make the Church the concrete
reality it is. Every one of us is affected by Peter's brother
Andrew and John's brother James, and Philip and Bartholomew and Simon Zelotes and Thomas and Matthias. In that
sense what they had to give is truly part of what Christ committed to his Church, though it has not come down to us
traceably. Apostolicity means among other things, or above
other things, that they have bequeathed us their vital experience of Christ and of God revealed in Christ. What we have
in the New Testament is what Christ gave them as it flowed
into writing and has been preserved for us.

How do we know that the New Testament contains the
inspired record of the Apostolic teaching, contains it as no
other book does? The New Testament does not say so. Indeed it says nothing of itself as a *New* Testament, a continuation of the Old, nothing of its own superb adequacy. In plain
fact it shows no awareness of itself at all. It does not contain

a list of its own contents. No book of the New Testament refers explicitly to another, save only 2 Peter, which combines a tribute and a warning about one particular letter of St. Paul (2 Thessalonians, perhaps) and "all his letters": "There are passages in them difficult to understand; and these, like the rest of Scripture, are twisted into a wrong sense by ignorant and restless minds, to their own undoing." It sounds like what would now be called a Papal Monitum.

It is the Church that guarantees the New Testament to us; she alone tells us that it is inspired. She has been accused of teaching things not in Scripture: this at least, the inspiration of the New Testament, is certainly not there. We accept the New Testament books, their authority and their inspiration, on the word of the Church—the Word in his Church testifying to the Word in his Scripture.

Yet people do accept the New Testament, and indeed the whole of the Bible, who do not believe in a Church which has the authority thus to constitute and guarantee it. I happen never to have met anyone who has come to accept Scripture from zero. Most people have in fact received it from the Church, but at one remove. Their ancestors brought the certainty of Scripture's inspiration with them when they broke from Rome, and the certainty has been simply accepted through the generations, till they find themselves reading it in the light of Christ's teaching as it has been given them by their own Church—and finding it good. There is a natural tendency to build everything on this last, "finding it good," and to forget the rest.

And the goodness found in it is very powerful. If no question were ever raised, it might very well suffice. Certainly it was easier to accept Scripture in the power of it when in-

spiration was simply taken to mean God using a man, as a
player might use a plectrum to pluck music from the strings
of his instrument. But the questions have begun, and have
mounted to a whirlwind. And the Christian may find that he
is basing a belief so immense simply upon the effect Scripture
produces upon himself, thus making himself the test.

So he is forced to analyze. He may base everything upon
an overwhelming sense of the spiritual genius of the authors.
As I have seen it expressed, God touches us in Scripture as he
touches us in all great literature. Yet this means that Scripture is inspiring, but not that it is inspired. It is much the same
with those who place their certainty in the value of the message. Standards of value change from age to age, and it would
be hard in any event to judge from the value we find in any
book that only God could have inspired the writer. To com-
plicate our judgment, we cannot help finding different levels
of value—from almost infinite to almost nil—in different parts
of Scripture, just as we find some of the writers—Amos, for
instance, and John, and Paul—a great deal more "valuable"
than most of the others.

There is more than a hint of subjectivity in all this, of which
a man might well grow conscious when the challenge is strong.
There is a movement towards objectivity in finding Scripture
"verified" in one's own day by day experience. This judgment
has force in the moral order, but less obviously in the order of
revealed truth: who has *experienced* the Blessed Trinity? Or
the life after death? Or the mind of God as it purposed this
universe and brought it into being? And indeed one sometimes finds that the inspiration in which belief is "experienced"
is diminished to a point that would have startled Luther or
Calvin. As that towering Congregationalist scholar, Dr. Dodd,

has phrased it: "When we observe that the thing they (the prophets) think they receive from God acts creatively in human life . . . then we may fairly conclude that they are not wholly self-deceived in thinking so" (*The Authority of the Bible*, p. 252).[2] Dr. Dodd's book is a brilliant statement of reasons for accepting Scripture which do not include the Church's teaching about it.

For a very different belief in the inspiration and the authority of Scripture we note the words of St. Augustine, himself a man of no mean spiritual genius: "The plain truth is that I would not believe the Gospel unless the authority of the Catholic Church impelled me" (*Contra Epist. Manichaei* V.21.6). This may not be "the plain truth," but rather the truth with one element emphasized: Scripture *does* need the support of an authority other than our own response to it.

And yet how glorious Scripture is, all unsupported.

4. The Word in His Church and the Word in Scripture

By the end of the first century the New Testament was complete and the last Apostle was dead. It was the end of an age, the age of personal contact with the Christ of this earth. Did men feel it so? Are we to imagine them as counting the Apostles, as one after another they died? Saying at last, "There's only John left"? And at his death breathing an almost desperate "Thank God, we still have their writings"? There is nothing whatever in the New Testament to suggest this. It tells of the death of James, and nothing could be more matter of fact than the mention of it in Acts. If the death of

[2] New York, Harper, Torchbooks, 1958.

any other caused a ripple at the time of its happening, it has never reached us. Everything goes to show that to those early Christians and their children and grandchildren, the Church was what mattered, for the Church was a society of men living in Christ, in-lived by the Holy Spirit. It was what St. Paul had called it to Timothy, "the pillar and the ground of truth."

The Church had been born of Christ on Calvary, baptized in the Holy Ghost and in fire at Pentecost. When we meet it in Acts—nourished by the Blessed Eucharist, nourished too by the Old Testament but not by the still unwritten New Testament—it is already the Church we know. We can recognize the character, temper, tendencies, muscularity, certainty, ways of receiving light and food, digesting and assimilating. By the time the last Apostle died, the Church was in its sixties, and it was already itself, so that today's Catholic feels totally at home in it. Reading St. Paul's criticisms we find "the primitive Church" only too much like the Church as we know it ourselves, its closeness in time to its Founder has not conferred the perfection on it that we might have expected.

At any rate its personality was established—the incommunicable, unpinpointable something which, in the Church as in the individual, is ultimately decisive. "It has seemed good to the Holy Ghost and to us," said the Apostles gathered in Jerusalem (Acts 15.28). "If certain persons should be disobedient to the word spoken by him through us," wrote Clement, Bishop of Rome, to the Church at Corinth in St. John's last years.

The Apostles had gone, the Church remained, the New Testament remained. How early did they see the New Testament as *Scripture*, comparable with the Old? In 2 Peter 3.16, we find St. Paul's Epistles linked up with "the rest of Scripture." But there seems to have been no instant recognition that there were now two Testaments. After all, the Gospels contain no hint that Our Lord had told his Apostles to write— they were to *go* and teach all nations—"Be witnesses to me ... to the ends of the earth" (Acts 1.8). Even the Apostles' Creed, developed from one used in Rome in mid-second century, goes straight from the Holy Ghost to the Holy Catholic Church, without mention of Scripture.

It probably dawned upon men only slowly that the Church had one more treasure—not only written by men close to Christ, but inspired by God, true Scripture. Round the middle of the second century—say sixty years after John's death— St. Justin Martyr tells us in his First Apology, "The Apostles, in the memoirs composed by them which are called Gospels, have handed down to us what Jesus had thus enjoined on them"; and he adds, "These memoirs are read together with the Prophets at worship on Sundays." (Justin's disciple Tatian made a "Harmony" exclusively from our own four Gospels.)

In the second half of the second century we get the inspiration of the new writing stated fairly clearly by St. Irenaeus. And in the document found by the Italian scholar Muratori we find practically the whole of our present New Testament listed. This takes us to somewhere between 180 and 200: for our whole New Testament we must wait another century or more after that. As Dr. Trevor Jalland says (in his Bampton Lectures, *The Church and the Papacy*[3]): "It was not till towards the close of the second century that a collection of Christian writings came to possess a generally acknowledged canonical status." It was a hundred years after its last book

[3] Napier, Ill., Allenson, 1944.

was written that the New Testament was accepted by the whole Church for what it is, its contents fairly completely established. Not till then did the practice begin of quoting it in support of disputed doctrinal positions—two doctrines to receive the new treatment were Trinity and Papacy.

There were now two, an infallible Church and an inspired New Testament. No one asked Why two?—so clear was it that they were different ways of enriching men's contact with one same Redeemer and Teacher: as Dr. Jalland says: "Among the criteria by which the claim of a particular document to canonization was judged, was included that of conformity with a pre-existing body of doctrine." And there was no sense of rivalry, of either-or. Nor should there be. The question is not whether men get revealed truth from the Church or from Scripture any more than whether they get Sanctifying Grace from the Church or from the Sacraments—which themselves are also ways of contact with Christ. Church and New Testament are simply two energizings of the one Word and the Spirit he sent.

So Christ, living and functioning in the Church, is living and functioning in the New Testament. The Word in the Church presents us with himself in the Scripture, the Word in the Church guaranteeing through the Spirit the revelation of himself written under the inspiration of the Spirit. The Church is not the custodian of a library, but the wielder of a sword, the sword of the Spirit which is the word of God.

FIVE

The Inspiration of Scripture

"All Scripture inspired of God" was St. Paul's phrase (2 Tim. 3.15). He uses a new Greek word, *theopneustos*, God-breathed—*pneustos* being from *pneuma*, the word Our Lord used for the Holy Spirit.

1. Inspiration Defined

What does Inspiration mean? The Old Testament constantly has God moving men to do his will—the actual word "inspired" is not, I think, used in this context. He moves them to action and speech. We hear David saying, "The Spirit of the Lord speaks by me, his word is upon my tongue" (2 Kings 23.2). What of writing? We have Moses (Exod. 17.14 and 34.27), Isaiah (8.1), Jeremiah (30.2), Habakkuk (2.2) commanded to write, but to write things already revealed or

commanded by God. Of inspiration to write, inspiration flowing straight into writing, we do not find mention in the Old
Testament.

Nor is the command to write explicitly attributed to the
Spirit of God. Upon this last point the New Testament is
clearer. Of the first verse of Psalm 110 Our Lord says, "David
in the Spirit calls him Lord." Of Isaiah 6, 9–10 Paul says (Acts
28.25), "The Holy Spirit was right in saying to your fathers
through Isaiah the prophet. . . ." And, in 2 Corinthians 6.16,
with the words "God said" he introduces not a particular
passage from the Old Testament but a conflation of things
written in Leviticus, Ezekiel, Isaiah and Hosea. The clearest
statement of all is "No prophecy ever came by the impulse of
man, but men moved by the Holy Spirit spoke from God"
(2 Peter 1.20)—this given as the reason why "No prophecy
of Scripture is a matter of one's own interpretation." Late in
the second century Theophilus of Antioch said that the writers
were "spirit-borne and spoke by the Spirit of God."

Given Paul's determination to free the Church from the
detail of the Mosaic Law, we might have expected the Old
Testament to be relegated to an inferior level of inspiration,
but neither by him nor by the Church as a whole was this
even hinted at. Marcion, who wanted the Old Testament and
its God thrust out of Christianity, was declared a heretic. The
first "official" list of canonical books, issued by the Council
of Carthage in 397, names the Old Testament books without
comment, as a matter of course.

For the appearance of Inspiration in an official document
of the teaching Church we must wait till 1441. In the
Decretum pro Jacobitis, the Council of Florence says: "One
same God is author of Old Testament and New, that is of the

Law and the Prophets and the Gospel, since the Holy Men of each Testament spoke under the inspiration of the same Holy Spirit"—*eodem sancto Spirtu inspirante.* A century later the Council of Trent has *Spiritu Sancto dictante*—this last word we may translate "prompting," not "dictating" certainly.

But of what Inspiration is, there is no explanation of this official sort by the teaching Church until the nineteenth century. The First Vatican Council begins by dismissing a couple of insufficient theories: Inspiration does not mean that the books of Scripture were composed by men without the special aid of God and then approved by the Church's authority; nor does it mean only that they contain Revelation without error. It means that, being written under the inspiration of the Holy Spirit, they have God for their author and have been entrusted to the Church as such. Leo XIII's Encyclical *Providentissimus Deus* (1893) goes into further precisions:

"God so stimulated and moved the authors to write and assisted them in their writing

"that they rightly conceived in their mind, willed faithfully to write down and expressed fittingly within infallible truth

"all those things, and only those things, which He Himself commanded."

Of further clarifications in the twentieth century—especially the Encyclicals *Spiritus Paraclitus* and *Divino Afflante* and the Constitution on Revelation of the Second Vatican Council—something will be said as we proceed further with our study of Inspiration in the concrete. Here it may be worth noting that the Second Vatican Council (Ch.5.19) rejects the theory (about which more will be said in Volume Two) of "a creative power emanating from the primitive community"—the writers are chosen by God and inspired by him individually.

The question for us is how God operates on human minds and wills while yet leaving them true human minds and wills. And there is no complete answer. I have had correspondence about it with theologians and Scripture scholars: most of them, having made their statement, open the next paragraph with "Whatever inspiration is . . ." Inspiration is mysterious, not (or not only) as the Trinity is, by containing more than finite minds can cope with, but because we cannot see the whole process in operation. Yet there is a good deal that we *can* see.

2. *Inspiration Existentially Various*

One thing at least seems evident, namely that Inspiration is not all one undifferentiated thing. Essentially it is one, in that it always means that God saw to it that what he wanted written by men was in fact written; but existentially it is various. God is the only unchanging "factor."

There is the *subject matter*, what is being written about— God's action on mind and will could not be the same (existentially!) on John writing his Gospel, and on the author, whoever he was, who extracted the second book of Machabees from five volumes written by Jason of Cyrene, and on the men, whoever *they* were, to whom we owe the book of Genesis as we now have it; or on Paul writing his letter to the Romans which thrusts as deep into doctrine as man can

go, and on the same Paul writing to Philemon about a run-
away slave. If the scholars are right who tell us that Psalm 104
was adapted from an Egyptian hymn to the Sun and Psalm 28
from one chanted in the Baal worship at Ras-Shamra, the
inspiration to include them would have been different; and
the inspiration to include existent documents in the Historical
Books different again. Above all God's action must be different when—more rarely—Revelation is involved: the illumination of the writer's mind to know truth which could not
otherwise be known is different from guidance in handling
matters already known to him, or discoverable by the ordinary
ways of investigation.

Then there are the men whom he has chosen as his writers,
and the readers for whom he and they were to write. Like
every writer who knows what he is doing, God takes the
readers into account: he makes all allowance for realities they
had not mentally grown up to, experiences they had not had,
all the things that had not yet happened: yet he could make
his own kind of provision for very different readers who
were not yet, but would one day be!

In this context of existentiality, the *writers* mattered even
more. God did not take just anyone, as one might pick up a
pen from a desk. That comparison has been used (as the plectrum in the hands of a harpist has been used); but no one calls
a pen the author, and authors these men of Scripture really
are. He selected the ones who, while remaining genuinely
themselves, would yet serve his purpose and be more richly
themselves for having served it. We get something faintly
analogous in the choice of Mary of Nazareth to be the
mother of the Second Person of the Blessed Trinity. God did

not pick someone, anyone, who happened to be of the right age and available: he chose Mary. The Child was like Mary, the writing was like the human author; but in neither instance was the human author the sole author.

The men he chose differed vastly one from another. To take one instance of their variety—Amos was a herdsman with a herdsman's education, Isaiah (the first, not Isaiah II or Isaiah III whom the scholars have discovered for us) was a highly educated man of an established family. At some of the choices we may marvel, others we feel we might have chosen ourselves—and the omissions surprise us too, Elijah, the greatest of the prophets, has no book to his name.

But God knew the men before he inspired them to write, knew their minds, temperaments, backgrounds, words, ways of speech. The resultant writing was all in God's plan. It was no more a surprise to him, so to speak, than was the human race, Creation and Inspiration having a good deal in common. God, operating in nothingness, produced the human race; God, operating in human minds and wills, produced Scripture: into God's Creation nothingness introduced elements quite notably un-divine; so did all these finite minds and wills into his Scripture.

In Inspiration, as in so much else, God submitted his action to human limitation—ignorance in particular, the things they did not, could not, know. He could, of course, have eliminated all limitation. But he could have done so only by treating the men as un-men, their human activity only a token or fiction, with his power alone truly operative. In the Incarnation he was not pretending to be man, he became man; so in Inspiration he was not pretending to use men, they *were* men, acting throughout as themselves. They received certain special gifts from him, charisms we call them; but these they could receive without any diminution of their humanity, as we can receive and respond to actual graces.

How God influences a mind while leaving it free is his secret. The fact that we cannot see *how* is quite irrelevant. After all, we do not really know how any writer's mind works or any artist's; we hardly know how our own minds work, still less how God's grace works in them. If Mark had lived long enough to find his own Gospel listed with the inspired books of the Old Testament, he might well have been startled: that Peter was inspired he did not doubt, but that he, Mark, was—that possibly surprises him still! It may have been like that with Luke too. He tells us how he wrote his Gospel, mentions the other people he consulted, and so on. It is quite clear that he had not a suspicion that God was inspiring him. As far as he was concerned, he was writing his own book.

As far as God was concerned, too. There is a balance we cannot see, a line too fine for us to draw, between what the men wished to write and what God wanted written; or rather, between what God wanted the men to write *as theirs*, and what he himself, *as himself*, wanted written. Whenever the New Testament speaks of things in the Old Testament as having been said by God, one usually has the feeling, I think, that we are hearing things of this second sort.

That the men thus moved by God should write what they wanted to, God did most certainly want, because that went with their manhood, their writerhood, so to speak: God was not muzzling them. As the Encyclical *Divino Afflante* puts it: from the books, as we find them, we may learn "the distinctive genius and the individual characteristics of each author"

—"Let the interpreter, using light derived from recent research, try to determine the peculiar character and circumstances of the writer, the age in which he lived, the sources written and oral to which he had recourse, the forms of expression he used." The Encyclical *Spiritus Paraclitus* tells us that Inspiration does not prevent the writer from expressing himself in a manner consonant with his own talent and cultural background.

3. The Problem of Inerrancy

How far, then, did God engage his responsibility for all that they wrote? In one sense, totally. As we have seen, what they wrote contained all that he wanted written. But there has to be a difference between what he wanted them to write for *his* reasons, and what he wanted them to write for their own. He allowed them to write within their own limitations of vision and of utterance (the things, I mean, that they did not see or saw wrong) in so far as their limitations did not impede his purpose.

Since God is principal author of Scripture, the absence of error would seem to follow inevitably. Yet there are things stated in Scripture which were not so. I mean not only the use of poetry, drama, parable, story. Nor only certain ways of speech, for instance that numbers—like the 969 years of Methuselah or the couple of million Israelites who left Egypt for the desert (Exod. 12.37)—are freqently symbolical not arithmetical. Nor only the use of literary conventions then recognized—as when the Book of Wisdom (7.5–10; 8.14–15; 9.7–10) presents itself as written by King Solomon, dead a good eight hundred years. But there are things stated as fact which are not fact.

We find them in the first chapters of Genesis, when recorded history had not begun—Noe is called (9.20) the first tiller of the soil, whereas Cain had already been called a tiller of the soil (4.2); and the author has interwoven two stories of the Flood, differing in details. Père Benoit, O.P., of the Ecole Biblique in Jerusalem, treats some of the explanations of place names as clearly fictional. As we move into the period of history, there is again an interweaving of two stories with details which do not match in the account of the conspiracy of Jacob's sons to be rid of Joseph (Genesis 30). The author knew he was writing contradictions, clearly he did not think they mattered—they were not what he was concerned to teach but only part of the framework.

But when the prophet Ahijah says to Jeroboam's wife that God said of David that he "kept my commandments . . . and did only that which was right in my sight" (3 Kings 14.8), we have what sounds like flat contradiction, and it cannot be lightly written off as not mattering. For the prophet knew, and the writer of Kings knew, of David's sins. Evidently they saw no contradiction: we may learn something by dwelling on that.

There are many things-not-so in prophecy. Isaiah (ch. 13) and Jeremiah (chs. 50 and 51) foretell in blood-drenched detail, as told them by God, how the Medes will destroy Babylon: the Great City will become "a heap of ruins, the haunt of jackals, a horror and a hissing, without inhabitant" (Jer. 51.37). But we know that the Persian Cyrus, when he captured the city in 539, decided to leave it standing. What went on in the minds of the two prophets we cannot see: but the two essential things they foretold did happen—the fall of Babylon and the release of Israel from captivity in Babylon: the rest, however consoling to the oppressed Jews (and we may think to the two prophets), did not. Did they mean it as framework only? What went on in their minds we have no way of knowing. They had experienced the act of God in the depths of their souls and they had responded in their own way, perhaps clothing the naked revelation with the richness of prophecy's well-established, and very effective, imagery.

Perhaps, I say.

There is a distinction to be drawn between what the writers affirm and what they see as accessory, with only the former guaranteed free from error. In this sense Dr. Vawter can say, "What the author of Genesis intended to teach us is the meaning of Genesis . . . while Genesis undoubtedly contains errors it teaches none."

The student must be on his guard here against the temptation to regard anything in Scripture *that he personally finds difficult to accept* as merely accessory, part of the framework, belonging to the envelope not the message—and so write it off as not affirmed by the writer. This might well be a great simplification: but it could leave us with a pretty desiccated Bible.

The simple fact is that we have here an unparalleled use of the word "inerrancy"—though at that we might think the word closer to the reality than "a certain cogent persuasiveness" which one scholar uses instead. In any event, we must not fool ourselves into thinking that the distinction between what the writer merely writes and what he affirms for its own sake is a complete solution of the problem of God as author of things-not-so. I have known Catholics who maintain their belief in the inerrancy of Scripture by happily assuming that if a statement is proved not to be a fact, then the writer was not affirming it for its own sake. They are in for a bad shock the first time they try this on an intelligent unbeliever.

The distinction is really there, but it is not always easy to apply. Especially as *Divino Afflante* warns that Scripture's freedom from error is not restricted to matters of faith and morals only, with the rest simply obiter dicta, things uttered in passing. The perfect statement of the distinction has not yet, perhaps, been found. One imagines that it may be on the lines of the definition of evil—not the absence of good, but the absence of *due* good, the good appropriate to, required for integrity by, a given nature. If we think of error as the absence of *due* truth we shall be less troubled by its apparent presence in God's inspired word. For we remind ourselves of the Church's teaching that the whole of Scripture is inspired. God wanted the human author to say everything that he says.

As we try to see deeper into Inspiration, we wonder why God should inspire those two prophets to say that he foretold something which did not happen. "Inerrancy does not apply," says Père Benoit, "to details which are not affirmed for their own sake." But Divine Authorship does, says the Church. Inspiration *is* mysterious. But at least it is clear that God does not make everything his own in the same way. God does not, so to speak, *say* everything that the human author says. For this, that or the other thing in Scripture which is not so, Père Benoit has the phrase "The Holy Spirit has not shed his light on this point or guaranteed the truth of it in the same way that he does in other matters immeasurably more important" (*Initiation Biblique*, p. 27). Again he says, "The entire work builds up to a full revelation which disengages itself from the whole; but though each detail is inspired not all of them command the assent of faith."

The writers of Scripture serve their own purposes, but to the service of God's. What their purposes were we can study by the ordinary way of the critic, but not what *his* were.

There is always a residual there, whose possibility we can never forget. A computer might perhaps tell us which books were written by St. Paul, but cannot contribute anything to our knowledge of what books were written by the Holy Spirit. God's ways are unsearchable, that is one fact. And God wants us to search, that is the other. We may not always find, but if we conduct the search with a full awareness of God's omniscience and our own inadequacy, we are certain to find *something* to our profit. The Constitution on Revelation of the Second Vatican Council, allowing for the problem as we see it, assures us: "an infallible teaching flows from it."

Whether we can trace God's action or not, the fact that he has acted in the production of Scripture is what matters. Even if a given man would have written exactly the same without Inspiration, the entry of the Holy Spirit makes it a different reality—as water with the Holy Spirit is different from plain water. The water of baptism remains wholly water. And some of the books of Scripture strike us as wholly human in this sense, that we can observe nothing in them that the men might not have written by their own power. It is the presence of the Holy Spirit that makes the difference. God abides in the inspired books and can still make new contact with the mind and the will of the reader, with the depth of his self. When we read, there is possible a communication between the Holy Spirit in us and the Holy Spirit in the writer. And that is the point.

4. *When the Writer Writes More Than He Knows*

How does God serve his own special and particular purposes, which are not consciously those of the writers? We do not know the answer, but there is light to be gained by simply looking at the question.

When we find in Scripture things that are certainly, or anyhow seemingly, beyond the knowledge of the writers, there are three obvious possibilities.

That a man should have his mind illumined by God does not lie outside his manhood, or in any way diminish or restrict it. We are all capable of receiving light, God made us so. When prophet or inspired writer knows that he is inspired, there is not even a problem: God has revealed some truth to him, and he has accepted it. Again and again we find this kind of revelation-known-as-such in Scripture. The Old Testament is filled with it, especially the Prophetical Books, and in the New Testament we think instantly of the revelation God made to St. Paul on the road to Damascus.

When the writer does not know that he is receiving divine inspiration, we have two situations—he may know the fullness of what he is saying; or what he is saying has a meaning, later to be shown, which is hardly likely to have been in his mind.

The first of these is only one example of an experience all of us have had, in our response to Actual Grace. We think things out for ourselves, and arrive at decisions in light which is in fact given us by God, ourselves never suspecting the source of the light in which we have come to see the situation so clearly, and have come to feel so clearly the desirability of a particular line of action. It is so, surely, with writers of Scripture.

An example *may* be in the opening of Genesis. The writer's mind, working on existent stories of the creation and of man's beginnings on this earth, produces something wholly unique, in its richness and profundity beyond anything produced by men. Even if the Church did not say so, we could not help feeling that God was very much in action; yet the writer may have been aware of no such special aids, so completely was his mind moving with what he wrote. Similarly when we read what God said to the serpent about the feud between him and the woman and of how the woman's offspring was to crush his head, the writer may simply have arrived at a certainty that, God being God, the conflict would end with the triumph of God's people and expressed this certainty in those terms. And in this he need not have been aware that God was guiding his mind to the truth, still less of what the fulfilment would be.

With this last example we are face to face with the other possibility—that the writer is saying something that means more than he is likely to have known. The theologians talk of a "*sensus plenior*" known by God, present in what was written because God saw to it, with the writer all unaware not only that God was aiding him but of the full meaning of what he was writing. And the Encyclical *Divino Afflante* speaks of a spiritual sense of Scripture which "God alone could know and which He alone could reveal to us." Again and again we find phrases which totally fit a revelation not yet made, a revelation which we may feel could not have been known to the writer. The truth thus so miraculously expressed did of course exist in the mind of God. Was something of this communicated to the mind of the author? If so, how?

Who knows? *Sensus plenior* is sometimes discussed as though it were a cut-and-dried process, with one answer excluding another. But there is far more mystery about *any* kind of utterance than some of those who discuss Scriptural inspiration allow for.

To begin with is the elementary fact that when we have

said something we have made something. And *it* has a meaning. When we have said something, we have started something. Words have their own meaning, their own energy. The thing said goes its own way, lives its own life. It no longer means only what the speaker meant by it, any more than a child means only what its parents meant by it. If it is true to begin with, its life-giving power will grow. Yet the speaker did say it, it is really his. All this is the fact about any utterance; it applies to inspired utterances too: they do not lie dead on the page, all their vitality forever exhausted in the breath that caused them to be.

Again, there is a kinship in all things that come from God, family likenesses which show one mind at work throughout— for example, the one we have already noted between God creating the universe, and God inspiring the writers of Scripture: or between God operative in Scripture, operative in Sacrament, operative in the humanity of Christ. There seems to be one formula at work on a great number of levels. You say something wholly true on the level at which you are speaking. Exactly the same set of words would be true on a higher level altogether: so that *meaning* what you say, you are in fact *saying* far more. To take an obvious example: With no revelation at all we might arrive at the conclusion that man's destiny must be to know and love God: with the revelation of Sanctifying Grace and Beatific Vision, we can still say that man's destiny is to know and love God, but with what a new depth of meaning.

A sense fuller than the writer is likely to have had in his mind, fuller anyhow than lies on the surface of his words, may emerge in all sorts of ways, but in two especially. Of one we have already spoken, namely that by living any truth men grow deeper into its meaning. The other is that later revelation casts light upon earlier. This one is worth a longer look. It may operate in things that Scripture tells us *happened* later—in the fulfilment of the prophecies, as Dr. Vawter reminds us, we see more than those to whom they were first committed.

It may operate in things *said*. When Paul says (1 Cor. 5.7), "Christ our Paschal Lamb has been sacrificed," he is enriching beyond all measure the commandment given by Moses about the establishment of the Passover ritual (Exod. 12). Yet we feel that the original words are fulfilled, not distorted.

This was the sense surely in which Paul told King Agrippa and Festus (Acts 26.22) that he was "saying nothing more than what the prophets and Moses said would come to pass: that the Christ must suffer and that, by being the first to rise from the dead, he would proclaim light both to the people and to the Gentiles." Did Moses, did the Prophets, know they were saying that? Whether they did or not, Paul heard them saying it. As Peter heard David saying things apt to the Judas situation. As the disciples at Emmaus, with Christ to guide them, found things said of him by Moses, and the Prophet, and the Psalmist.

To summarize, we find countless examples in Scripture of this aptness of words at two levels. In Psalm 50 we read "I was brought forth in iniquity and in sin did my mother conceive me." Yet the writer was not likely to be thinking of the doctrine of Original Sin, of which the men of the Old Testament had at best only the sketchiest notion.

And when the Psalmist says, "Thou wilt not give thy holy one to see corruption" (Ps. 16.10), he might simply have been uttering his conviction that for the man who serves God the breaking-up of the body at death will not be the end—very much the same principle that may have caused the writer of Genesis to be sure that the serpent's victory over the human race would not be final. But the phrase the Psalmist used applies in its totality—as Peter told the crowd in Jerusalem (Acts 2.27) and Paul told the synagogue congregation at Antioch in Pisidia (Acts 13.35)—to the death and resurrection of Christ. God knew this. Did the original author?

Of course God could have revealed it to him. We may feel it more *suitable,* and it is the mood of our day so to feel it, that God should not thus have revealed it. But there is a danger in this, the ever-present danger of deciding what we should have done had we been God. Yet we can at least say that it does not seem necessary that the writer should have known all that was contained in what he had said. God knew what the fulfilment was to be, and could see to it that the writer, while uttering his own meaning, did not so express himself as to exclude the fuller meaning which was later to emerge.

5. *Special Problems of Old Testament Inspiration*

The Jews thought that the first five books of the Bible were entirely from God, the books of the Prophets less wholly so, the rest simply written by men variously aided by God. We need not follow them point by point in this, but there is a sound instinct behind it. As we have already seen, Inspiration is essentially one, but existentially various. It varies from book to book, it varies much more between the Old Testament and the New Testament.

To treat the inspiration of both Testaments as one undifferentiated reality would, in the first place, ignore the subject matter; as Father Alexander Jones says, "There is all the difference in the world between the committal to writing of a seven-hundred-year-old tradition about Abraham, and a written account, perhaps as early as fifteen years after the event, of the main outline of Our Lord's career" (*God's Living Word*, p. 100).[1]

But the misunderstanding of Inspiration involved in it would go deeper still. It would treat God's action as the sole factor, ignoring the writers *through* whom and the readers *for* whom he gave the Scriptures. To treat as irrelevant the difference the coming of Christ made to both readers and writers would be as gross a failure of vision as if we were to regard Sanctifying Grace as existentially the same reality in the souls of Christians as it had been in the souls of men before Christ, even the mightiest of them. Christ made all things new—Sanctifying Grace, of course, by his life and death, Revelation by his teaching: and in its newness Revelation made Inspiration new, made Inerrancy new, just as it gave teaching authority the newness of Infallibility.

He made not only things new, but men too—new in knowledge, new in grace, new in their offering of the new sacrifice, new in all the ways of contact with God. The Old Testament was written by and for men as they were, in a situation as it was; the New Testament by and for men as Christ had changed them, in the changed situation made by him. A Scripture for angels, if it existed, would be different again; the angels might find our Gospels as primitively expressed as we find so much of the Old Testament and Prophets.

[1] New York, Sheed and Ward, 1961.

Let us look at the people of the Old Testament. We remember that the books as we have them cover some eight hundred years of writing and some fifteen hundred years of historical happenings back to Abraham, with a glance at what lay before him. At the beginning of that time the people were indeed primitive, at the end of it the same adjective can still be used, though there had been continuous development.

In the order of morals, they had thought polygamy right, concubinage too and the enslavement of defeated enemies, to take only the most obvious examples of what I have called primitive. And even in their ideas of God and man and the meaning of life we find them at their starting point very far indeed, and at the high point of the Old Testament still a long way, from what by Christ's revelation we now know. Human sacrifice probably disappeared early, but polytheism and idolatry and ritual prostitution, male and female, were an abiding temptation, which again and again they failed to resist over the greater part of the period covered by the Old Testament. Only after the return from their captivity in Babylon can we feel them safely, irrevocably, monotheist, monotheist to the marrow of their bones.

But their knowledge of the one God, whom alone in the world they upheld, lacked so much. Not only did they not have the Blessed Trinity—that great reality can be known only by revelation, and God had not yet revealed it. Nor do we get more than a hint of the approach to God by way of mystical union, nothing like the union with the personal God attained by such men as St. John of the Cross or even with the impersonal God of Hindu mystical experience. They lived in the conviction that God was to be known only in his actions, not in himself—not till the period between the Old

Testament and the New did Jewish writers, under the influence of Greek thought, begin to give their minds to the ultimate question what God is in his own reality.

They concentrated on God's dealings with men. To the end, their failure to use their minds upon God blocked the fullness of progress possible to them. And it made all sorts of errors almost inevitable. Thus it is not possible for men to talk of God without using human language. Provided they know what they are doing and are capable of making allowance for all that their way of speech prevents them from uttering, there is no harm in this. But there is a danger of anthropomorphism, of simply treating God as the highest kind of man, and those early Jews did not always escape it.

Thus only too often they simply assumed in all unconsciousness that if a course of action seemed to them right, then God willed it, so that in carrying it out they could see themselves as obeying God's command, and could say so in total conviction. The trouble is, of course, that as civilization develops, men's minds change upon the right way of handling other men, if only as a result of growth in understanding of human psychology. Cruelties which at an earlier stage appeared normal can come to appear revolting. But before that stage is reached, their rightness is not questioned—all the less so because, with their total acceptance of God's will as the law of man's action, they had not come to the distinction between his will decisive and his will permissive.

So we find the really appalling massacring and enslaving of the Midianites (Numbers 31) regarded by Moses as "wreaking the Lord's vengeance" on them. We find the same ferocity even in some of the Psalms we value most. Psalm 109, for example, has the phrases "Thou art a priest for ever" and

"Thou art my Son, born like dew before the day-star rises." But it also has "The Lord will pass sentence on the nations, heap high the corpses, scatter far and wide the heads of the slain." And the most moving Psalm 136, which begins "By the waters of Babylon we sat down and wept, remembering Sion," ends with "Blessed be the man who will catch up thy children and smash them to pieces against the stones."

Love is in the Psalms undoubtedly, but the balance is different from what Christ has shown us. If we take the two great Commands, we can find love of God most wonderfully uttered, but love of neighbor in nothing like the same power, and of love of enemy not a trace. Similarly, the Book of Wisdom tells of the word of God carrying out the slaying of the first-born of Egypt—"Thy word omnipotent leapt down, thy word that could spread death everywhere": that *feels* a long way from the words of the Word, "I am come that you may have life and have it more abundantly."

From an insufficient concentration upon what God himself *is* flowed naturally an inadequate idea of man and his destiny. The supernatural life of Sanctifying Grace, which is the very key to life here and hereafter, is scarcely to be found. And there is almost nothing about the next life. Redemption is primarily of the race, and the golden future is for the race and not for the individual, very much indeed as in Karl Marx: and though the emphasis they placed upon community can be a corrective of our own individualism, they saw the community as made by shared blood not by shared love (though Jeremiah was feeling towards this). We do find a sense of some kind of continuance after death, but without detail or great emphasis. Resurrection comes quite late. Daniel has the first clear statement perhaps (12.2,3) though Ezekiel's vision of what happened in the valley of dry bones used it powerfully as a symbol of national resurrection. Of the Beatific Vision there is not a hint. And there is no awareness that knowing where the road of life leads has any relevance for the living of life here on earth.

Yet, with all that we know to be true and fail to find in the Old Testament, the story of development is wonderful for those who have the skill to trace it, or to follow it when traced by men more skilful than themselves. We see the full doctrine of Christ marvellously, miraculously, on the way to formation—provided we know the fulfilment in Christ. This we may feel was God's object in inspiring the writing of the Old Testament. He wanted it written, which meant that he wanted it read. But we may phrase this rather differently: He wanted it reported, which meant that he wanted it preserved. If he thought it valuable for men throughout the ages to follow the story of Redemption, then he would see to it that the stages would be written down for us. Reading it, we see the point men had reached at a given moment, see the slow advance and another point reached. The prime value for us may be that, with God abiding, men have passed that way.

SIX

Scripture in the Church

1. Guidance in Reading Scripture We Must Have

Scripture has been given by God to the Church, and by the Church to us. What would it be like without the Church?

The one thing certain is that we could not read it effectively without aid from someone, a great deal of aid. It was written roughly from 900 B.C. to 100 A.D. There are over seventy individual books, so that in one sense it is a library. But more profoundly it is a single book, one part of it throwing light upon another, so that only in the whole book do we get the wholeness of what God is telling us in it. Yet none of the writers, save John, perhaps, could have read the whole book. That at least we can do. But not unaided. And, even with aid, not easily. In the Bible as a whole there is no evident system. At first it seems more like a jungle than a garden, more for exploration than instant delight. And how shall we explore?

As we have noted, there is the question of the religious knowledge, outlook, practices which the writer is taking for granted in his readers. It is difficult enough for us to know with certainty either what these were in themselves or what they meant in the living fact, even for the half century within which the New Testament was written. It is more difficult still for the centuries that came and went as the Old Testament books grew to their present form, and quite immeasurably difficult for the ages into which they reach back.

Then there is the history of all that thousand-year period: the writers assume knowledge of events now forgotten, situations long vanished. Consider the Gospel only. The trial and death of Our Lord are almost incomprehensible if we do not know how the Romans came to be ruling Palestine, what Herod's position was, what rights the religious leaders of the Jews had.

His relations with his own people are wholly incomprehensible if we do not know that the Sadducees were the dominant party and stood for collaboration with Rome, if we attach no idea to the Pharisees save hypocrisy; if we do not know all the complex of ideas bound up with "the multitude," what the Jewish expectation of the Messiah was *at that time*, what the Jewish feasts signify, what a synagogue service was, what the phrase "Son of Man" suggested to those who heard it. Without all this knowledge the reader can get an impressionistic sketch of a good man misunderstood and maltreated, but he cannot pretend to know what is really happening.

There is a difficulty of another sort than the historical knowledge which the Bible assumes and does not provide.

We, differently formed, are reading a book written by Semites for Semites. We have to be told just about everything. Of ourselves we should not know that the tremendous words of the prophet Joel, used of Christ's death by Peter in his first Pentecost speech, about the moon being turned into blood and stars falling out of the sky—were quite normally used, right into the Middle Ages, about the death of any outstanding Jew: they were not astronomical at all. When, as we have already noted, the writer of the book of Wisdom talks as if he were the centuries-dead King Solomon, he was not being guilty of a forgery, he was using a literary device conventional in his world. And for many a century men read the Book of Jonah without any suspicion that it might be a kind of extended parable, directed against racial arrogance.

There is the question of the languages in which the Books were written, the meaning of the words. We find ourselves watching, lost but fascinated, the battle between the philologists who specialize in language and the exegetes whose concern is with the message. For words are only a part of the problem. What was in the mind of the author, what was he setting out to do or show? What did he regard as primary? What did he affirm, what did he simply take in his stride? Where is he using a document that has come his way? There are, as we have seen, prophecies unfulfilled. And the prophets themselves show great changes of outlook and teaching—the collapse of all that David and Solomon had built, followed by the forty years of the Babylonian Captivity, made an immense difference to them. How is the ordinary reader to evaluate all this or even know it?

The whole thing is too vast. The details are myriad, but even to know them all—which even the greatest scholar could not possibly do—would not be enough. Prophecy must be taken massively. Yet the totality of prophecy is harder for us to make our own than the myriad details. It is not too much to say that Israel itself was a prophetical fact—prophecy incarnate in this one people—as Christ was the Word, incarnate in this one man: Christ was the Word which prophecy existed to utter.

Without guidance we are first confused, then discouraged. Even those who persevere do not get a tithe of what is there to be got. One can, of course, read Scripture in a state of pious coma, feeling that the general experience is uplifting and not expecting any very specific meaning—rather like listening to a lovely voice singing in a language we do not know. But this is fooling oneself. To read the Bible without external aids is to fail to take it seriously. "The word of God is living and effectual and more piercing than any two-edged sword": is Scripture so to us? A two-edged sword is not meant for playing with. Aid in using Scripture we must indeed have: the Bible read without commentary is like a landscape before sunrise; it is all there of course, but not to the eye: and if one does not accept the Church, there are only the scholars.

Do not let the word "only" suggest that the scholars are not doing a mighty, and mightily valuable, work. Their work on the texts we should know to be essential, even if *Divino Afflante* had not told us so. Their work on the languages, and on the shifts of meaning of individual words from one age to another, has made passage after passage of Scripture a new thing. And linguistics is not the whole, or even the main, of it. Their discoveries of similarity, of religious episodes and ideas, to be found in the religions of paganism before we find them in Scripture is the most moving reminder that God did not leave men at any time without his help, unless they themselves refused it. We have noted that the Egyptians honored the Sun with a hymn which could become Psalm 104, and that a great part of Psalm 28 had been chanted for Baal. There was a great flame of prayer going up from men to God all over the world, and God has his own ways of responding, appropriate to their powers of acceptance.

But we must approach the scholars with care all the same, in the religious field especially, but not only in that. It is possible to know every word in the dictionary and even be able to add one's own supplement to the dictionary, and yet be unable to write a living sentence oneself, or even to respond to the life in the writing of other men. A given scholar might study Shakespeare, for instance—vocabulary, grammar, scansion, sources, the age in which he lived, and every first-rate critic who has ever written on him—and simply not "get" Shakespeare at all. It is for us to learn what the learned have to teach us, and then read Shakespeare. We lend them our ears, but not our mind. We bring to our reading the self that we are. Shakespeare must find us responsive. So must God.

There are of course great commentators, whom we are the richer for reading. Yet even the greatest cannot do otherwise than bring to the reading and interpretation his own philosophy of life, the experience life has brought him as he has lived it. And that means that he brings not only strengths but limitations, his own limitations and those of his age. Today's scholars see the weaknesses of yesterday's, but only the greatest of them see that today will soon be yesterday. They feel that they have transcended earlier thinkers, but only the rare ones see themselves as transcendable in their turn. Only the exceptional teacher takes absolutely for granted that his best pupils will outgrow him—indeed that his function is to help them to. But if the scholars seem to forget it, we who read them must not.

And there is something else. The man who does not believe in God *must* read Scripture differently from the man who does. Or again the man who accepts God's existence but whose every instinct shrinks away from God's intervention in human affairs, reads Scripture differently from one whose mind is open on the matter. For all practical purposes the man who believes that Christ is God and the man who does not are reading two different books: a discussion between them as to the meaning of the New Testament is as though one were discussing marriage with a eunuch.

When Peter's Second Epistle (1.20) says, "No prophecy of Scripture is a matter of one's own interpretation," it is saying that one needs aid from the teaching of the Church, not from the consensus of scholarship. But without the Church, men are at the mercy of scholars, who have so little mercy on one another.

2. Doctrine and Scripture Not Simply Different Arrangements of the Same Material

There is endless conflict, and no referee. And in the nature of the case there can be no merely human referee. Revelation is a matter not only of light seen, but of a seeing mind enriched in its very substance. "May the Father grant you a spirit of wisdom and insight, to give you a fuller knowledge of himself. May your inward eye be enlightened" (Eph. 1.18). While the conflict goes on, men are un-nourished, left in darkness.

That may be regarded as St. Paul's commentary on the words of Our Lord: "Anyone who is prepared to do his will shall know of the doctrine, whether it be of God or whether I speak of myself" (John 7.17). Our Lord is not saying that teaching is unnecessary if one does God's will, but that the doing of God's will is an essential pre-condition for the understanding of God's word. And this not solely because obedience deserves so great a reward, but that doing God's will is nourishing, muscle-building, health-giving, an enriching of the self to whom God's word is addressed. Père Congar, O.P., speaks of "the fundamental error of believing that by an exegetico-historical study it can be decided what Christians should hold." And his fellow Dominican, Père Benoit, writes: "How are we to know that we have not substituted the exegesis of our spirit for the exegesis of God's spirit? Only a public authority divinely guided can spell out without error a public message divinely revealed." (*Initiation Biblique*, p. 55)

Masses and masses of the truth God wants us to know here on earth can be drawn out of the Scriptures, but not necessarily by the individual reader, or by any number of individual readers. The Word in his Body not only bears witness to Himself in Scripture, but watches over the teaching, the interpretation, the application, the whole immense process of unfolding.

Even one who believes none of this does see that there has been an unfolding. The Jews have had one—within the Old Testament itself and subsequent to it, Mishna developing Torah, Talmud developing Mishna. To quote Père Benoit again (*La Prophétie*, p. 357): "The very words of the inspired ancients have received, in the vast perspective of the divine plan, a richness and fullness that their first authors have not conceived, but by which future readers were to profit—e.g. those who centuries later could compare one with another the messianic prophecies of an Isaias, a Jeremias, a Daniel, and could compare them with their fulfilment in Christ had a more lucid and deeper understanding than those to whom they were first revealed. Or again, the knowledge of the mystery of the Trinity enables us to read with a new eye the words of the Old Testament on Wisdom. Thus God has commented His own word by itself, illuminated the old utterances by new, giving them a wider reach, which one calls the *sensus plenior*."

Our Lord fills the Old Testament themes of King, Son of Man, Servant, Redeemer, with a content of which the Old Testament gives only glimpses. To read the Old Testament without knowing the New means to miss this rich content. Similarly if we know the New Testament without knowing the Church's long meditation on it, her long labor on it, in the power of the Word whose Body she is, then equally we are missing richness that God means for us. There is so much that the Old Testament writers had not. It is all in the New Testament, of course—but rather as the whole truth of God is in the phrase of Deuteronomy "I Am": it is all there, but we cannot unpack it. To dismiss what the Church, living in Christ and in-lived by the Holy Spirit, has made of it in near two thousand years, is to impoverish ourselves.

Not that the Church comments on Scripture, verse by verse. There are, indeed, only a handful of verses to which she has attached an authoritative interpretation. She is there to teach of God and of man's way to God *in the very fullness of our present knowledge.* Her subject matter, in fact, is Reality as it exists. But in this teaching she is continually nourished, and nourishes us, upon Scripture and Sacrament—we may feel that to be nourished by the Eucharist without the Scripture is better than to try to nourish oneself by Scripture without the Eucharist, but either course would be a putting asunder of two that God has joined. The same Holy Ghost by whom the Word of God was conceived in the body of Mary caused the Word of God to be conceived in the minds of the writers of Scripture. Thus nourished and living in the truth, the Church sees and tells us more of Reality, and thereby casts further light upon the Scripture from which she has already drawn so much light.

The doctrine she teaches does not necessarily decide what given passages of Scripture mean. Doctrine and Scripture are not simply different arrangements of the same material. *They are two approaches from different angles to one same Reality.* There are elements in Scripture which the teaching Church has not yet crystallized in doctrine, and there are elements in the doctrine which are not explicit in Scripture. Each sheds light, but the two may not always combine—for us—in one single luminous stream, any more than the elements in a given dogma do. We may twist the meaning of texts in an effort to force them to support a particular doctrine; but it will be rather like the oddity called Concordism round the turn of the century, the effort to make Genesis say what the newest scientists were saying about Creation and Evolution. On the relation between Scripture and the Church's teaching, Newman stated the principle: "The question," says Newman, "is not whether this or that proposition of Catholic doctrine is *in terminis* in Scripture, unless we would be slaves to the letter, but whether that one view of the mystery, of which all such are exponents, be not there."

3. The Unfolding of Revelation

We have already discussed what this unfolding of the truths contained in the Deposit of Faith involves. It is carried out by scholars, by the men who have to conduct the daily running of the Church, by the mass of ordinary people living by the truths. There are the Fathers and Doctors, not possessed of all the knowledge that the modern savant has, but saints every one of them, and as such entitled to that insight which Christ has promised to those who do God's will. There are whole armies of theologians and Scripture scholars. What emerges from all this work may find universal acceptance, so that it may fairly be said that the Church teaches it: some of this universally accepted doctrine reaches definition by Pope or Council. But there are always elements which are accepted in one place or another, so that to masses of Catholics they seem plain matters of faith, yet time winnows them. All this we must look at more closely in Volume Two when we come to consider the Church.

But we shall not understand the whole process of unfolding if we think of it as simply a means of drawing the *logical* consequences from the elements first committed to the Apostles. That is one way, but not the only way. There is another way, which we may call *organic:* This really *is* impact. (See the Constitution *de Revelatione* 2.18.) Christians, living in and by the truths, living them in Christ, come to the certainty that other things must be true too, although the connection could not be stated mathematically. An example is the clearer light in which Christ's Mother came to be seen, as men grew into, and grew in, the explicitation of the reality of Christ himself. Living in the truth that Mary had conceived a son who was God, and in those other truths concerning sanctifying grace and God's plan for the restoration of the fullness of manhood by the resurrection of the body at the end of time, men grew to see it as unthinkable that she should ever have existed without sanctifying grace or that she should not now be present with her Son in the fullness of her humanity: this sort of certainty does not perhaps exclude all possibility of error, though the possibility dwindles to vanishing point when the new truth is held by all over a very long space of time. In these two instances, the Church settled the matter with the defined dogmas of the Immaculate Conception and the Assumption.

The Old Testament writers had not heard the truths that Christ was to reveal, had not received Christ sacramentally; they had been in-lived by the Holy Spirit indeed, but not as he in-lived Christ. And quite apart from the supernatural realities, they had not had the widening of natural mental outlook which would have come from long-continued mental and spiritual contact with cultures very different from their own. The Jews are a remarkable people, but they do not exhaust either the mental or the spiritual resources of the human race. Already in the Old Testament we can see something of what they drew from Babylonian and Persian culture; as well as a bare beginning of what the Church was to gain in enrichment from the Greeks. There are other cultures still—Hindu and Chinese, for example—and who knows what still remains for them to give us, who knows what development of our understanding of Revelation there would have been if the Church had moved Eastward instead of Westward? Or indeed if the Word had been made flesh in Asia, not in Asia Minor. . . .

But in the providence of God it was the Greek enrichment that the study of Revelation has most notably had. And the Old Testament writers did not have it. We must not canonize their limitations or be congealed in them. To repeat a point already made about one of these limitations—they thought that God could be known only in his actions and not in his innermost self. They would have listened uncomprehending to St. Paul's clear statement that man's mind can see even the depths of God (1 Cor. 13.2; 10.16), just as they did listen uncomprehending to the words of Our Lord upon which Paul is here making his own comment—"No one knows the Father but the Son, and him to whom the Son shall reveal him" (Matt. 11.27).

The New Testament writers did not share this first limitation of their predecessors, for they had the revelation of Christ. Yet certain things, and these immensely educative, they had not had. They had not had seventy generations of living in and by the truths Christ revealed and of receiving the life that comes from him. They had not seen the truths challenged by new situations—one wonders, indeed, if any writer of either Testament had ever had an argument with an atheist. And there are all sorts of other experiences they had not had, experiences which would have taken them deeper into the revelation they had received. St. Peter had not met, or possibly dreamed of, some of his successors in the Papacy —John XII for instance; St. Paul had not seen the Inquisition —he lists his own sufferings in no awareness that some of his successors would inflict these same sufferings on others. Our Lord learnt obedience by the things he suffered (Heb. 5.8): his Church has learnt a great deal by the things she in her turn has suffered, and something perhaps from the sufferings she has caused other men to undergo.

One way or another there has been a continual growth of realization of the truths Christ entrusted to men. The Deposit of Faith was not a talent to be buried in the ground or wrapped in a napkin for fear of contamination. It is closer to reality to think of it as a seed—and in no seed is all the fruit that is to grow from it plainly contained.

Infallibility, guaranteed by Christ to his Church, is a reality, just as the Inspiration of Scripture is a reality. Uncertainty as to what Scripture means—that is as to what the words meant to the man who wrote them—does not keep us in uncertainty as to what God has revealed, if the Church has defined it. Our deepest concern must always be not with as much of the truth as the original writer saw, but with what God can bring to light *in us* upon the reality of himself, and ourselves, and our way to him.

But if one does not see the Church as the Mystical Body in which the Word is continuously in operation, this channel of light is not known to be available—above all, when there is question of a development of what I have called the organic kind as distinct from the purely logical. We saw this very clearly after the definition of the dogma of the Assumption of Our Lady into heaven. Those men did not fall behind us in devotion to Scripture who at that time said that their Church "refuses to regard as requisite for saving faith any doctrine or opinions not plainly contained in the Scriptures."

Three comments suggest themselves. (1) We have already noted that fruit is no less from seed because not plainly contained in it: unless you are a botanist you might look long at a seed with no notion of what fruit was meant to come from it;

even a botanist cannot know all of what soil and sun might do to it: and this seed was unique like none that botany knew. (2) A thing may be quite plain, yet not to us—because of a defect in our vision; and there are areas of obscurity which can grow luminous as the Holy Spirit gives increase of light. (3) Leaving the Church out of it, but considering only what the scholars have had to say, one wonders how many texts of Scripture are left with a meaning so plain that all sane readers must accept it.

Let us look longer at the phrase "requisite for saving faith." Actually the question whether a given truth or practice is necessary for salvation cannot possibly be the primary test. God being merciful, we can be saved on such a bare minimum of knowledge of what he has revealed. But even if great numbers of truths were necessary to be known if we are to be saved, that would not be the principal reason for knowing them. To hold that it is would make ourselves central instead of seeing God as central. Truth is still worth having because it is true, even if we could be saved without knowing it.

And what about the necessity of truth for love? Each new thing learnt about God is a new reason for loving him. Can we imagine anyone saying, provided he was really listening to what he was saying: "We don't need to know any more about God or his work, we know enough already for our salvation"? Love of God, as of our fellow men, craves knowledge and is fed by it.

4. The Two Testaments Need Each Other But Not Equally

Christopher Dawson has said that a society which does not know its own history is like a man suffering from amnesia.

We cannot really know where we are, if we do not know how we got here. This applies to the Christian community. As we have already noted, one value of following the story of Redemption in the Old Testament is simply that men passed that way, and that we should not be where we are now if they had not.

This does not mean that we should begin our study of Revelation with the Old Testament and work forward: that would be rather like beginning the study of astronomy with —say—the Chaldeans, passing on to Ptolemy, on to Galileo, making a detour to study the Mayans, arriving at last at the structure and operation of the heavens as we now know them to be. A ship should be steered by all relevant knowledge now available, so should man's life. To begin with the most primitive and work forward would be a strange way of study in any field. In the redemptive field it would involve us in two difficulties special to itself.

The first of these is that most of what is called salvation history is in fact *not* history as modern scholars have conditioned us to understand the word. It is true, but in its own order. Adam, for instance: we do not know what his name was—Adam means "man"—or where he lived, or what language he spoke, or (within half-a-million years or so) when he lived; the account of him in Genesis was written a few hundred years before Christ, we do not know by whom, or what authority he had. With Noah as second ancestor of the whole race, with the flood, the Ark and the animals, even conservative believers will hardly assert that we are in touch with history in the modern sense. As Ronald Knox writes (in "Absolute and Abitofhel"):

First Adam fell, then Noah's ark was drowned,
And Samson under close inspection bound.
For Daniel's blood the critic lions roared
And trembling hands threw Jonah overboard.

Samson and Daniel and Jonah matter less. But how much
do we know of those key figures, Abraham and Moses? What
are the credentials *as history* of Deuteronomy?

It is becoming clear that there is more sheer history in the
Old Testament than men thought round the turn of the century, but only one trained in the relevant highly specialized
disciplines can evaluate the arguments for the historicity of
any given statement. Any text can prove to be a battle-
ground, and the battle is not for beginners.

I imagine scholars, hearing the phrase "salvation history,"
might ask, "Don't you mean salvation midrash?" "Midrash"
is a Hebrew word used of episodes or teachings valuable for
their spiritual meaning but not meant as statements of historical fact: Our Lord's parables are examples.

But with the word "meaning" we come to that other profounder reason for not beginning our study of Revelation
with Salvation History. It is that the true beginning is Christ:
"No one comes to the Father but by me." That other word
of his, "I am the door," has a wider application than entry
into the Church here and now. It means entry into the whole
Christian inheritance—including the fulfilment in which the
Old Testament receives its meaning. To one who did not
know the New Testament, the line of Salvation History we
trace would seem highly artificial, just too selective.

For the understanding of the Old Testament we need the
New, for the understanding of the New we need the Old

Testament. But the two "needs" are not equal. The New Testament is fulfilment, luminous in itself but yielding more light still if we know what came before. Whereas without knowledge of the fulfilment, the Old Testament has too much of its light locked up within it. One might find it a maze rather than a road. As we noted earlier, to one who came to it unprepared, it would be more like a jungle he was not equipped to explore than a garden for present pleasure. Pleasure? Only the toughest manage to read it from beginning to end—a fact of some pedagogical bearing. In all honesty most of us admit weariness to the heart in great tracts of it, and revolt in the heart at some of it.

Though the New Testament writers revel in the Old Testament prefigurings, we do not find them urging those first Christians to read it. Timothy is approved of (2 Tim. 3.15) for having read it, and it is worth noticing the terms in which its value is expressed—"*profitable* for teaching, for reproof, for correction and for training in righteousness, that the man of God may be *complete, equipped for every good work.*" The Constitution on Revelation of the Second Vatican Council (4.15) says: "The books of the Old Testament, even though they contain much that is temporary and provisional, are of *importance* even to Christ's faithful in setting down the divine teaching."

"Profitable," "of importance." To Old Testament lovers the words sound a shade measured, they would have liked something stronger, closer to the vehemence of the phrase about Scripture as a whole in the Encyclical *Humani Generis*, "Without Biblical theology dogmatic theology becomes *sterile*." Certainly for the serious student of theology the Old Testament is essential.

A fuller discussion of Scripture will come in Volume Two, *God and the Human Race*. But it may be helpful to summarize certain principles here.

(1) The weariness of spirit and the horror may never, for some of us, wholly cease; but they will not be dominant. We shall find a growing excitement as we recognize the first shadowings of realities we have met in the New Testament—the kind of phrases or happenings which cause the New Testament writers to attach to so much of what they are recording the words "that the Scripture might be fulfilled." These may be vast things like Passover and Pasch, or simply verbal felicities—like discovering that a couple of words in Luke's first chapter had already been used—and so fittingly—in the Greek version of the Old Testament. The same Greek verb is used in Exodus for the cloud that *abode* upon the meeting-tent of Moses when the glory of the Lord filled the tabernacle, and for the power of the Most High *overshadowing* Mary of Nazareth when the Lord entered her womb. Similarly the Greek verb used (2 Kings 6.14–16) for David *dancing* before the Ark (which contained the written word of God) is used again for John the Baptist *leaping* in his Mother's womb when Mary entered Elizabeth's house.

The Old Testament is full of such excitements, smaller and greater. We must indeed be on our guard against a danger which sounds improbable but continues to take its toll. In an essay in *Theology and the University*, Father Charles Davis writes a warning: "Biblical theology can become as remote as Egyptology and as irrelevant for the life of mankind today. . . . If the biblical revival hardens into an exclusive biblicism, it will peter out into an ineffectual anachronism." Short of "an exclusive biblicism," it is possible to develop an unbalanced interest in the prefigurings, to the point where we can see no value in the fulfilment till we have found something in the Old Testament which we can feel that it fulfils.

Paul warned the Colossians (2.16) about due proportion—"These are only a shadow of what is to come, but the substance belongs to Christ." As Shakespeare said in another context, "The best in this sort are but shadows." The primary importance is in the thing Christ did or suffered or said—there is always more in that than in its prefiguring. Christ brought us salvation, but we hear no word from him of Adam's sin which lies at the beginning of the road that leads to himself. Paul shows us Adam as a type of Christ, but we hear no suggestion of this from Christ's lips.

The Old Testament has a power to fascinate—I have known Catholic scholars so much in the grip of its fascination that the whole New Testament seems to them only a postscript to it. There are commentators who to all appearance find nothing worthy of attention in the New Testament save texts from the Old misunderstood by the writers who lacked the equipment of modern scholarship!

They did lack it of course, but they had a different approach as well. In any given thing they could see the whole story of Redemption, and often enough that is all they are saying with the phrase "that the Scriptures might be fulfilled." When Matthew spoke of the return of the Holy Family after the flight from Herod as a fulfilment of the text of Hosea "Out of Egypt I called my son," he knew of course that Hosea was talking of Israel's Exodus from Egypt. But the mere aptness of the words to the present situation delighted him, especially perhaps because of the words preceding those he quoted—"When Israel was a child I loved him."

(2) If we accept Scripture and the Church as two ways of the Word's utterance we do not force either to say what the other is saying on any given point, we simply do our best to find what each *is* saying; but we do reject any interpretation of either which would make it contradict the other. The Church cannot contradict Scripture, Scripture cannot contradict the Church.

Both these statements are true, but one is easier to apply than the other. We can see at once if an interpretation of Scripture is irreconcilable with Catholic doctrine. Those who see Christ's words "Why do you call me good, none is good but God?" as an assertion that he is not God, are plainly denying the doctrine of the Incarnation. Those who see his words "He that believes and is baptized shall be saved" as forbidding the baptism of infants are plainly denying the doctrine that the grace given in baptism is for all.

But those who feel that a given Catholic doctrine is irreconcilable with Scripture have to face the difficulty we have already noted—that more than one interpretation is possible for practically any text that is not a simple statement of simple fact. Thus, I imagine, Catholics have always taken for granted that Simeon's words in the temple, "Thine own soul a sword shall pierce" (Luke 1.35), refer to what Christ's Mother is to suffer. But the learned Dominican Père Benoit argues that they are not about her at all, but about Christians generally, very much as Christ's words from the Cross "Behold thy mother" gave Mary as Mother not to John only but to Christians generally: and that the "sword" does not mean suffering but is "the word of God, sharper than any two-edged sword, piercing to the division of soul and spirit . . . and discerning the thoughts and intentions of the heart" (Heb. 4.12). This is one text out of thousands, where any one interpretation may be challenged by some other.

The Church's teaching, being formalized and organized, is less subject to a variety of interpretations. And when it is, we can ask the Church to clarify as we cannot ask the Bible. The answer to the question with which I began this chapter is in two sentences: Without the Church what I could do to the Bible. But with the Church what the Bible does to me.

The possibility that they can be asked for a fuller explanation must always be a difference between the living teachers actually present and the books written by men long in heaven. The difference is more strongly marked today. As Karl Rahner has noted in *Nature and Grace:* "It has never been so easy to know clearly what Christ teaches as it is in this, our modern age, when the Church (above all since the First Vatican Council) has developed her understanding of herself to the point of formulating precisely and finally the nature of her teaching authority and the way in which it functions."[1] The Second Vatican Council has shown that there are still problems to be examined; but, as to the mass of the Church's teaching, there are no great problems, only the invitation to thrust deeper, to widen the area on which the light falls.

5. Reading Scripture for Vital Equivalents

The Old Testament tells the story of the preparation, but it is not a blueprint, not history written in advance. If you had only the Old Testament, you could not possibly see in advance what the fulfilment would be. But study what Christ in fact was and in fact did, then re-read the Old Testament

[1] New York, Sheed and Ward, 1964.

and you will find it incredibly fulfilled, fulfilled beyond all measure and all possibility of foreseeing, but fulfilled all the same, and unmistakably. We have just glanced at 2 Tim. 3.16 —about the profitableness of the Old Testament. But we may not remember the verse immediately before: "From your infancy you have known the Holy Scriptures, which can instruct you to salvation, *by the faith which is in Christ Jesus.*"

To have lived generation after generation in Christ and in the light of his revelation makes a difference beyond all measuring. Yet we can still go back to the New Testament writers who had had the experience of Christ only so newly and so recently, and to the Old Testament writers who had not had the experience at all. Why?

There is a way of return to Scripture which is a kind of self-indulgence. The plain truth is that there is a burden in the thought-structure which, under the guidance of the Holy Spirit, his Church has erected in nineteen hundred years. To bury oneself in the inspired books can simply be a way of un-shouldering the burden. If we select carefully, there are lovely words and deeds in Scripture which set the emotions vibrating without calling upon the mind for labor and sweat, and in these vibrations we can luxuriate. And indeed we should: there is health in occasional luxury.

But that must never be our sole way of return. There are profounder reasons. For in the first place God is in them as in no other writing. They are a permanent presence of God communicating and energizing. Every reader has had the experience of coming upon phrases which say something special to himself, as if they had been written for him alone. The Holy Spirit abides in the inspired writing and our souls can still make contact with him: nor is there anything written since in which we can have so present a consciousness of God's majesty and our own nothingness. It aids in *our* concrete situation to see what a particular Prophet made of *his*— with all that we have and he had not of revelation and sacrament, his intensity does something for our pallor.

To return to an earlier distinction, we shall be reading for vital equivalents as well as mental. Thus we might very well learn the whole doctrine on the Virgin Mother of Christ as the Church gives it to us, then re-read all that is relevant to her in the New Testament. If then we go to the Old Testament and concentrate not only upon her as we find gleams and glimpses of her there, but also upon the rich thread of teaching on the Virgin Israel, then, however much or little the original writer saw, what he has written operates in us most powerfully not for illumination only, but for vitalization. And so with every element in the Revelation—Scripture enriches, gives life, widens the horizon. So St. Paul told the Romans (15.4): "What things soever were written, were written for our learning: that through patience and the comfort of the Scriptures, we might have hope."

Remember that for St. Paul hope and vitality are inseparable. And remember, too, that "comfort" has not our modern meaning: it means strengthening. To cope with some of what we shall meet in the Old Testament, that strengthening will be needed.

SEVEN

The Experience of God

The Chosen People knew God as they experienced him. So must we. We listen to his words, build them into our minds, translate them into action, live by them, fail to live by them, see others living by them or failing—the living and the failure each bringing its own evidence of their validity. We are shaped by them; react emotionally to them, agonize in them and draw strength from them, rage against them sometimes and outgrow rage, grow in understanding, in intimacy with God, and in love. Without such depth and variousness of experience, the truths of revelation lie in the mind, shedding the tiniest light, communicating no excitement, energizing scarcely at all.

But there is another way of experience, the mystical, which is an awareness of some sort of direct contact with God. It is not the certainty faith or reason can give that God is, in fact, everywhere: his presence is somehow "felt"—as really as we feel heat and cold or the beating of our heart. E. I. Watkin calls it "as it were a touch, even an embrace, in the dark."

An impression exists that in comparison with mystical experience, Theology is only a second best, a kind of talking down to the average man's immaturity. Dionysius the Areopagite, whom we have heard called The Father of Christian Mysticism, says in *The Celestial Hierarchy* that it would be truer to deny than to affirm that God is good and wise: the first time we meet this, we wonder what is left of the Christian revelation. His translator, the ninth-century Scotus Erigena (both words mean that he was Irish), seems to dot every i and cross every t of that statement when he says that God's Unity and Trinity alike were taught by theologians to give the faithful something definite to contemplate.

All this may sound to us like raving, if only because Our Lord does teach us of Father, Son and Holy Spirit, and does teach us that God is good. But Dionysius knew his Bible, and knew it to be inspired. It is worth our while to find out what so famous a mystic was trying to say. Scotus Erigena we can leave for another time, he was no great theologian, not a very good translator for that matter, and perhaps not a mystic at all. But what of Dionysius, always spoken of so respectfully by Thomas Aquinas? We must look at Mysticism —not a full-length study, but only to see what its relation is to the Theology we accept as the God-guarded working out of the Revelation God has given.

1. The Basic Mystical Experience

"In the beginning was the Word, and the Word was with God, and the word was God. All things were made by him." So St. John's Gospel opens.

All things whatsoever were created by God: there was no matter already existent of which he might make them, he created everything. Apart from everything, what is there? Nothing. That is what we mean, as we reminded ourselves in Chapter One, by saying that God made all things of nothing: and the Will which alone brought them into being must still operate to keep them in being.

We concentrate our mind upon the point at which we (like any created thing) emerge from not being into being, from non-existence into existence: we may call it the root from which the whole of our self grows upwards, or the center round which the whole of our self develops. At that point, root or center, we know that there is God—not simply God's power or God's action but God himself, since in him there is no distinction between what he is, what he has, what he does. If he were not there nothing at all would be there. God's presence then is essential to our being. I do not mean that without him we should be incomplete. We should not be at all. Without God we should be meaningless, because we should have no being to mean anything. God is essential to our meaning as to our being: and to the meaning and the being of all things whatsoever—ourselves, angels, cats, oysters, specks of dust.

These are plain facts about the universe and ourselves. God is at once Infinite Meaning in which our meaning has its origin, and Infinite Energy by which we exist and act. To be such as we are, in such a universe as we are in, and never "feel" anything of it at all, would be an eerie insensitivity. Yet, even if we know these things, we take for granted that the area of reality to which the mass of men ordinarily respond is the totality to which they *can* respond. But why should it be? The universe is, of course, mysterious, but we are inside it; God is mysterious, but he is inside us.

For most of us there are at least moments when Reality breaks through. For artists the moments are commoner. They are not planned for or trained for, not usually understood as what they are. The power to respond to the divine life at the center of all things seems to be inbuilt—the artist is simply taking things as he finds them, and suddenly it is as if he were on a new wave length. There is nothing consciously religious in this: what happens is that the depth of the man, with God energizing there, responds, vibrates, to the depth of things, with the same God energizing in them too.

The mystic does not leave the response, the vibration, to chance, but tries to bring it about. He turns his attention inward, concentrates all his powers in the effort to reach his own ultimate depth, to make contact and "feel" contact with the central point of his being—the point, in fact, where nothing is made into something by God. The training for this journey into depth is arduous, the journey is arduous. Bodily desires must be brought under control, for they belong to the surface and hold us there, they distract, and concentration must be total. The body has no contribution to make, it must somehow be eliminated—if not yet from existence, at least from consciousness; even its existence must suffer diminution, the life-giving energy the soul normally pours into it must be withheld almost to the point of death because the soul needs all the energy it can muster to reach that uttermost depth.

All who have had the mystical experience agree that when it is reached, there is an overwhelming, utterly certain, sense of contact with a Reality beyond ordinary experience, vast beyond ordinary measure; utterly real but utterly beyond, vast to the very limit of vastness, different to the very limit of difference. The difference is so total that there can be no question of *seeing*, all is darkness. The intellect, the knowing faculty, is out of normal action; "touch," "feel" are the mystic's words, not "see." Yet, in spite of difference, the soul feels that in some way it belongs, almost that it has come home but has ceased to be its own individual self in the homecoming. It is "overwhelmed"—in a sense comparable to the literal sense—submerged, drowned in this other Reality so deep that all distinction seems to be lost. A Christian mystic, St. Catherine of Genoa, phrases it: "My me is God, nor do I recognize any other Me but my God Himself."

This, roughly sketched, is the basic mystical experience. In both its elements—the vast beyondness of the other Reality, the sense of some kind of belonging, of returning to one's origin—the experience matches what we know by revelation to be the facts. If mystics do actually make the contact they claim, why should it not be like this? Even if one accepts Karl Barth's view that the depths in himself reached by the mystic have nothing in common with God, yet some special contact with God there may be. There seems reason to doubt neither the *fact* of the experience nor the mystic's *certainty* that he has been in realized contact with the Absolute, the Infinite, the Supremely Real. But the interpretation the mystic gives the experience is not necessarily valid. It is not part of the experience but subsequent to it. It has to be weighed more carefully. It depends to a great extent—at least it cannot help being strongly colored by—the theology or philosophy he already holds.

2. Indian Mysticism

The great Indian mystics believed in Brahman, an impersonal Absolute, the Ground of Existence. The word is neuter —so is pneuma, of course, but Christ gave the Holy Spirit a personal pronoun, He. About Brahman nothing meaningful could be said: yet a great deal was said. There are diverse schools of Indian Mysticism, I follow what seems to be the main line. Brahman was not a person, not He, It; they could not allow It knowledge, or life, or being—or existence even. Because all these attributes, *as known by us*, imply differentiation, limitation therefore, and multiplicity which would break the utter oneness, infinite stillness of the utterly undifferentiated One. The Absolute, they say, is totally beyond the reach of our knowledge; yet of what the absence of differentiation implies in it, they speak as confidently as if they had the Absolute under their microscope. They assert that It cannot know anything at all, even Itself, because *knowing* implies a distinction between the knower and the known; cannot be a *person*, because personality means the consciousness not only that I am I but that I am not someone else; cannot have life, because life is a process, so that it implies the distinction of one stage from the next; *being* similarly would imply finite relations, since one being must be distinguished from another; even *existence* cannot be allowed, for it is to be contrasted with non-existence.

Yet It alone is real, It alone abides: existence cannot be attributed to It, but It is the Ground of Existence. The universe is a kind of bubble heaved up from It and in due course to be sucked back into It, only for the Absolute once more to bubble out and once more re-absorb, and so on without end.

This is their solution of the problem of the One and the Many —how from infinite Oneness can come multiplicity which is its complete contradictory: the solution God has revealed we shall discuss later.

Having that concept of the ultimate Ground, they would assume that it was with this that they had made their lightless, ecstatic contact. I say "assume," for they had no way of being certain that what they "touched" was the Absolute, only that they felt It vastly, inconceivably, greater than their own soul or any other being known to them. If they were in fact in contact with ultimate Reality, then they were in contact with God himself, the God of Our Lord Jesus Christ. Why did they not realize it, why did they not recognize him, the personal, the tri-personal? Why did they rise no higher than Brahman?

Because in the mystical experience their intellect was not in action, so that there could be no conscious experience of a person—"touch," "feel," "taste," can give a certainty that something is present, but only understanding can give certainty that the something is a person. And the necessary absence of any utterable reality in their own sense of contact would not contradict what their philosophy told them of the Absolute's infinite negativity. If their conviction of ultimate un-knowableness, un-sayableness, had been based solely on their inability to see God here below, it would be pathetic, making the creature's seeing-power the measure of the Absolute. But it was profoundly in their philosophy too.

What of their certainty that in the moment of contact their own individuality ceased to exist, was fused with, merged with, wholly lost in the impersonal Ground of their existence? There could be no experience of the individual self's having actually passed out of individual existence, for there would be no self left to have the experience. Pantheism can be held as a philosophy, but it cannot be experienced. Obviously there could be a complete vanishing of their *consciousness* of self; they could be so overcome by the immensity of the Reality with which they were now in felt contact, that they would not have a thought to spare for their own selves (that is what ecstasy is, being made to stand outside oneself).

And there is something else. The mystic, as we have seen, like all other created beings, exists eternally as known by God: in direct contact with God, there may be some reaction of the created self to the Uncreated Self eternally existent in him. Christian mystics have experienced it, and the greatest have known it for what it was: the English Julian of Norwich writes: "I *saw* no difference between God and our substance but as if it was all God—my *understanding* took it that our substance is in God, that is to say that God is God and our substance is a creature of God." Or as the Epistle of Privy Counsel phrases it—"He is thy being, but thou not His."

The Hindus had not had the revelation to enable their understanding to go so deep. But in their philosophy they found an explanation which satisfied them. The Absolute, Brahman, is the only reality. Creatures are simply the Absolute expressing itself in the transient, unnumberable elements of the universe of daily experience, and this is the truth of our transient, unnumberable selves. Individuality, plurality, distinction of any sort are not in the wholly undifferentiated One. Therefore we, like all things else, are only appearances. In felt contact with the Absolute, the soul "undergoes" in advance that reabsorption into the Ground of Existence which awaits all beings whatsoever—including the Gods of the Hindu pantheon.

It is impossible fully to understand a religion one has not

practised, or a religious experience one has not had. I can but report my feeling that philosophy alone would not account for this universal emphasis upon individual extinction—that some profounder appetite underlies the philosophy, a love of darkness as an end in itself, an exaltation of nothingness. In the writings of the Hindu mystics, as in that of some of the Christians, one senses an intoxication with nothingness. Chesterton has noted that the phrase "I want nothing" can have three depths of meaning. It may mean "I have all I desire"; it may mean an absence of desire; it may mean a positive desire for extinction. At the root of our being there is God and there is the nothing which, but for his action, we should be. The mystic may react to one or other, and react with ecstasy. There can be a yearning for God, but there can likewise be a craving for nothingness which is like a nostalgia for the womb, a weariness of the burden of selfhood as the sin at our origin, the source of all finitude and misery. The first temptation recorded in Genesis—"You shall be as Gods"—carries this sort of divinity as a tempting possibility within it. For the Impersonal Absolute, into which men are to re-merge, can present itself as wholly lightless: has indeed nothing that can *by men* be conceived as anything, no utterable— that is no distinguishable—content whatever.

The greatest of the Mystics of the Impersonal could hold firmly to, and be nourished by, the certainty that the negatives were a way of indicating the Beyond—that non-existent was not less than existent, that lifeless was not less than life. One of these was Plotinus (205–270 A.D.) the founder of Neo-Platonism, which was the last stage of Augustine's journey to the fullness of Christian faith. It was Platonism as seen, six hundred years after Plato, by a man of great holiness, who had himself experienced the mystic ecstasy.

He had studied Hindu mysticism and he knew Christianity as well: in Alexandria he had for fellow-pupil that great Christian genius Origen. We may wonder if two men of comparable genius ever met in one class: someone should write a Dialogue between them, though he would need to be a genius too. St. Augustine said of the philosophical school Plotinus founded: "The Platonists, with the change of a very few words and opinions, would become Christians" (*De vera religione* 7). But, as Augustine also tells us, one of these words was Incarnation. There was nothing in the teaching of Plotinus to exclude the Trinity. But matter, the body, he could not conceive as capable either of union with divinity or as partner in the soul's everlasting life: resurrection was to be *from* the body.

Great or less great, the mystics of the Impersonal find ecstasy in a contact without communication, a contact with an Absolute which does not even know they exist, which is experienced rather like a drug—for a drug also knows nothing of the addict yet means everything to him. The ecstasy itself only the mystic could know, there is no way of conveying it to another any more than the idea of color could be conveyed to a man born blind. But, even from outside the experience, we can see one positive value in it—namely that the self shrinks toward life-size. The shrinkage may go too far perhaps: but selfishness is at the source of all the evil men do.

3. *Dionysius the Areopagite*

We come now to Dionysius, whose assertion that it would be truer to deny than to affirm that God is good and wise started us upon our inquiry into the mystical experience. We know nothing about him, not even his name. He was writing round the year 500, but he wrote as if he were Dionysius the Areopagite, mentioned in Acts (17.34) as one of the few converts from St. Paul's fiasco on the Areopagus. This was not necessarily forgery: pseudepigraphy was a sufficiently respectable practice, we remember that the author of *Wisdom* writes as if he were King Solomon, so long dead. But our Dionysius does it with thoroughness, bringing in references to Timothy, for instance, to Bartholomew, and to his having —in the company of Peter and James—stood by the dead body of Christ's mother.

In the ninth century Scotus Erigena, an Irish scholar living in France, translated him into Latin; and the French fused him with that other Dionysius who was their own St. Denis. To the end of the Middle Ages it was not questioned that he was St. Paul's convert, which won for his books—especially *On the Divine Names* and *Mystical Theology*—a quite special reverence: We have Thomas Aquinas, for instance, making the considerable effort necessary to reconcile some of his statements with Catholic orthodoxy.

His mysticism is formed by the Neo-Platonism of Plotinus. If one goes straight from reading Dionysius to reading Plotinus, one is not always certain afterwards which said which; and indeed the Christian writer embodies without acknowledgement sections from Proclus, who had been lecturing on Plotinus in Athens a few years earlier. Augustine, we remember, said that Neo-Platonism could have been Christian but for the Incarnation: Dionysius shows how difficult it is to interweave the one with the other; that his own theology of the Incarnation had a Monophysite tinge made it no easier.

Neither as Neo-Platonist nor Monophysite could Dionysius find a real place for Calvary or Redemption.

But his effect upon the Christian mystics has been immense. Augustine lived and died before him, and Gregory the Great before his invasion of the West. St. Bernard owes little to him. But thereafter Dionysius seems almost to have taken possession of great numbers of Christian mystics, and none are wholly unaffected by him. Was he himself a mystic? Only another mystic is equipped to judge. I can but record my own impression that—as compared, say, with Ruysbroeck—he reads rather like a fervent student of mysticism than a practitioner!

Why did he find it preferable to say "God is not good"? In fact he saw no contradiction between that and Christ's "Who is good but God?"—which we find him quoting. He would wholeheartedly have accepted Our Lord's "No one comes to the Father but by me." But for Dionysius the Father is not the Ultimate Reality. Beyond God lies the Originating Godhead, *thearchia*—"the Cause of all things and yet Itself nothing, because It super-essentially transcends them all."

What then of the Trinity? Here Dionysius is under a special difficulty. As a Christian he accepts Father, Son and Holy Spirit. But how is he to identify them with the originating Godhead? The essence of the super-Essence is that in It there is no differentiation or distinction of any kind: It must not even be called "Deity" or "existent"—save "symbolically and inadequately." The problem is beyond him. He meets it —or rather avoids meeting it—in two ways.

The first is by lavishing all his art in praise of the Blessed Trinity. The second is by making it almost impossible to know what he is actually saying. He leads into it with a promise of clarity—"free from all dubiousness and obscurity." He goes on, "The Initiates of our Divine Tradition designate the undifferenced attributes of the Transcendently Ineffable and Unknowable Permanence as hidden Incommunicable Ultimates, but the beneficent differentiations of the Supreme Godhead they call Emanations or Manifestations. . . ."

He would be a bold man who would undertake to set out Dionysius' doctrine of the Trinity. My own feeling is that he is closer to orthodox Catholic teaching than some of his admirers assume. But I *think* he holds that just as God is subsequent to, resultant from and less than, the Originating Godhead, so too is the Trinity. Is it perhaps the face worn by the Absolute, which has no face? One could find expressions to support this, others to contradict it.

The most famous of those who learnt from him, the fifteenth-century Dominican Eckhart, could say, "Heaven stands a thousand miles above the earth, even so the Godhead is above God"—which is as far as a Trinitarian could get from the orthodox statement of the mystery, namely that each of the Persons *is* the divine Nature. I find it hard to believe that Dionysius would have said what Eckhart said, or thought it. But the Trinity *is* a philosophical embarrassment to him. His Absolute is not Father, Son and Holy Spirit. It is ultimate as these are not. It is the Originating Godhead Itself.

Indeed even the word "Itself" is misleading. For "self" is transcended along with every other limitation, distinction, attribute, even existence, even being. It is the ground or source of the Many, but It is undifferentiated Oneness. All distinctions—between men and things, men and men, the Persons of the Trinity—are contained in It, but not *as* distinctions, not as distinct. Dionysius uses the word Super-Essence, not Essence; but in his determination to exalt the difference between the Ultimate Reality and all those beings which have emanated from it, even "super" is not enough, exaltation is not enough, only negation will suffice. "It has not the power of perceiving or being perceived. It does not know existent beings as they actually are. . . . We cannot apply to It either affirmation or negation." (*The Mystical Theology*, Chapters IV and V.) We are back at Brahman (that word, we note, is neuter).

Dionysius cannot be content with simply saying that nothing that can be asserted of us or even of Christ can be asserted of It. He must make the statement an absolute lyric of negativity. In Chapter V of *The Mystical Theology* we have: "It is not soul or mind or endowed with understanding—not immovable or in motion or at rest—has no power, is not power or light, does not live, is not life; is not personal essence or eternity or time—nor is it one, nor unity, nor Godhead nor goodness—nor does it belong to the category of non-existence or to that of existence. . . ."

There is here a kind of intoxication with negativity which comes to the very verge of that intoxication with nothingness which we have already seen as a possibility. Yet Dionysius—more perhaps than some of his followers—can balance intoxication with sobriety. He says, for instance: "It is surely truer to affirm that God is life and goodness than that he is air or stone; and truer to deny that drunkenness or madness can be attributed to Him than to deny that we may apply to Him the categories of human thought." In other words, though nothing that can be said of us can be said of the Absolute, there are still levels of unsayability. Though all are inadequate, there are levels of inadequacy. One could list more statements of this sort, but they have not the same impetus as the lyrical. Sobriety as such is not exciting.

We have already noted that neither his great denials nor his great assertions could be mystically experienced. Dionysius, and those by whom he was introduced to his mysticism, and those who have been introduced to theirs by him—all make the contact with the Absolute to be something akin in the spiritual order to touch or feel or fragrance in the bodily. That no personality—one or threefold—is experienced tells nothing as to its presence or absence in the Supreme Being: an experience thus limited is not responsive to personality: nor to most of the views Dionysius has of Godhead. They are his own personal geometry of the Infinite. The mystical experience has no geometry.

This does not mean that his views are of no value, but it does mean that they must be seen for what they are—a product of the human intellect operating with great brilliance, a tour de force of the discursive reason. Operating on what? On what Dionysius received from a variety of sources, including the Christian revelation as it had reached him. Each one must test them for himself by reason and revelation: the mystical experience can neither prove nor disprove them.

By one type of mind Dionysius is simply dismissed because at times he seems to contradict himself, as when he says that "the Super-Essence passes outside of Itself even while It remains all the time wholly within Itself." But this is an occupational hazard of all who try to utter the unutterable. Why do they try? Because the unutterable is a continual challenge to utterance which no man can refuse without loss: God wants to be known by us, we must not deny him. Knowledge in him finds utterance in the Word; and we are made in his image.

We cannot know him as well as he knows himself—in any truth revealed to us there will be elements whose reconciliation lies deeper than we can see. But this does not mean that we need not bring the full power of our mind to bear on what theologians or mystics are saying, mystics especially. They may glory in the intoxication of their experience, it would be no glory in us to be intoxicated by them.

Dionysius writes, at the beginning of *The Mystical Theology:* "The simple, absolute, and unchangeable mysteries of heavenly Truth lie hidden in the dazzling obscurity of the secret Silence, outshining all brilliance with the intensity of their darkness, and surcharging our blinded intellects with the utterly impalpable and invisible beauty of glories which exceed all beauty." According to our temperament, we may find this splendid or inflated. But St. John of the Cross, I think, found it splendid, and so do great numbers of lesser masters. Whichever mystic captivates us, we may easily be experiencing *him* and think we are experiencing That which he experienced.

We must at all times make the effort to find out what the mystics are saying, never dismissing the possibility that in a given sentence they may be saying nothing at all. Even that is no reflection on them, the unutterable might well produce an occasional stammer of words.

But one trick of speech in Dionysius is not occasional, a trick which, as it seems to me, the Infinity of God neither demands nor is served by. I mean his use of the negative. He says (*The Divine Names* IV, 3): "In it alone Not-Being is an excess of Being, and Lifelessness is an excess of Life, and

Its Mindless state is an excess of Wisdom." Like the Hindus and Plotinus, he uses negatives to convey superabundance; but, in language as spoken by men, they do not convey it. A mystic schooled by Dionysius, the seventeenth-century Benedictine Augustine Baker, says of the ultimate mystical contact: "This is the state of perfect unity, termed by some a state of nothing, by others—with as much reason—a state of totality." One feels the intoxication perhaps: but sobriety could have conveyed more. After all, the word "nothing" already has a meaning. When Dionysius himself tells us that it would be better to say God is not good, he does not mean that God is bad: but that is what the words mean. One feels it would be better not to say things which (as Newman said in another context) can be explained only by being explained away.

There is indeed no attribute that can be used alike of God and of creatures. If we make man the standard of personality, then God is super-personal. If we make God the standard, then as applied to us the word person is diminished. So with existence, goodness, wisdom, love and the rest. It would seem more logical to make the Original the standard than the image. And that is what Our Lord did: "Why do you call me good? Who is good but God?" And he knew no Absolute beyond his heavenly Father.

4. Christian Mysticism

What I have called the basic mystical experience was established, codified so to speak, by believers in an Impersonal Absolute—a belief which can range from all-but-atheism, by way of agnosticism or pantheism, to acceptance of an all-but-personal Deity. For all of them the starting point of religious philosophy was the Absolute—remote, abstract, in their minds essentially an Idea. The Christian mystic begins with the living God "made flesh and dwelling among us" in Christ, save by Christ no one comes to the Father.

We have already noted that the mystic interprets the experience according to what he already holds, so that between Christian mystics and mystics of the Impersonal there must be a difference in the interpretation. But there is also a difference in the experience itself. There *must* be, because Christianity has made a difference in the person who has the experience. He has already experienced God in the context of daily life, received him sacramentally, spoken with him, pleaded with him, grown in intimacy with him, loved him, before ever coming to the mystical contact: like St. Augustine, he has known what it is to talk with God "as friends talk." He knows that the Living God *is* the Absolute: but this means equally that the Absolute is the living God—a mystery, but not a void. When the immediate contact—touch, feel, fragrance—is at last made, it involves no diminution of that other kind of contact already richly existent. The intellect may lay aside its normal modes of action, but the will is wholly energizing in loving *and receiving love*.

The difference between Christian mystics and mystics of the Impersonal can be noted, once one is alive to it, in Dionysius the Areopagite, who has a foot in both camps. To him the utter indifferentiation of the Absolute is the primary fact. God is the great Solitary: it was his teacher Plotinus (*Ennead* VI, 9) who described the mystical experience as "the flight of the Alone to the Alone"—a romanticization of solitude which is natural enough in one who knew neither our membership

of the Mystical Body at one end of the flight nor the infinite
un-aloneness of Father and Son and Holy Spirit at the other.
For Dionysius it was not easy to see the Originating Godhead
taking part, so to speak, in the mystical experience, responding to man's love, returning it.

Indeed it is on the side of God's love that Dionysius is fur-
thest removed from the Christian mystics whom he was to
influence. For most of them the mystical experience would be
interwoven of the infinite Godhead and Christ, in the humanity which suffered and died and rose for our redemption: it
was an entry into union with the God Christ had revealed. In
The Ascent of Mount Carmel St. John of the Cross writes:
"In the highest state, general loving knowledge of God is
necessary. If the soul were without this knowledge or sense
of God's presence at that time, the result would be that it
would have nothing and do nothing." There are Christian
mystics, we have seen, who would use the word "nothing"
as if it were a kind of ultimate glory. But the difference is
mainly verbal; of most of them, that can be said which
Jacques Maritain said of St. John of the Cross (in his Introduction to Father Bruno's Life): "The wisdom that intoxicated him was derived from a loving union with the Blessed
Trinity."

"Loving union" is not the key phrase for Dionysius. In *The
Mystical Theology* love is not mentioned at all; and though
elsewhere he treats of love, he is inhibited by the impossibility
of harmonizing it with the indifferentiation of the One. And
what he says of love—"a sincere, spontaneous and entire sur-
render of yourself and all things"—is correct but there is not
much passion in it—there is more in Plotinus!

Christian mystics in general had much more than the basic

sense of contact with the unknowable. We need not go as far as Julian of Norwich, who had so vast a wealth and variety of "showings." But Ruysbroeck speaks of the soul, emptied of all images and concepts, being shown the operations of the Three divine Persons, being transformed by them and raised to a union with them of great closeness—though, in the actual union, the soul was no longer aware of the distinction of Persons, but only of the Oneness of Being.

St. Teresa perhaps went deeper. In *The Interior Castle* (*Seventh Mansion*, Ch. 1) she tells how, in the "ground" of her soul, she apprehended the Three Persons as distinct, yet "all these Three realized as one Substance, and one Knowledge and one God alone." Thus the two elements in the Mystery were apprehended by her as one same Reality. It was God—One and Three—that she "saw in a point."

Whether these "apprehensions" of revealed truths are part of the mystical experience proper; or special graces given by God to the mystic over and above, for the enrichment of the union; or a stimulation of the powers of the mind to insights normally beyond it—these questions would have to be discussed if this were a full-length study of Mysticism.

But our concern is only with its relation to Theology, particularly with the question whether it reduces Theology's importance: and the rather different question whether our own study of Theology would gain from it.

On the first question, the overwhelming answer of the Catholic mystics is that there is no such reduction. The Mystical Experience is not a competitor with, or a substitute for, Theology; it is of a different order. It is aided by the truths the Church has taught—no mystic ever had mystical apprehension of the Blessed Trinity who did not already know the doctrine. And it confirms the mystic's faith in the truths.

Augustine Baker speaks for the majority when he writes: "In regard to the understanding, there is a divine light communicated, *not revealing or discovering any new verities*, but affording a most firm clear assurance and experimental perception of those verities of the Catholic religion which are the object of our faith. . . . No thanks to those that believe after such sight, which is more evident than anything we see with our corporal eyes." (E. I. Watkin reminds me that "the experience in which Augustine Baker claims to have received this assurance of the 'verities' was a passive contemplation, the ultimate—the only one he received until the eve of his death.")

Abbot Cuthbert Butler mentions, among great mystics who have this heightened awareness of the truth of Catholic doctrines, Ruysbroeck, St. John of the Cross, St. Teresa, St. Ignatius. St. Augustine (*De quantitate animae*) says it clearly: "When contemplation has been achieved . . . we shall know how true are the doctrines of faith, how well and wholesomely we have been nourished by Mother Church."

The second question is as to the value of mystical experience for the study of Theology. I do not mean its value for the student, as Christian or as man, but for his advance in the *understanding* of Reality.

The Teaching Church has not had much to say officially on mysticism. But there is clear acceptance in the Bulls of canonization of St. Teresa of Avila and St. John of the Cross. The one speaks of St. Teresa's "many books of mystical theology full of true piety from which the faithful must draw abundant fruit for their souls" (Gregory XV, March 12, 1622); the other speaks of St. John's "books of mystical theology full of divine wisdom" (Benedict XIII, December 27, 1726). Two hundred years after his canonization St. John was declared a doctor of the Church.

It is hard to think of any statable knowledge of God or ourselves which has come to us from the mystics and not from the teachings of the Church. We may go further and say that we actually know more of the things that concern us from the teaching Church. Theology tells us more about the union with God in heaven than we—or the mystics themselves—can learn from mystical union with God here upon earth.

Mystics have expressed the ecstasy of that union—the touch, the feel, the fragrance, the song—as a foretaste of the bliss of heaven. But what does "foretaste" mean in this context? Our ultimate goal, as the Church tells us, is the union of the whole man, soul and body, with the Blessed Trinity: the union is effected in the Beatific Vision, the intellect brought into a realized contact so total that there is nothing between God and itself, God taking the place in the intellect of the idea of God which is the most it can attain on earth: seeing God thus face-to-face, man will attain a new immediacy of love, no element in him will not be brought to a new level of blissful activity. How much of this could we—or the mystics —learn from the mystical experience? The whole man is not involved in it—neither body nor intellect "belongs"; the direct vision which is the basis of the life in heaven is not in action at all. The mystic himself is still *here*, seeing as in a glass darkly—not yet *there*, where the seeing is face-to-face (1 Cor. 13.12).

Yet upon the testimony of those who have known it, the

experience is immeasurably worth having. It is worth having for the joy of it—a single touch, says St. John of the Cross, is more than compensation for all the sufferings this life can bring. It is worth having for the enrichment it gives at the very root of man's being: God is everywhere, of course, but he is uniquely present *to us* only at that one point. There the soul is in direct contact with God, not as Infinite Meaning certainly, but as Infinite Energy; and no earthly experience is comparable.

But, to return to the opening of this chapter, it does not exhaust the meaning of experience. There are mystics who dismiss the intellect and its powers as meagre and inconsiderable. One feels that they must have rested in the *words* of Theology, not brought the full power of the mind to the development of mental equivalents, not known in themselves the *energizing* of vital equivalents. St. Augustine would not have agreed with them. While in the utterance of the ecstasy of his experience he equals the greatest of the mystics, yet scholars dispute whether he was a mystic at all. So much delight did the intellectual apprehension of revealed truth bring him, that it is not evident that mystical contact would have brought him more. Upon that large question I have nothing to say. But no one who has made a serious beginning of the kind of study I speak of would assume that he *must* have had mystical experience in mind when, in the Tenth Book of the *Confessions*, he wrote: "What do I love, when I love God? Light, melody, fragrance, food, embrace."

GOD IN HIMSELF

EIGHT

The God of Both Testaments

The problem for the unbeliever, so we tend to think, is to know God, for the believer to love God. But if we mean by this that the believer has solved the problem of knowing God we are wrong. To have the assurance that God exists is only a beginning; its value depends on how much we know of him. It is for us to enter into a living relation with him, and the relation will be closer and more living as our knowledge of him grows. Great evils have come from God believed in, but wrongly seen! Those who saw him only as Power came to worship him with human sacrifices. Those who saw him only as life-giver came to worship him with phallic rituals. The fusion of such groups meant that he was worshipped with both. And the variations were endless. Those to whom he is little more than a name, arousing a feeling of awe but bearing no light, will tend in the practical running of their lives not to think of him at all.

The more we know of him the more elements in us will respond to him, the more of ourselves we can bring into the relationship.

1. *"Thou Shalt Love the Lord thy God"*

Christ Our Lord tells us that the First Commandment is to love God, with our whole heart, mind, soul and strength (Luke 10.27). We are so accustomed to hearing the phrase, that it hardly has any effect upon us at all. But if, just for once, we pause to ask ourselves whether we *do* love God, our complacency might well be shattered. What, in fact, does loving God mean? None of our ordinary experience of loving either things or people seems to apply readily to loving God. We analyze the word love a little more closely, and we see that it must include a desire to come nearer, at the very least some sort of movement towards the loved object. How much of such a movement towards God do we ordinarily detect in ourselves? As a small boy I was taught a prayer which ended: "Grant that I may love and enjoy You for ever in Heaven." I think I had already reached middle age before I was brought up short by the word "enjoy." I had to admit that I had given very little thought to God as enjoyable.

The Commandment Our Lord chooses as the first is, in fact, a quotation from the Old Testament (Deut. 6.5). But the Jews found it at least no easier than we to give God their love. We and they can love him for what he has done for us, which is gratitude; we may love him for what he can do for us in the future, which might easily be no more for us than gratitude in the classical, cynical definition—a lively sense of favors to come; but loving God means loving him not only for what he does, but for what he is. And this involves some sort of *knowing* what he is.

How are men thus to know him? "The heavens show forth the glory of the Lord"—to one who already believes in the Lord, of course. Does the earth? The universe he has made is not inarticulate or in itself meaningless; it is crammed with meaning and utters it in its own way to whoever has eyes and ears, which itself has not. Eyes are for seeing, ears for hearing, but it is the mind that sees and hears, making its own selection and arrangement of all that flows in through eyes and ears. And the minds of men have not often seen love as the meaning.

There is joy in the universe, evidently; and there is pain. But mankind's tendency is rather to see the pain and blame God for it, than to see and thank God for the joy. It is not that pain outweighs joy in quantity, though we see anguishing individual cases where pain seems an ocean and joy hardly visible at all. It is much more, I think, that in their beginnings pain's impact is keener than joy's; and in their continuance, we easily grow used to joy, and ultimately callous to it: never to pain. If we had nothing but the experience of life as it meets us, I doubt if it would occur to us to cry out in an ecstasy, still less to utter as sober judgment, the words of St. John—"God is love."

The mass of the world's suffering can lead men either to rage against God or to deny his reality altogether. Even where it does neither, it can cool men's approach to God, setting a vast question mark against his love! Men feel that if they had the power that he has, they would do something about the world's pain . . . doubtless, he has his reasons . . . and so on. "What is necessary to know of God has been manifest; for the invisible things of him, his eternal power and divinity, are evident when considered from the creation of the world" (Rom. 1.20). So much they can accept—power, divinity; but there is not much warmth in the acceptance.

The warmth in our religion, indeed, is more apt to be kindled by Christ dying for us on Calvary. But an inclination to turn with relief from the distant majesty of God to the loving-kindness of Christ simply means that in us Christ is frustrated. His whole reason for coming into the world was to bring man to the Father, he himself was only the way. There would have been no love in him to utter its ultimate word on Calvary, unless infinite love was in God eternal. And infinite love is love itself: finite love, even the love of Christ's human heart, is at once immeasurably less than infinite love and owes its whole being to it.

We have just heard St. John's word "God is love." Remember that he had witnessed love of God triumphant over suffering permitted by God. John had been on Calvary when Christ, dying, cried out, "Father, into thy hands I commend my spirit" (Luke 23.46). In that cry, Christ was giving himself to the same Father to whom he had prayed in Gethsemani to remove the chalice of suffering. John had been there for that, too. To know suffering unto death, yet not love God the less for it, we must somehow see, as John did, the God that Christ saw.

2. Yahweh

"No man comes to the Father save by me," says Christ. And Christ takes the God of Abraham, Isaac and Jacob wholly for granted as his. When the Sadducees challenged

him about the resurrection of the dead (Matt. 22.32) he
answered by quoting God's word to Moses (Exod. 3.6): "I
am the God of Abraham and the God of Isaac and the God of
Jacob," and adding his own comment: "He is not the God
of the dead but of the living." In his duel in the desert with
Satan, he answered Satan's three thrusts with three phrases
from Deuteronomy: "Man does not live by bread alone, but
by whatever proceeds from the mouth of God"; "Thou shalt
not tempt the Lord thy God"; "Thou shalt adore the Lord thy
God and him only shalt thou serve." These are simply examples of that total acceptance by Christ of the God of the
Old Testament which is the sufficient cause of our own acceptance.

The text he quoted to the Sadducees comes at the beginning of the episode in which Moses, ordered by God to go
to the Children of Israel in bondage under Pharao, had asked
God to tell him His name, that he might be able to tell the
people Who it was that sent him.

God said to Moses "I am who am" . . . "Thou shalt say to
the children of Israel 'I am has sent me to you.' " The opening
words are variously translated. Besides "I am who am," we
find "I am who I am," which could mean "It is no business of
yours"—a refusal to answer, an interpretation based on a
notion found in some of the paganisms that to know the name
of a god gives men a hold over him. We find also: "I am that
I am," which does not seem to say anything at all. And there
are other translations. There has been a great outpouring of
scholarship on the text, with instances adduced of the same
phrase in other contexts.

I do not pretend that I can settle a matter so learnedly disputed. But it seems to me that it is settled for us when Exodus

has God going on to use "I am" as his name without any modifying or qualifying addition: "Say to the children of Israel: 'I am has sent me to you.' "

To the Semitic peoples a name was not simply a label, having no higher purpose than to distinguish one person from another. It uttered the reality of the person. In English we still have odd phrases like "What in Heaven's name does he think he is doing?" But these are relics of a dead habit. With the Jews the habit was intensely alive. The Temple was built to the *name* of Yahweh (2 Kings 7.13): He wished his *name* to dwell there (Deut. 12.5): Whoever blasphemed the *name* was to die (Lev. 24.16).

Because God's name bore such richness of content, its own meaning matters vitally. His "I am" is of importance beyond measuring, since it is the name by which he chose to be announced to the people he was calling into being as especially his. The text continues "This is my name forever, thus shall I be remembered from generation to generation." He would hardly have given them "My name is not your business" as his name forever. Even though no name he might give them could wholly utter his reality, the one he did give them was not all darkness.

God called himself "I am"—Ehyeh. His people responded "He is"—Yahweh (or perhaps in an earlier form Yahiweh). Yahweh was the sacred name. It occurs over five thousand times in the Old Testament, but not written out in full—they wrote the four consonants only, the tetragram, Y H W H. The word was uttered by the High Priest on the Day of Atonement, and in the blessing the priest gave after the daily sacrifice in the Temple—but by him, so we are told, in a low voice not heard above the chanting. Because of its sacredness, it was not to be cheapened by common utterance.

"I am" sounds as though God were asserting existence as the primary fact about himself, the fact by which he is willing to be named. To men of the Catholic tradition, who see God as Self-Existent Being, it seems that this is what the name of his choice is telling us about him. Could it have seemed so to Moses? Or even to the men who wrote the account in Exodus as we now have it, two or three hundred years after Moses—round the year 1000? The great Greeks did not arrive at self-existence as the ultimate truth about the Supreme Being for another six centuries after Exodus. Could a primitive people have seen it, even with a spiritual genius as their leader?

In considering these questions we must distinguish between the possibility of their arriving for themselves at so profound a concept—which seems unlikely—and their ability to understand it when it was offered to them. Whatever Moses thought God meant, whatever God himself meant, it is quite clear that the Old Testament does present God as the Self-Existent Being—the one who owes his existence to no other, to whom all others owe their existence. We remember "In the beginning God created heaven and earth" (Gen. 1.1). In the last book of the Old Testament we have "Look on heaven and earth and all that is in them and consider that God made them, made mankind too, out of nothing" (2 Mach. 7.28). And in between the first book and the last the same truth is repeated over and over. Any suggestion either that God owed his existence to any other being, or that any being existed not made by God, would have sounded to an instructed Jew like a blasphemy inconceivable, stoning would not have been bad enough for the blasphemer. And this *is* Self-Existence.

Certain other truths flow from the fact of self-existence which only the philosopher can expound but which anyone at all can *see*, really if unphilosophically. One is infinity, God is totally without limitation. The word "infinite" is not a favored word in the Old Testament, the word they prefer is "perfect," but the meaning is the same. They would instantly have denied any limitation in God that anyone might have had the temerity to suggest. Omnipotence was his, for there was nothing he could not do, we find the word seventy times in the Old Testament; he was omniscient, for there was nothing he did not know; and he had life without limit, too: "eternal" is a word always on the lips of his people.

But would the words "I am" have meant all this to an Israelite so long ago? What indeed do they mean? After all, when God said, "I am," Moses might very well have said, "I am too." But at least he would have known that when God said "I exist," which is what he *was* saying—he must have been affirming something special about his existence, something that neither Moses nor any man could affirm of his own. Whatever may have been his instant reaction, it is hard to believe that he would have been incapable of seeing the link between the words by which God named himself and the fact that God owes his existence to no other. We too can exist, we can say "I am": but only to God do the words wholly belong. When they have been said of him there is no more to be said! Everything has been said. Whereas, uttered by any one of us, "I am" needs every sort of addition; and every addition subtracts from fullness of being—e.g. "I am but I was not always," "I am because my parents met," "I am this but not that."

It is a strange name, "I am." The idea remained in the Jewish mind as an assertion of divinity. The prophet Isaiah accusing Babylon, the prophet Sophonias accusing Assyria, of arrogance swollen beyond the human level—both make the people they are condemning say of themselves "I am, and there is none else beside me." But we do not come upon God's own name for himself, "I am," actually used of him by his people. They used "He is," as we have already noted.

The words "I am" in the ordinary sense are everywhere in Scripture, as they are scattered all over our conversation; but for a second extraordinary use, by its strangeness forcing our attention, we must wait until Our Lord utters them of himself: "Before Abraham was made, I am" (John 8.58). It is as strange a phrase as "Say to the children of Israel *I am* has sent me to you." Moses had never heard "I am" used thus strangely before. Those to whom Our Lord was speaking had—in that one place in Exodus. What else could they do but take up stones to cast at him?

Thinking over it since, with a certain guidance from the philosophers, we have come to see that more is involved in God's "I am," in Self-Existent Being, than is likely to have occurred to Moses. Existence, of course, is a primary. It cannot be defined, because definition relates the thing defined to some other thing, and for existence there *is* no other thing, since there is nothing to which it does not apply. In fact what existence does not apply to *is* nothing! to exist is to be something, not nothing. So far we are considering existence as an abstract idea, which men have arrived at from their experience of all kinds and levels of existent beings. But with God's "I am" we see (or half-see, or glimpse) existence not as an abstract drawn by the mind from things, but as a reality in its own right superior to all things else—the reality, in fact, to which they owe their existence. It has an existence of its own!

Existence exists! and it is not just something, it is someone. It is God.

Someone, in fact, is what the Greeks did not reach. They could see Self-Existent Being; but their Self-Existent Being could not say "I am." Ours can. When we speak of God as "He is," we have uttered the whole truth about him, though we cannot, yet or ever, know all that we have said. But there is one level deeper still, a level so wrapped in darkness for the finite mind that we can hardly be said to see more of it than that it must be there. For we realize that, to utter the Infinite, two words are still one word too many. One of the two words is in some way repetitive. There is not one reality expressed by "I," another expressed by "am," and the two joined to make God: for there was none beyond to join them. There is one single reality: "I" and "am" are two ways of uttering it.

3. Religion Before the Exile

Is all this what God meant by uttering himself as "I am"? Certainly, no two words could better assert self-existence. It would be strange if he used them while deliberately excluding a meaning so apt to the whole Old Testament revelation, so capable of receiving all that Christ was to tell of God and all that the Church was to develop of the telling. There has never been one single phrase more *capax Dei*.

But whatever the phrase *can* mean, whatever God did mean by it, we still ask ourselves what the Israelites made of it. What indeed in their beginning did God mean to them? How early did they see Yahweh not as the High God, El Elyon, Supreme over all gods, but as the One God, the Only God?

In its depth, this is a matter for Old Testament specialists, but certain things are obvious.

To Abraham, Isaac and Jacob God made himself known as especially concerned with themselves and their families. In the Exodus from Egypt the descendants of the Patriarchs were formed into a people. Every people had a god, much as every man had a face: a people without a god was unthinkable, so indeed was a god without a people. And the god of a people must have a name. We hear God say to Moses (Exod. 6.2): "I appeared to Abraham, to Isaac, and to Jacob, as God Almighty—El Shaddai—but by my name Yahweh I did not make myself known to them." To the New People, he spoke the name.

A god's greatness was measured by what he did for his people: the conflicts of peoples were the test of their gods. And the God of the Israelites had shown his power by bringing them out of Egypt, and would show his power again (though only after forty years) in the victories which gave them the land of Canaan: for a people must have a land of its own.

Were they as yet monotheists? It would be hard to prove that they were. They had been told that they were not to have "strange gods"—that is, the gods of other peoples—befor him. But they do not seem, fully anyhow, to have realized that they must have no dealings at all with those other gods. We may summarize centuries of development in their transition from seeing other gods as weaker than Israel's God to realizing that other gods had no existence, were mere emptiness, human inventions.

In Canaan they found Baal, or the Baals—for every village, every notable tree or rock could have its Baal. And there were a host of lesser deities. Baal had a wife Ashtoreth, and their worship involved child sacrifice and ritual prostitution, male and female. There was a temptation to adorn the worship of Yahweh with elements from the cult of Baal. And of Ashtoreth, his wife. "There were male cult prostitutes in the land, Judah did according to all the abominations of the nation which Yahweh drove out before the people of Israel" (3 Kings 14.24). This was in the time of Roboam, Solomon's son. Centuries later Jeremiah could write (11.13): "Your gods have become as many as your cities, O Judah; and as many as the streets of Jerusalem are the altars you have set up to shame, altars to burn incense to Baal."

These insertions into the religion of Yahweh were made not only by the mass of the people and the more corrupt of their leaders. Consider Solomon. When he dedicated the Temple in Jerusalem, he uttered the prayer: "O Lord, God of Israel, there is no God like thee, in heaven above or on earth beneath, keeping covenant and showing steadfast love to thy servants who walk before thee with all their heart. . . . Will God indeed dwell on the earth? Behold, heaven and the highest heaven cannot contain thee; how much less this house which I have built! Yet have regard to the prayer of thy servant and to his supplication, O Lord my God, hearkening to the cry and to the prayer which thy servant prays before thee this day; that thy eyes may be open night and day toward this house, the place of which thou hast said 'My name shall be there' . . . And hearken thou to the supplication of thy servant and of thy people Israel, when they pray toward this place; yea, hear thou in heaven thy dwelling place; and when thou dost hear, forgive." (3 Kings 8.23ff.)

There is splendor and profound understanding in this

prayer. But we have only to read three chapters on to find the same Solomon building "a high place for Chemosh the abomination of Moab, and for Molech the abomination of the Ammonites, on the mountain east of Jerusalem. And so he did for all his foreign wives, who burned incense and sacrificed to their gods" (3 Kings 11.7–8).

In reading the minds of men of another civilization, another millennium, one feels the folly of confident assertion. Yet I think we may feel sure that Solomon did not feel guilty of apostasy from Yahweh—any more than the Jews did who built a temple at Elephantine, an island in the Nile, where they had altars to two other gods and goddesses: it is clear from their correspondence with the authorities in Jerusalem that they felt themselves to be in perfectly good standing. As we read carefully, indeed, we find it difficult to be certain of any early revelation from Yahweh that the other gods did not exist. All the texts assert his superiority—for example, "Who is like thee, O Lord, among the gods?" (Exod. 15.11); "Now I know that Yahweh is greater than all gods" (Exod. 18.11). But the question of the *existence* of those other gods does not seem to have arisen for a good many centuries.

Even texts which might be taken to assert that there is only one God—like "The Lord Our God is one Lord" (Deut. 6.4) —do not necessarily mean more than that he is God in a sense especially his own. And when the Jews of old read "See now that I, even I, am he, and there is no god beside me" (Deut. 32.39), the preceding verse might still have been read as leaving the pagan gods existent, though powerless—"Where are their gods, the rock in which they took refuge, who ate the fat of their sacrifices, and drank the wine of their drink offering? Let them rise up and help you."

Texts declaring Yahweh's superiority to the gods would be read monotheistically by monotheists, so that we find Psalmists using them as a matter of course—e.g. "There is none like thee among the gods, O Lord" (Ps. 86.8). Once at least the Psalmist takes care to guard against the misunderstanding which might come from too literal a reading: in Psalm 95, the words "The Lord Our God is to be feared above all gods" are followed instantly by "for all the gods of the peoples are idols, but Yahweh made the heavens."

We need to remind ourselves that the Books in which we read the Mosaic legislation attained their present form long after Moses—Exodus perhaps three hundred years after, Deuteronomy a couple of centuries after that. I am not raising here the question whether either book gives us God's law point by point as Moses received them: I note merely that for centuries the Israelites did not have these books as we have them. We cannot know for certain what even Solomon had read. How did the ordinary Israelites learn the teachings and the laws of Moses?

About the laws, we read (Deut. 31.10) that every seven years at the Feast of Tabernacles, "you shall read this law before all Israel in their hearing." About the teachings, we can only speculate. As a boy I had a vivid mental picture of those ancient Israelites reading their Bible as assiduously as I was urged to read mine. But the Old Testament itself does not, as far as my memory goes, record a single occasion on which anyone sat down to read a Book of Scripture as spiritual reading—as it happens, the word "Scriptures" is not found in the Old Testament.

There were altars for sacrifice to Yahweh—at Gilgal and Bethel and Dan for instance. But until the Exile—say round

500 B.C.—there were no synagogues for prayer and Scripture reading and instruction. It seems probable that the teachings reached them piecemeal, mostly by word of mouth, with an occasional copy of some of the Books of our present Old Testament reaching the more learned among them in an earlier form. Monotheism may not have stood out as clearly to them as to us who have not only read the Pentateuch, but have read it with minds formed by reading the later Prophets. It is not only we of the Christian world who read them so. The Jews of Our Lord's time had come to their ideas about God and man's relation to him with minds similarly formed.

What were these ideas? Of God's dealing with men I shall treat in Volume Two. Here our concern is with what they made of God himself, with the picture which emerges from the Old Testament of the God they could not picture.

4. Monotheism in Possession

From the Exile onwards, monotheism was in strict possession. Yahweh was God and only he. The pagan gods were more and more seen not only as powerless, but as unreal, figments of the imagination, non-existent. Not that existence was a primary for Israelite thought. Men knew, of course, that things existed, came into existence, went out of existence: but what really mattered was action. Existence was taken for granted but not much thought about. Yahweh existed because he showed his presence by his actions. This is almost certainly the explanation of the text with which two Psalms, 15 and 54, open—"The fool has said in his heart, There is no God!" The fool in question was probably not in our sense an atheist: he simply felt certain that God would not interfere!

Only with the Prophets of the Exile do we come to clear
and repeated assertion of monotheism. "Thus says Yahweh,
the King of Israel and Israel's Redeemer, the Lord of hosts:
'I am the first and I am the last, and besides me there is no
God'" (Is. 44.6)—a text which we meet again in the last
chapter of the Bible, the twenty-second of Apocalypse—"I
am the Alpha and the Omega, the first and the last, the beginning and the end." Along with that assertion of God's total
uniqueness we have the dismissal of all the rest—"The gods
who did not make the heavens and earth shall perish from the
earth and from under the heavens."

Yahweh was utterly transcendent, not natural forces personified, but a Person; not emergent from the universe but its
Creator—the opening verses of Genesis could have been
written of no other deity, by no other people. Other nations
had made their gods but Yahweh had made Israel. The others
had made gods in their own image, only too horribly and
sometimes ridiculously like themselves. But Yahweh had made
men in *his* image and his whole shaping—wooing, hammering
—of Israel was to restore their damaged likeness to himself.
No people ever invented a god so fiercely and continuously
critical of themselves, critical of every sin to which they were
tempted.

Yet though Yahweh was the Creator of all men, he was yet
peculiarly their God: they did not easily or soon find a balance between these two truths. They had begun with the
idea that every people had a God and Yahweh was theirs—
that he should in any conceivable circumstances favor others
before them was against the order of nature. All peoples felt
like this about their God and Yahweh had given Israel special

encouragement—"You shall be my peculiar possession above all peoples; for all the earth is mine" (Exod. 19.5).

With them, as with others, the idea of *their* god and *their* land were bound close. Could he operate at all outside? We find hints of the feeling, or fear, that he could not—Canaan was his territory, outside Canaan one was out of God's protecting reach, out even of his knowledge. When David was in exile he pleaded with Saul: "They have driven me out this day that I should have no share in the heritage of the Lord, saying Go, serve other gods. Now therefore let not my blood fall to the earth away from the presence of the Lord" (1 Kings 26.19–20).

This "localization" of God did not survive—he was Creator of all the world, he had made his power felt in Egypt. "Can a man hide himself in secret places so that I cannot see him? Do I not fill heaven and earth?" (Jer. 23.23).

But the notion that he was exclusively theirs did not die so easily. It was given a stronger hold on life when the Prophets began to talk of the relation between Israel and its God in terms of marriage. This figure, especially as we find it in Ezekiel (16.8), could not have been used earlier, it would almost certainly have resulted in phallic rituals. By the time it came, that danger was less. But it strengthened the sense of racial exclusiveness. The idea of marriage between Israel and Yahweh gave vividness to the injunction that they must not go whoring after other gods. But Yahweh, they felt, must not go whoring after other peoples either.

With Jeremiah and the Second Isaiah God's care was shown as extending to the whole of mankind: but for the mass of Jews this could only be a secondary interest for him, Israel was his people and he Israel's husband. That Israel was to grow, not by physical descent but by rebirth in grace, how could they have seen?

Of the "personality" of the God who meant so much to the Israelites something has been said in Chapter Five (3), Chapter Six (3), and we shall see more of it in Volume Two. Here we may pause upon certain ambiguities in their mind about him which only Christ could clarify. When we come to their "mind," we must go carefully. Much is now written of the Semitic mind, so different from our own, and of the necessity of entering into it. We must do our best, and the scholars can help us. But only to a point. We cannot enter into the minds of those long-distant spiritual kinsmen of ours—that is, we cannot think and feel as they thought and felt. No width and minuteness of study is a substitute for being an Old Testament Jew. But at least we can find them uttering certain problems they had not solved. In especial there were two pairs of contradictories which they could not bring into one vision.

The first was the certainty of God's transcendence as against the certainty their faith gave them that he was close to them. On one side was the immeasurable beyondness, the majesty that they could contemplate only with stricken awe. On the other side was their need for union with him, the need to feel his closeness. He had come very near to Israel *as a people*, had shown his care for them. The individual Israelite could love him for it and utter his love as the Psalmist did. The Prophet could tell him of God's presence within him— "I the Lord search the mind and test the heart" (Jer. 17.10). But he wanted to feel God's presence, feel him close. This surely was what drew many to the idols and to the sexual rituals.

The second "irreconcilability" which troubled them, and

still leaves ourselves not wholly untroubled, was between God's Justice and his Mercy—how can perfect Justice co-exist with limitless Mercy?

Again and again we find the Mercy expressed with total conviction, but with Justice to shadow it.

Yahweh had proclaimed himself to Moses as "merciful and gracious, slow to anger and abounding in steadfast love and faithfulness, forgiving iniquity and transgression and sin, but who will by no means clear the guilty, visiting the iniquity of the fathers upon the children and the children's children, to the third and fourth generation" (Exod. 34.6). Moses reminds God of this, both the mercy and the punishment of the innocent (Num. 14.18). We find the merciful part quoted again by Ezra without the rest (Neh. 9.17). We find it in the New Testament (2 Peter 3.9). "The Lord is not slow about his promise as some count slowness, but forbearing toward you, not wishing that any should perish, but that all should reach repentance." We get heart-warming statements of God's love and mercy; but we get, too, such phrases as "Yahweh will not have compassion on their fatherless and widows" (Is. 9.17).

For a quick glimpse of a mind which has not seen through to the reconciliation of Mercy and Justice, a mind which does not seem even to see any problem, one might read Psalm 139. The first eighteen verses show God as all-seeing, all-knowing, all-provident. They culminate in "How precious to me are thy thoughts, O God! . . . When I awake, I am still with thee." But then comes "O that thou wouldst slay the wicked, O God, and that men of blood would depart from me. . . . Do I not hate them that hate thee, O Lord? And do I not loathe them that rise up against thee? I hate them with perfect hatred."

I think I am not alone, as I read the Old Testament, in sometimes feeling the absence of Christ almost physically, sometimes feeling him most wonderfully present. But at all times one feels the mystery—the precious light, the darkness, God always realized by the men who wrote the Books. The writer of Ecclesiasticus speaks for all of them (43:29ff.): "We shall say much and yet shall want words. But the sum of our words is: He is all. . . . Glorify him as best you may, glory is still lacking, such is the marvel of his greatness; praise him and extol him as you will, he is beyond all praising. . . . Who can magnify his eternal being? Much more lies beyond our knowledge; only the fringe of Creation meets our view; and of all things the Lord is maker."

5. The New Testament Shows Us the Same God

We have already noticed Our Lord's "Before Abraham was made, I am," which may quite well have been uttered soon after he had spoken to the Sadducees of the God of Abraham, Isaac, and Jacob.

He had a fondness for the words "I am" used where we would not expect them. "I am the light of the world," "I am the Way and the Truth and the Life," "I am the Resurrection and the Life"—these are, if not grammatically monstrous, at least improbable enough to force us to look deeper into them. We might have expected him to say: "I know the Way and can show it you"; "I have Truth, and Life, and a Food to nourish Life, and can give them to you"; "Into the world's darkness I can cast light"; "I have the power to rise from the dead and, united with me, you too can rise." But he said: "I am." "I am" seems to have been a continuous theme in his mind. And we can see why. If one *has* existence, one *has* all the perfections that go with it; if one *is* existence, one *is* those perfections.

Consider what Our Lord has to tell us about God.

He is the one only God, to be loved with all the power of mind and heart (Mark 12. 44; cf. Deut. 6.4). He is good, and he only is the plenitude of goodness (Matt. 19.17). He is perfect (Matt. 5.48). All things are possible to him—even the salvation of the rich (Matt. 19.26). He is continuously in operation (John 5.44). He is the God of the living not the dead (Matt. 22.23). He is hidden, dwells in secret (Matt. 6.6). In a wealth of adjectives and verbs, he uses one noun—"God is a spirit" (John 4.24).

All these are statements directly about God. In statements about God's ways of acting upon us, Our Lord shows him as knowing, hearing, listening, caring, loving, giving himself, withdrawing himself. He clothes the grasses of the field. No sparrow falls without God seeing. We do not find the actual phrases "God is love," "God is light" on Our Lord's lips; for these we must wait, John has them in his First Epistle; but there is no question where John heard them.

Read through the items of this list one by one. There is nothing that need have surprised the Jews of that day. In twelve hundred years of such a closeness of relation with God as no nation or people had ever known, they had come to a most wonderful sense of intimacy with him. Our Lord takes God as someone to whom they need not be introduced afresh. He corrects and develops some of their notions of man's relation to God—especially of God's care not for the Jews only but for all men alike; but for the rest he is simply giving shape and proportion to truths about God already known.

The movement into God's innermost life—the life of Father and Son and Holy Spirit—is the one new reality which it is his to reveal: apart from that it would be hard to find any feature in the portrait of God drawn by Christ Our Lord with which they were not already familiar. We sometimes have a feeling that the God of the New Testament is a God of love, a great advance on the Old Testament God of justice. But this means only that we have not been reading the Old Testament recently. God's love is all over it.

Indeed one of the joys of coming again to reading the Old Testament is to find word after word of Christ already uttered in it. The Gospels tell of God's mercy, for instance; so does the text already quoted of Nehemias—"Thou art a forgiving God, gracious and merciful, patient and full of compassion, and thou didst not forsake them." Our Lord loved children, and the Psalmist had called God "Father of the fatherless" (67.6).

In the absence of a clear notion of re-birth in Sanctifying Grace, we should not expect to find an awareness of our supernatural sonship, but they did feel themselves God's children. We have it in the Song of Moses (Deut. 32.6): "Is not he your father, who created you, who made you, who established you?" To address God as Father was not Israel's habit, but the comparison was always in their minds, and often enough on their lips—"As a father pities his children, so the Lord has compassion on those who fear him" (Ps. 102.15). St. Paul compares marriage with the union of Christ and his Church, but, as we have noted, the Old Testament had developed the idea of Israel as the bride of God to the point where straying after strange gods was "whoring."

And God's love was returned by men. "As the stag pants for the fountains of water, my soul pants for thee, O God. My soul has thirsted for the strong living God" (Ps. 41.2). These words are a reminder that in each Testament we come upon things that cannot quite be matched in the other. The Psalmist pants and thirsts for God, for instance: we do not find the new Christians saying that (perhaps because they had Christ in the Eucharist). God's care for every sparrow that falls to the ground is special to the Gospel. But while both Testaments see God as Father, only in the Old is his love compared to a mother's—"Can a woman forget her infant, so as not to have pity on the son of her womb? Even if she should forget, yet will I not forget thee" (Is. 49.15).

The difficulty is that, as we read the Old Testament, the phrases I have drawn out for quotation do not leap to the eye; in its forty or so books there is so much else. As we have seen, the Chosen People were developing their understanding of God, guided by him in their development. We meet many things in our reading which seem to force us back upon this fact. We remind ourselves that the Jews of long ago did not know about the *permissive* will of God and would therefore assume that whatever happened was willed by him in the strictest sense. We may be surprised to discover that the Old Testament can walk step by step with the New in the matter of God's love. But at least, we feel, the Old is filled with the anger of God as the New is not.

So indeed it is. But look closer. All our lives we have known that God said: "Vengeance is mine, I will repay." We look up the text in Chapter 32 of Deuteronomy, and we find the whole chapter glittering with threats. Still, we tell ourselves, it represents an early stage in God's tuition of his people, an early stage in their pupillage. There is truth in this explanation, but it does not cover everything. Particularly, it does not cover the fact that the text is quoted twice in the New Testament. St. Paul (Rom. 12.19) uses it as a reason why we ourselves should take no vengeance for wrongs done to us. But in Hebrews (10.30), we find it carrying the same threat of divine vengeance as in the original. And it continues with one of the most blood-chilling sentences in all Scripture: "It is a fearful thing to fall into the hands of the living God."

The truth is that God is not simply the personification of our own best self. We construct an idea of a God of whom we can wholly approve, a God as enlightened as we, in fact what we should be if we were God. And so often the God of one Testament or the other does not conform. There is not only mystery unfathomable in himself; but, as St. Paul reminds us, his ways are unsearchable: the unlikeness to us, which the Fourth Council of the Lateran finds greater in him than the likeness, affects us even more in what he does than in what he is.

And it is not simply that we find some of his actions inexplicable—as when he chooses two nobodies, like Abraham and Peter, for the mightiest offices ever entrusted to men. It is much more that we find ourselves trying to defend particular actions of his which look like a flat contradiction of love. Later we shall discuss the pain of the world and the question why God allows it to continue. What concerns us here is not the suffering he allows but the suffering Scripture shows him as inflicting or threatening—eternal punishment above all.

We try, I say, to defend these; and we find ourselves wondering if they are defensible. It is our own defenses that need strengthening. What defenses have we? Two, principally: the certainty that God knows the whole of every situation and we only a fragment, so that his judgment is surer than ours; and the certainty that we can trust his love. In these two certainties we can cling to belief where we cannot see, cling to love even when we cannot feel it.

Why are we certain that we can trust his love? For one reason, because Christ, whose love we can trust, did so wholly trust it. For another, and profounder reason, because God gave us his Son: "He that did not spare his own Son, but gave him up for us all—will he not also give us all things with him?" (Rom. 8.32). If he can give us his Son with so total a giving, what can he refuse us? There is no refusal in God. The refusals are ours. In this truth the contradiction vanishes between Infinite Mercy and Infinite Justice. Repentance is acceptance of God and changes the man, so that Mercy can have its way with him, Justice content. There is no ultimate loss for any man save in his ultimate refusal of God. But let us not pretend that this truth is always easy to see. Or to show.

6. *"No Adequate Philosophy"*

With all the agreement in detail the Jews, even at the highest point they reached, did not see God as Christ Our Lord saw him. We find St. Paul saying (Rom. 10.2): "I can testify that they are zealous for God's honor, but it is with imperfect understanding." At the root of this imperfect understanding was the deep-lying instinct we have already discussed against any effort to probe the mysterious reality of God himself. We have already quoted Dr. Dodd's comment: "Judaism failed because it had no adequate philosophy behind its faith and practice." The men of the Old Testament could experience God's action and react with joy or anger, but they did not give their whole mind to the God whose action they were experiencing and reacting to.

Two key truths of the religion of Christ are "God is" and "God is a spirit." The Jews had them both, but not as key truths. As we have seen, they had God's own name for himself, "I am," but we cannot feel that they had developed in the understanding of the reality those words uttered. In regard to "spirit" the position is in a way even stranger.

We are so accustomed to the phrase "God is a spirit" that when we hear Our Lord say it at the well to the Samaritan woman with the five husbands, its newness may not strike us. It is not in the Old Testament. Spirit is there. But, as we have seen, it was only at the very end that they had developed beyond the literal meaning of the word they used, namely "breath"—God breathed and man lived. But "breath" was not strong enough or rich enough to support all the realities that could flow from the true meaning of Spirit.

They could speak of God's eternity, omnipotence, omniscience: but, lacking the concept of spirit, they could not see deeply enough into any of these. Their notions were not anthropomorphic, exactly, but we are left with the impression that for all save an intellectual and spiritual elite their God tended to be only man writ large, man writ immense. But God is not man writ large, writ infinite even, any more than man is his statue given life. What God's infinity meant they could have known only if they had analyzed self-existence. But, though they had all the elements of it, they had not the actual word: and the fertility that certain great words have in themselves simply by being words was not for the Jews of that time.

Because they were not really thinking about God himself, there was too much that they necessarily missed in man's relation to him—about which they were most certainly thinking. Their concentration was on man's duty to serve their insufficiently comprehended God. This led them to attach what seems to us (and sometimes seemed to the Prophets) a swollen importance to ritual actions of every sort. And there was a result more serious still: they did not know the supreme truth about man, that the everlasting destiny of every man is to come into the fullness of union with God. So that their notion of redemption had to remain meagre, very much of this world. At the beginning of this chapter I said that the prayer "Grant that I may love and enjoy thee forever in heaven" is one that we do not say with any very vivid realization. There is not much indication in the Old Testament that anyone would have said it at all.

A great wealth of truth about God is contained in the concept of spirit, and this concept they had not unlocked. Towards the end, indeed, under the influence of the Greek philosophers, they did make a beginning of the unlocking—in the Wisdom books and in the books written between the two Testaments. When one remembers what the Jews gained from their enforced contact with Persian thought during the forty years of the Babylonian Captivity, one cannot help wondering what might have been the outcome had Alexander the Great removed the whole people to Greece when he had them in his power a couple of centuries later.

NINE

God and Philosophy

1. Revelation and the Philosophers

Pascal has told us that the God of his longing was the God
not of the philosophers, but of Abraham, Isaac and Jacob. I
met this for the first time with a shock, which only after a
while became a shock of recognition. Yet it is plain common
sense. It is the simple rule for all who would have God for
their own.

The God of the Patriarchs is, we have seen, the God of
Jesus Christ. What Pascal's soul craved for was the living
God, God coming to us, in action and utterance among us,
not the God whose existence is the end of a chain of reason-
ing however flawless, whose nature has been explored for us
by thinkers superb in intellect but with only a minimum
experience of him. Above all, Pascal wanted the God with

whom we can enter into our own personal and incommunicable relation, the God who, as we cannot too often remind
ourselves, is not a problem to be solved or a solution to be admired, but a reality to be possessed, contemplated, conversed
with, enjoyed, loved.

An ounce of revelation is worth a ton of philosophy. Yet
philosophy has contributed to our growth in the knowledge
of what God has revealed of himself. Theology and philosophy are different disciplines, but they are ways of growing
into knowledge of one same reality. The Ten Commandments
are for the most part a codification of moral insights that men
have arrived at by using the natural powers of their minds
upon the experience of living. The minds of men have similarly been occupied with ultimate meanings, and not fruit-
lessly. Guided by the Holy Spirit, the Church has built many
of their insights into the teaching God has given, and we are
all nourished.

St. Thomas, we say, baptized Aristotle. In the same way
Augustine can be said to have baptized Plato, or rather to have
carried Plato with him into the font of his own baptism. Our
religion reaches us the richer for those two men. There would
have been a different richness if Augustine had baptized Lao
Tse, dead a couple of centuries before Plato, a different richness again if St. Thomas had baptized Shankara, dead three
centuries before himself. The Chinese thinker and the Indian
could have been built into the living teaching of the Church
as the Greeks were—perhaps it is not too late, even now, thus
to baptize them.

We must not exaggerate our debt to the Greeks. There is a
tendency to talk as though Greek philosophy had taken over
the Christian revelation, a tendency sufficiently controlled in

the learned, but apt to produce very odd comments from lesser men who cannot tell Philo from Plato but happily dismiss every development of Christian doctrine as a Greek adulteration: they really do fear the Greeks especially when the gifts they bear are philosophical. In fact, while the debt must not be exaggerated, there *is* a debt. On a foundation unknown to Plato and Aristotle, the foundation laid by Christ, we can use their insights and their vocabulary, develop them, correct them, supply their omissions.

To take a single example of these last—they never did arrive at a definition of "person" or make any serious examination of personality as distinct from individuality: so that for them, and for the men formed by them, the one was as essentially a limitation as the other, and much about God himself remained dark. But, with whatever they failed to see, they still saw enough to help us enter more deeply into realities which they could not have revealed to us. The rest of this book is concerned with the realities and our deeper entry into them.

2. How Can the Finite Know the Infinite?

Because God is a spirit, we take our own spirit as a starting point. In an earlier chapter we considered the disadvantage that comes from its being embodied; but as against that we feel that it has the enormous advantage, for our present purpose, of being made in the image of God. What could be a better starting point than an image of the original that we are seeking to see more clearly? Yet it can be a tricky business.

One cannot proceed as a matter of course from the image to the original. Otherwise we might deduce from a man's photograph that he lacked depth, or from his statue that he was inconveniently rigid. In other words we have to allow for the material in which the image is made—there may be elements in the original which cannot be reproduced in that particular material (it would be hard, for instance, to represent steadfastness in jelly). And there are qualities in the material which cannot be eliminated in the fact, but must be eliminated, or at least allowed for, by the mind. How does all this apply to ourselves who are images of God made by him of nothing? Obviously, nothingness has no qualities of its own to get in the way of such likeness as can be produced in it; but what likeness of an infinite being *can* be produced in nothingness? And given that the likeness is found primarily in the mind, what understanding of the infinite original can the finite image have?

We have already considered the answer given by Dionysius the Areopagite, who was so possessed with the total unknowability of the Infinite that he could say that it would be truer to deny than to affirm that God is good and wise. A better phrase is "We do not know what God is, but only what he is not." Scripture does not say this, not very clearly at least; nor does the Church in her official teaching; yet there is a great weight of theological learning behind it, and it is full of meaning for the learned. But those who come new to it can find it confusing. They are inclined to ask, If we do not know what God is but what he is not, what do we love? Evidently, the word "know" is used here in a somewhat truncated sense, as though the only knowledge were conceptual. Even here we feel that the statement is too compressed.

It is true that when we come to analyze what God has told us about himself, we find that to enter into the meaning we must be constantly cleansing our concepts. We must cleanse them especially of the finitude that is necessarily in them insofar as finite beings that we are have arrived at them by our experience of life as we finitely live it. In that sense we are negating limitations. But limitations are themselves negations, and negating negations is not being negative, but positive; and it is by positive knowledge that we negate them. We use a profusion of words negative in form—in-finite, in-dependent, im-mense, ab-solute—which assert that God is not finite, not dependent, not spatially contained, not tied by any chain of any sort. Our language is naturally soaked in the finite, because that is what it has to cope with in its daily work; but it also has the word "not," which always negates but is not always negative; it can negate upwards as well as downwards, and the upward negation is positive.

We can speak of a *point* as not in space, and we have reached almost the limit of negation; we can speak of a *spirit* as not in space, and our statement is wholly affirmative—not a negative, but a kicking away of the springboard of material reality by which the mind leaps upwards. Even more clearly we see a word like "infinite" not as negative, but as a kicking away of created reality, so that the mind soars upward to a being wholly self-sufficient, self-existent, self-explanatory, self-possessive. To say "A man is not his photograph" is only verbally negative; and that is what every "in-" before all the modes of finitude comes to.

The finite is a necessary springboard, our feet rest on it. To change the figure, its value for clarification is very great. We can define "creation" as making a being according to its totality, which is an entirely positive definition; but it helps us to know what we have said if we re-state the definition as making without the use of any material, which sounds negative, but is not.

We can see why the great philosophers are concerned that we should not lose awareness of the gap between infinite and finite. But there is such a thing as letting the infinite paralyze us, where it should simply awe us; and this is rather like letting the ocean frighten us. In fact, if we decide to take the plunge, we discover that it is easier to swim in the ocean than in a pool, we feel that there is so much more of it to support us: it is easier to let the intellect swim in God, provided it is letting God support it—which by revelation and grace he does.

It is true that the likeness between the creature and the Creator is, in the phrase of the Fourth Council of the Lateran, far less than the unlikeness; the same might be said of my photograph and me; but, in the first case as in the second, the likeness *is* a likeness. We were made in the image and likeness not of what God is not, but of God. It would be a strange image that gave no *positive* hint at all of the original, a strange likeness in which there was not one gleam of the original to be caught.

In this field Christ Our Lord is a better guide than the greatest philosopher or theologian, if for no other reason than that he had at once an intimacy and an identity with God that no other has had. He uses all sorts of words about God without giving any hint that it would be better to deny them. He speaks of God in human language with superb freedom, giving no effect as of one merely stammering negatives, hobbling about in negatives. He not only uses the great words— spirit, life, knowledge, love, work—of God, but he constantly uses the same word about God and about man within the one sentence. Thus: "God is a Spirit, and they that worship him must worship him in *spirit* and in truth" (John 4.23); "No one *knows* the Father but the Son *and* him to whom the Son shall reveal him" (Matt. 11.27; Luke 10.22). "If anyone *love* me, he will keep my word and my Father will *love* him" (John 14.23). In no way could Our Lord more clearly have shown that from our own human concepts we can proceed to positive knowledge of God and his attributes. With all their imperfections, we get more aid out of the truth in them than hindrance out of their limitation.

Our Lord's human nature truly bore the infinite Person of God the Son—he who had seen him had seen the Father, as he told Philip at the Last Supper. Similarly, Our Lord's human concepts and their utterance in human words bore the infinite. So that we who receive them have true knowledge—that is, true beginning of knowledge, including the realization that there remains an endlessness of knowledge.

The Incarnation, indeed, is more than a reassurance that the concepts Christ utters are meaningful: it is our best guide into the depth of their meaning. It is not "what God is not" that became man. The infinite, incarnate in our nature, is no less infinite because we can love It, enter into personal union with It, receive It bodily. It is immensely worthwhile to examine such words as spirit, knowledge, love, life as the philosopher does by the sole power of the mind, making no direct appeal to what revelation teaches. But it would be mere folly to study them exclusively in that way, as though we had not this deeper access by revelation.

In fact it would be dangerous to do it too long at a time without returning to Scripture to meet the living God. The concepts are rich, but they are still abstractions; to stay too long only with them would be rather like studying skeletons without looking at people, which might result in losing all notion of humanity, especially of humanity's attractiveness. Philosophy is indispensable, yet the philosopher at best is only pressing his nose against the window and straining his eyes into the blackness on the other side. No "pure" philosopher ever saw love as one of the Infinite's attributes; if any of them had, the love could only have been frigid with the Infinite's own frigidity, to which a response of love by the philosopher would have seemed like an impertinence, or at best an irrelevance.

But for us, and for the philosopher too if he chooses, Christ is there whom, as St. John says, "we have seen with our eyes, whom we have looked upon, whom our hands have handled" (1 John 1.1). As beginners we are apt, in the first excitements of philosophy, to forget that the Infinite whom we are philosophically studying is the same Infinite whom we meet in the Gospels and whom we receive in the Blessed Eucharist. And there is more to be learned about the Infinite by studying Christ than by studying the concept of Infinity, or even by entering into ecstatic contact with the Infinite as mystics do.

None the less, while striving to grow in intimacy with Our Lord, we must make our own exploration of spirit, knowledge, love, life—treading, as the Church herself does, the path philosophers have blazed for us, studying the paths philosophers are still trying to build into the darkness around us. We do so, not to discover whether God is all these, for he has already told us what he is and we have accepted his word and found it good, but to go deeper into their meaning in order to know him better. Here above all we must get mental equivalents which, God aiding, may become vital equivalents. It is not much gain to hear Christ tell us that God is a spirit, if we think spirit is some kind of astral matter, shaped like the body but thinner.

3. God Is Not Infinite Indifference

The exploration starts with our own spirit. We may follow some such line as that suggested in Chapter Six. We begin by stripping away the body, tracking down and eliminating from consideration all those elements in our own spiritual being and activity which flow from the spirit's embodiment. We must hush imagination to quiet, quicken intellect to reluctant activity. We must concentrate the whole force of our mind upon the being we have already considered, partless, spaceless, living its own life of knowledge, love, power. That effort we may find hard enough, yet we cannot rest in it, we must proceed to a harder still. We must try to strip away finitude. Such a being as we have been contemplating, but infinite, is God. He is an infinite spirit, infinitely simple, utterly spaceless therefore, living his own life of infinite knowledge, infinite love, infinite power.

Strip away finitude. It sounds such a simple, direct, no-nonsense formula. If only it were possible. Once again we must make what beginning we can. We must develop an ever more piercing eye for the limitations in our own spirit, and negate them. The first trouble is in the process—how *can* a finite being be sure that it has discovered every element of its own finitude?

The second, graver, trouble is in the result—let us be as successful as man has never yet been, and what we arrive at after all this stripping and negating is something of which we have no personal experience: we can be frightened of it, or lost in it, or left cold by it: above all we can be misled into thinking we comprehend it. We are working in, or working from, abstract concepts; and abstract concepts can become as great a tyranny for the trained mind as imagination for the untrained. It is possible to fall so much in love with one's mental formulation of God as to be annoyed by some piece of God's revelation which does not fit.

Nowhere is pride of the mind greater folly; the most we can hope for is a flash of light here, a glint there, tiny in total compared with the darkness: but immeasurably precious, provided we bring them back to illumine our knowledge of Christ Our Lord. The first test of our thinking is whether we are seeing Christ closer and clearer, and growing in desire for union with him. The ultimate test—which it would be discouraging, perhaps, to apply too rigorously at first—is whether we are being drawn towards God *as* God. Is there some movement in us towards him, some beginning of meaning for "joy in him," some first taste of bliss in the thought of the total union for which we are destined in the Beatific Vision? Is the word "Beatific"—which means happy-making —beginning to be more than a word for us?

Unless we grow in love for God, we are taking no advantage from his offer of love. With this we come to a mystery which looks at first like utter contradiction. God is infinite, creatures cannot affect him, says philosophy. God is infinite, creatures *can* affect him, says Scripture. It is philosophically unthinkable that the Absolute should react to, be affected by, beings he has made of nought; yet from end to end Scripture presents God as "reacting," with love or pity or anger, with reward or punishment.

The truth is that both statements are colliding with the limits of human language and human thought in the attempt to utter a truth. There is no contradiction provided we realize that each is at once a superb effort and a realized failure to utter the whole of a reality by us unutterable. To deny the one truth puts care and sorrow into the Infinite, makes the Infinite vulnerable to us; but to deny the other gives a monster God to whom it is a matter of indifference whether we suffer or don't suffer, sin or don't sin. Sorrow as men know it, transferred to God, would connote a defect in infinite beatitude; but indifference would seem to connote a worse kind of defect still, a defect in love.

To say of Scripture and Philosophy that each is an effort at utterance which must always fall short is not to place the two efforts on a level. Philosophy is the work of men seeking to know more of God, Scripture is the work of God seeking to be known by men. Scripture has God's guarantee of its truth, philosophy no guarantee save our own conviction that the philosopher has seen aright. There is no question which authority is primary. Aristotle's concept of God as Pure Act is one of the most splendid achievements of the human intellect; but if it dims our vision of the God who is Christ's Father and ours, then Aristotle has not served us. Aristotle had not much personal, as distinct from intellectual, contact with the infinite, less than Plato, much less than Plotinus. It was without Aristotle's consent that Aquinas baptized him: and one cannot feel that the baptism wholly "took."

Christ sees no Ultimate beyond his Father, union with whom is the goal for which all men were created: our ac-

ceptance is not unsettled when we hear Dionysius tell of a
God more Ultimate still, beyond the reach of our minds. One
sometimes gets a feeling that philosophers, paralyzed either by
the Infinite or perhaps only by Dionysius, are warning God
to keep his distance and warning us of his unsuitability for the
kind of union with us that he so evidently wants. Perhaps that
is why Pascal wished them away.

Christ leaves us in no doubt: God wants to be known by
us, wants us in the closest union with himself—and this not in
some future life, but here and now: "I in my Father," he says
at the Last Supper, "and you in me, and I in you." In the light
of that, indifference on God's part is unthinkable. "Like as a
Father pities his children, so the Lord pities them that fear
him" (Ps. 102.15): the words are inadequate, scaled down to
our comprehension, almost unbearably disproportionate, but
they are not meaningless.

They do not convey nothing. They do not convey infinite
indifference, they must convey a reality in God, not less real
because there is no adequate human utterance for it. God
thought it better that we should have it thus than not at all.
There is something within the changeless, infinite, absolute
God which, reduced to words that we can hear, is mercy or
pity or anger, which yet leaves him changeless, infinite, absolute in unbroken beatitude. And there are more surprising
phrases. No amount of meditation on the verse just quoted
prepares us for the shock of St. Paul's "the Spirit himself asks
for us with unspeakable groanings" (Rom. 8.26).

Here is mystery—God invulnerable, God vulnerable—two
realities barely glimpsed, their reconciliation beyond our gaze.
We respond to them not by concentrating on one while
ignoring the other as a problem, not by watering down both

until we get some shapeless combination in which what is left of each ceases to trouble us by conflict; we respond by accepting both, drawing light from both. By all means let us strain and strain further, pray and pray harder, for a little more light. But, once more, do not let us worry at not being omniscient; we must simply learn to live with the obvious fact that we cannot know God as well as he knows himself.

Let us return for a long moment to Our Lord's way of speaking of God. He is himself infinite, but he never uses the word, or indeed any of the great negative-sounding words we have been discussing. He places the negative where it belongs —with us: "None is good but God," "No man is to be called father, for one is our Father who is in heaven." Christ is, as it were, warning Dionysius in advance that these great positives—goodness, fatherhood—belong to God properly and it is only when used of men, as he does indeed use both of them, that they need qualifying or modifying.

Few, I imagine, think that Our Lord spoke like this because he lacked our metaphysical training. What people are more apt to think is that he was accommodating himself to listeners who lacked it. To which one replies that, if that is what he was doing, he certainly does not sound like it; all that he says of God is so wholehearted, spontaneous, from the very depth of his being, with no trace of fretting at the limits of language, or even at the limits of human understanding— he complains often enough of his listeners' slowness to understand, but not concerning God.

There is a stronger answer still: he speaks exactly thus when he is speaking to God the Father in prayer. Take what is perhaps the best known of his prayers—"Father, forgive them, for they know not what they do." That, of course, is reconcilable with the divine immutability in the way we have already suggested. What it cannot by any theological refinement be reconciled with is an infinite indifference, or with the view that what man does makes no difference. There is a reality in the Absolute which forgives men because of their ignorance, which acts differently according to whether men do or do not realize the meaning of their own acts, which can be asked in prayer to do these things. What this reality is *in* reality, so to speak, we do not know. It is utterly beyond our gaze.

Nor do we know what the reality is in the Infinite God which expressed itself to us as a longing to be loved by us. But there it certainly is: and its high point is his desire to be known by us. "No one knows the Father but the Son, *and him to whom the Son shall reveal him.*" The Son alone knows the Father, but he is not hugging that knowledge jealously to his own breast: he will reveal the Father; we must open our minds to the revelation.

TEN

"The Son Shall Reveal Him"

1. "No One Knows. . . ."

After the return of the Seventy-two Disciples (Luke 10.17) we have the solitary occasion on which we are actually told that Our Lord was joyful: "In that same hour he rejoiced in the Holy Spirit and said, 'I thank you, Father, Lord of heaven and earth, because you have hidden these things from the wise and prudent and revealed them to little ones." This leads into "All things have been delivered to me by my Father," and this into the supreme statement he was to make about God: "No one knows who the Son is but the Father; and who the Father is but the Son and him to whom the Son chooses to reveal him."

The "newness" of the doctrine of the Trinity abides. When Our Lord revealed it, it had to burst through human limitations. It still has. It did not fall within Jewish modes of thought in the thirties of the first century, within Greek modes of thought in the nineties, within any human modes of thought from then till now. It is wholly from above.

The text usually sets us to pondering upon the relation of Father and Son within the Godhead. But we must not overlook its assertion of the total newness of the revelation Our Lord here promises—"No one knows." He was to reveal something that the heroes and saints of the Old Testament had not had—not even Moses who had talked with God as friends talk (Exod. 33.11). "Blessed are the eyes which see what you see. For I tell you that many prophets and kings desired to see what you see, and did not see it, and to hear what you hear and did not hear it."

It is evident that what he was to tell them of his Father and himself was not something that merely happened not to have been mentioned before. The introduction is too splendid for that. We are not about to receive merely precisions and enrichments of what is already there in Scripture, not merely apter metaphors. There was something men were to be told about God which only Father and Son knew in their own right, something that could not be uttered until the Son had entered our world, something that could be heard for the first time only from the lips of God himself. In the nature of the case it must be something wholly, unguessably, new: anything else would have been anti-climax. No one can meet the text without asking what insight into the reality of God he himself has, for which those words would not be too splendid an introduction.

2. *The Innermost Life of God*

In the Old Testament we have the story of God intervening in the history of a particular people, shaping history, con-

ducting it towards a goal. There is nothing in the least like it
anywhere else. We might very well ask ourselves what was
left to be known about God, after so close, so intensely personal, a relation over so long a space of time. The people
themselves were not conscious, one feels, of any lack. Indeed,
if Christ Our Lord had not shown us what was lacking, we
might have been as unaware as they.

But once it has been shown it looms enormous. For with
all that the Old Testament tells of God's actions upon men, it
tells almost nothing of God's own life. The name by which
God named himself to them—I AM—is indeed the essential
reality of himself, who exists as no other exists, in his own
right. But this seems to have been rather felt by the Jews
than meditated on; and everything else concerns his actions
upon men, with no light shed upon what that existence might
be within God's own self. Even the holiness before which
they bowed does not seem to have cast any light—the word
"holy" is from a root meaning "cut off," so that it indicates
his utter beyondness, but says no more than that.

They seem never to have asked, they might even have felt
it unforgivable irreverence to ask, what his own personal life
is—to put it crudely, what was God doing when he was not
intervening in the affairs of the Jews? If he had not created
the world, with what would he have occupied himself, what
would his life have been? Even to ask such a question requires
a living awareness of God's infinity: without such an awareness one might easily think that the running of a universe as
vast and complex as ours would be sufficient occupation for
God. Not so long ago a very learned theologian, not of our
communion—an expert on Mysticism, as it happened—was
asked to comment on a statement made by a scientist to the
effect that our universe was coming to an end. The theologian

answered that the universe could not possibly come to an end, because, if it did, God would have nothing left to think about. His answer was given in haste, of course: it had to appear in next day's paper: he probably regretted it himself the day after.

But the question still stands. Our universe could never be sufficient occupation for the infinite God—he made it of nothing, he need not have made it. With all the vastness by which it towers over us, it barely touches—*does* it touch, however barely?—the fringe of his infinite knowing power. And what of that other great activity of spirit? That he loves men, the Old Testament did most wonderfully show. But men could never be the adequate object of infinite love. They cannot comprehend it, they cannot return it. Unless there is an infinite object, then infinite love must always be loving beneath itself, doomed never to bring itself to its own completeness in the utterance of all that is in it.

What Christ chose to open to us was the innermost life of God himself, the life he lives, not in relation to the universe but within his own being. And the essence of his revelation is that God's life is the life of Three who are yet One.

I have said that the question we are asking was not one that greatly preoccupied the men of the Old Testament, though occasionally one gets a wonderful phrase like "My soul thirsts for the living God. When shall I come and behold the face of God?" (Ps. 41.2). Even among Christians of our day there is a tendency towards the view expressed by that not very fervent Catholic, Alexander Pope:

> Know then thyself, presume not God to scan,
> The proper study of mankind is man.

Our Lord gave the complete answer at the Last Supper: "This is eternal life, that they know thee, the only true God, and Jesus Christ whom thou hast sent" (John 17.3): knowledge is not only one of life's activities at its own highest intensity, it *is* life, life eternal.

But if Christ had not thus settled the matter, what reason should we see for studying God—apart, of course, from learning his instructions for our own conduct? St. Thomas Aquinas says in one place that we study God in order to know ourself better; for it is in his image that we are made. And indeed there is a great deal to be learned about ourselves by growing in the knowledge of God, especially about our own shortcomings as we realize what a parody of the Original we are. Yet as St. Thomas knew—one has only to read the *Adoro Te Devote* to see how well he knew it—this could not be the sole or even the primary reason; there would be a sort of penuriousness in it, as if we were making God into a convenience for ourselves. Profounder reasons are so evident that they hardly need stating.

As God made us, there is in us a kind of instinct towards knowledge, a drive to know: to know what? Reality: That drive was never meant to stop short of the supreme Reality. And by his revelation we know why he made us so: for he made us for himself, made us therefore with all the powers by which every element in us is ultimately to take hold of him, and with all the appetites which will move us to set those powers in action. The power, moved by the appetite, to know God is built into us by him as really as the power, moved by the appetite, to adore him. If either were lacking, we could not obtain the goal to which he destines every one of us.

The urge to know may grow faint, lie motionless in us.

But it is always there, because God made us so. Having made us so, he treats us so. He wills to communicate with us. When he gives a revelation, he is telling us something, not just testing our capacity to swallow. *Fides quaerens intellectum*—faith must seek to understand what God is trying to communicate. A mere willingness to believe whatever God says—a kind of "Certainly, dear God, if You say so"—is a poor skeleton of the virtue of obedience, and no skeleton at all of the virtue of Faith. Here Our Lady gives us the precisely right example. When told that she was to be the mother of a divine child, she asks "How?" Without knowing that, she could not know what God was telling her.

3. Love Seeks Understanding

But it is not only Faith that needs to understand. *Amor quaerens intellectum*, love seeking to understand, is a reality too: to love God and not want to know all that we can possibly know about him would be a monstrous misunderstanding of the nature of love. And both the knowing and the loving end in frustration if they do not reach into the very life of God himself. But until Our Lord revealed the doctrine of the Trinity, there was no way in. Man could not have the first beginning of a notion of what the life might be of a solitary God, companionless in Infinity.

What his knowing might mean was dark enough, yet with a bearable darkness. But how bear the darkness that must ring his loving, if there were no adequate object of his infinite power to love? He could, of course, love his own Infinite Self —with "a love of infinite complacency," as the philosophers phrase it, thus providing a perfect example of the genius of the English language for adding a touch of comicality to the most serious technical phrases. *Love needs two:* if there were no second, we should be left wondering why God should have chosen the word "love." Till his own St. John, no one had thought to say "God is love." How *could* God be love if for him there were no possibility of loving at his own level?

The word I have just used, "companionless," points directly at what men have always found wanting in the solitary God. The pagans tried to supply it in a multiplicity of gods, which meant they had found the wrong answer; yet they were asking the right question. The Jews were tempted often enough by the pagan gods, and yielded to the temptation often enough. But in the end they were cured of that particular weakness; and to one deviation they were never attracted. They did not bring sex into their concept of God, at their worst they never provided Yahweh with a female consort. The Old Testament did not even bother to deny this particular abomination, so unthinkable was it: they had been in contact, as had no other people, with the living God—the loving God, therefore, the lovable God. Concerning Yahweh they could never have produced any equivalent of Aristotle's remark that it would be ridiculous to talk of loving Zeus.

They were sufficiently certain from their own experience as a nation that God loved them and wanted their love. Yet even for them there was some need that the solitary God did not satisfy. We find them tending towards the end to treat some of God's attributes, or activities—Spirit, Wisdom, Word, Utterance—almost as though they were persons. Consider some of the things we find them saying about Wisdom:

"The Lord possessed me in the beginning of his ways, the first of his acts of old. . . . When he established the heavens, I was there . . . when he made firm the skies above. . . . When he marked out the foundations of the earth, then I was beside him forming all things, and I was his delight, rejoicing before him always." (Prov. 8.22–30) The man who wrote this—like the writers of Ecclesiasticus (24.5) and of Wisdom (7.25 and 9.9)—did not know or even suspect in God a Trinity or any plurality; but the solitary God would not suffice for that in him which demanded utterance, he was driven to feel out in a direction whose end he could not see. In the beginning, God had said, "It is not good for man to be alone." Something in man told him that it was not good for God to be alone, either. And he is not alone. In the doctrine of the Trinity we see how Infinite Oneness can flower in Infinite Companionship.

How are we to study the revelation of Christ upon the inner reality of the life of God? What he said, we shall find in Scripture, or rather we shall find it quoted from, referred to, applied, rejoiced in, by St. John and St. Paul especially, as something already known to the first Christians for whom they were writing. Again, we shall find the doctrine given to us by the Church which he founded and guaranteed to be with us till the end of time. Either way, we are getting the Word of God, and we must study both.

But as a mere matter of pedagogy, it is probably more helpful to most people to begin with the Mystery as the Church teaches it, what we know of it systematized, organized, clarified by its relation to our own spiritual and mental operations, with "difficulties" seen and fitted into the statement of the Reality itself, with awareness of darkness not yet pierced which is Light too great for us.

Nor is it merely a matter of pedagogy. As it is taught by

the Church, there is built into it nineteen hundred years of growing in understanding of the doctrine by thinking about it, praying it, living it. Not only have men been thus studying the doctrine itself; but they have been drawing light upon it from two lesser sources—namely their growth in knowledge of themselves who image the Original, and in knowledge of the world the Trinity created: the early Christian could no more know modern Psychology than he could know modern Physics, and each has its own light to shed upon God.

None of this knowledge by living can replace what the men had who actually knew Our Lord. We remember what one of them writes at the beginning of his First Epistle:

That which was from the beginning, which we have heard, which we have seen with our eyes, which we have looked upon and our hands have handled, of the word of life . . . we declare unto you: that you also may have fellowship with us; and our fellowship is with the Father and with his Son Jesus Christ (1 John 1.1).

At the beginning of his Gospel the same disciple sums it up in a single sentence: "Of his fullness we have all received." They received of his fullness, we must receive of theirs. We must forever be balancing the study of Theology and the study of Scripture, remembering that, even where it is hard to see the reconciliation, reconciliation there must be: for the same Word is uttering himself in two ways.

The awareness must be strong in us as we embark upon the study that it is like no other we make. It is unique in three ways especially: (1) nothing else that we study is so high above us, so that without prayer we cannot hope to make much advance; (2) nothing else we study is at the very root of our being, providing the energy with which we make the study; (3) of nothing else that we study are we made in the image, so that we are gazing upon the Original which our own being and our own actions reflect.

4. Not for Desiccation

We begin this part of our study with God. What constitutes him God? Essentially his hold upon existence. He alone necessarily is, he alone cannot not-exist; and there is no perfection of existence that is not his in richness illimitable. That is the God of Scripture, Old Testament and New Testament. He is a spirit, says Our Lord, uttering the truth that the men of the Old Testament were feeling for. To him all things are possible (Matt. 19.26)—he is omnipotent; he knows all things, even the inmost thoughts of men's hearts—he is omniscient; he loves beyond the love of a mother—we do not find the word omni-amorous ("amorous" having associations less than divine), but we find the reality: and in John's "God is love," love finds its place as one of the three nouns which in Scripture follow "God is." The other two are "spirit" (John 4.8 and 16) and "light" (1 John 1.5). All three represent not only what he is to us, but himself simply and absolutely.

Revealing himself in Scripture, God wastes no words on the Impersonal Absolute, paying it not even the compliment of dismissal. From the beginning He is wholly personal: He is Someone not Something, still less is He Nothing. "The Infinite" is not in Scripture: it is one of the most splendid achievements of the human mind to have arrived at the concept of Infinity, but we can hardly feel that man has mastered it. Linked with self-existence, it is a key to the understanding

of God, but a key which too many have used not to open
the door, but to close it tight, forbidding all access.

It was philosophy that gave us God as Pure Act, God as
the Infinite. One marvels at the sleight-of-hand by which the
pagan Infinite—so close akin to the mathematical, and by no
pagan seen as personal—has been made to seem like part of
Revelation. Theometricians love it, fitting it with the features
of Father, Son and Holy Spirit: but the fit is not perfect,
the joins show. Philosophy is *ancilla theologiae*, Theology's
servant-girl, and the Infinite is part of the equipment she
brings to her service—but for Theology's use, not for its
desiccation.

Purely spiritual men have made one special mistake in this
order, probably because men are not pure spirits. As we have
noted, they are in such fear of making any statement at all
about the Absolute that they leave us with the impression
that self-existence more or less exhausts God's capacity, leaving nothing else to be expected of him. Behind this is the fear
of introducing the defilement of limitation, a fear so potent
that they see limitation where it is not. The word "person"
is held to be inescapably limiting, the word "self" falls under
the same condemnation.

"Escape from the prison of the self" has become a cliché;
the essence of personality has often been described as the
consciousness of not being someone else. For a finite being,
certainly, the self must be finite, but the finitude does not lie
in the selfhood; if there are other persons, then to know one's
self involves knowing that one is not someone else. But that
is not what "person" means: a person is a being who can
know and love: and if his knowledge and love are infinite,
then he is infinite with them. Nor does any limitation lie in

knowing, unless the knower happens to be limited: in itself it means only that reality is present to consciousness as what it is. And so with love, any finiteness in it lies in the one who loves. Inability to know, impotence to love—these are the limitations. And the Old Testament makes very clear that God is free from them.

The Old Testament had left no place for an Impersonal God. It was left for Christ to penetrate God's Oneness. He quotes Deuteronomy—"The Lord Our God, the Lord is one" (Mark 12.32). But it is clear that the word "one" for him is not simply the numeral that precedes "two," he is not saying only that God is unique, that there is not another. He is asserting God's totality, his all-inclusiveness: he is saying that in the light of this, two Gods would be meaningless: not simply that there is not another, but there could not be another, all is here.

The numerical oneness is real. Left to ourselves, we could not see beyond it, we could not see into it. But we are not left to ourselves. Christ tells us that within the oneness there is a depth of richness—three Persons, three Selves. The oneness is not tripled; in being triply one it is more one than ever.

That is the mystery presented for our light and our nourishment. That is the God presented for our adoration and our love.

ELEVEN

The Trinity
in the Church's Teaching

What remains of this Volume will be concerned with the Blessed Trinity, with the doctrine as we receive it from the Church and as it shows itself in Scripture—the terms, the mental equivalents, the vital equivalents. It is unfortunate that the vital equivalents come only at the end. Before we reach them there is a lot of theology to be read, wrestled with, built into ourselves. One to whom this level of theological thinking is new may find it a weariness to the mind in its multiplicity of concepts and processes and precisions. He may find it a trial to the patience too. Why not, he may feel, cut out all the theorizing and come straight to God in repentance or gratitude or adoration?

There is something similar in music. Merely to read through an examination paper in the theory of music can lower the blood's temperature: the contrast between the cut-and-dried theorizing and the glory of great music would strike one meeting it for the first time as verging on the comic. But we must remember that people have already had some experience of hearing music before they come to the theorizing; and the theorizing makes possible the composing of great music at one end and its richer enjoyment at the other. It is possible, of course, to dwell in the theory and lose the music in the process: the relation of means to end must be kept clear. Mozart could not have made his music if he had not mastered the theory, but he was not thinking theory as he made the music: it was a kind of habituation, the theory had become part of him. If a man decided to cut out the theory and go straight to the piano, he would never play like Paderewski or Horowitz; he would be more likely to play like me.

So with the Trinity. It is music each one must make for himself, not vibrating to someone else's vibrations—even to Our Lord's—but to the Reality. Without the Theology we shall know God very sketchily indeed; and since each new thing learnt about God is a new reason for loving him, without theology we must always love less than we might.

One further word before we move into the doctrine. I shall often use the past tense in talking of God's own life and actions. Eternity, we have seen, has no tenses—no past, no future, an abiding present. In speaking about God we ordinarily use the present tense. But occasionally the past comes more naturally. We have the highest authority for using it— "In the beginning was the Word and the Word was with God and the Word was God."

Not only that. We remind ourselves that even our present tense *is* a tense, a word of time. and has no more place in eternity than past or future. Whichever tense we use, we must remember that God's being and action are timeless and that we have no grammatical equipment for uttering them. Thus, if we say God *generated* a Son, it sounds like an action over and done with at some earlier stage of eternity! If we say God *is generating* a Son, it sounds like an action in process but not yet completed. We must move from one tense to another, hoping that in the depth of our mind a verb is forming, tenseless and by us unsayable.

1. The Word Who Is Son

With two different words, the Gospels tell us of a second person within the one Godhead. He is the Son of the first, He is the Word of the first. The notion of a pure spirit generating a Son is not luminous. So we shall begin with Word: there is less immediate darkness in it, and the Old Testament is filled with the utterance of God's word.

In the first eighteen verses of St. John's Gospel we learn that God utters a Word—a mental Word, evidently, not framed by the mouth, more akin to an Idea therefore. This Word is *with* God, abides, does not pass in the utterance. And this Word *is* God, all things are made by *Him*, *He* became flesh and dwelt among us. What these phrases may have meant in the mind of the writer we shall consider later. Here our concern is with the realities the Church has found in them.

Of what could God conceive an Idea which would *be* God? Not of any created thing, certainly, not of all creation in its totality, only of Himself. God, then—as we know from revelation and could not otherwise know—conceives an Idea of Himself. The Idea must be totally adequate. All the reality that is in God must be in it, every perfection: otherwise He would have produced an inadequate idea of Himself, which would be at once a flat contradiction of His infinity and a piece of sheer aimlessness—given that in His omniscience He is already totally present to Himself, what would be the point of His producing an Idea in which He is not?

Nor is the Idea totally adequate merely in the sense that every perfection in the original is represented by an idea within the Idea—that God's Idea of Himself contains the ideas of spirituality, infinity, eternity, divinity and the rest, omitting none. Total adequacy of this sort would have been as pointless as we have seen that any inadequacy would have been: God does not need an idea of Himself in order that He may know Himself better, for with His infinite knowing power He already knows Himself infinitely. His Idea of Himself is totally adequate because every divine perfection is in the Idea—not ideally, but really, *in the same way* as it is in God. It does not add to God's knowledge of Himself but utters it; and all these attributes will be in Himself-uttered as they are in Himself-uttering.

The Idea then does not only *represent* the original as spirit, infinite, eternal, divine: It *is* Itself spirit, infinite, eternal, divine. It not only utters the original as all-knowing, all-loving, all-powerful. It is Itself all-knowing, all-loving, all-powerful. It images God perfectly not as a looking-glass mirrors a man—his surface, and two-dimensionally at that; not as, by creation, God is mirrored in nothingness. This is God's living Image within His own infinite being. There is involved a total adequacy of Idea to Original such as man never could have conceived for himself; it is more than adequacy, it is equality; and equality carried to the very ultimate point beyond which there could only be identity, no longer two but one.

Maintaining that last point of distinctness—for the Idea remains the Idea and not the Thinker, eternally the Idea and not the Thinker—we know that God conceives an Idea of Himself which is everything that God is. Because God is a Person His Idea is a Person, Someone not Something, He not It—God as He is God, equal in every perfection, lacking no perfection—yet infinitely distinct, each Person knowing Himself for Himself. So we have two distinct Persons, two distinct Selves, distinct but not separate; for an idea exists in the mind of the thinker and can have no existence of its own separate from that mind. With this second Self, we get the answer to the question which has bothered the human mind even when it did not know what was bothering it: we now have Companionship within the Deity, we have the adequate object of infinite love, one who can receive the love with total comprehension and return it as totally.

We can now return to the word "Son." The pagan myths had plenty of gods with sons of their own. But the Jews never thought thus of Yahweh; nor could the pagans have thought thus had their gods been wholly spiritual. One who has brought his mind to bear upon the Thinker conceiving an Idea of Himself will find less difficulty in applying to God the process of a father begetting a son. In our own human experience both processes, thinking and begetting, are ways of producing likeness. The whole point of an idea is that by it an object is present to the mind in its true likeness; and it is of the essence of a son to be like in kind to his father—the sons of men are men as the sons of lions are lions.

But we may see the two phrases as more than merely alternative ways—both difficult, but one slightly easier than the other—of saying precisely the same thing. Begetting and conceiving, each adds something to the other. A human father begets a son in the womb of the mother; a human mother conceives the son thus begotten in her own womb. In this first birth, the divine archetype of every birth that was ever to be, God invites us to see both. The First Person begets a son by his generative power as a father begets, conceives a son within his own being as a mother conceives. All parenthood is in the birth of this first son, generation and conception in one single, eternal, act.

But there is another way in which the two phrases are not simply alternates. Each gives us something that we might not have found for ourselves in the other.

The Gospels are filled with the relation of Father and Son. His Jewish listeners were shocked by it, or at best puzzled. That we are neither may mean merely that we are accustomed to it: it has become a formula, giving the mind no trouble, because the mind is not engaged. We must look at it more closely.

The words Father and Son mean that we are confronted with a real distinction, a duality. "Son" is not just a figure of speech, "father" looked at from a different angle. A father and son are two. It is not only because of our finitude that a father cannot be his own son, not only because of our bodiliness. The terms demand duality, and the terms are Christ's. But then what of oneness? We can hardly say that it stands out clearly: it is implied, we feel, but tenuously. A son is of the same kind as his father, and the mind shudders away from two Infinities: there is no way in which it can see a second

Infinite not limiting the first: if there really are two, each of whom is infinite, then somehow it must be by virtue of one same Infinity. We are stumbling here, it would be idle to say that we are walking in the light.

The oneness is established for us by considering the Idea produced by the way of knowledge: if Son establishes duality, Word establishes oneness. The divine Thinker, knowing Himself with infinite knowing power, conceives a totally adequate Idea of Himself: but it is of the very essence of an idea to exist within the mind of the thinker. So that where Sonship emphasizes the distinction of personality, Idea emphasizes the divine oneness. Does a closer look show that Idea also implies distinction of personality?

As we have already noticed, there is a real distinction between our ideas and ourselves: the duality is not as obvious as between a father and a son, yet duality it is. But let us remind ourselves that the Idea has not the same function in God as ideas have in us. We know by means of ideas; and our knowledge of them varies with the truth or falsity, richness or poverty, of the ideas we have of them. Not so with God. As we have seen, He does not produce an idea of Himself in order that He may get to know Himself. We must not think that the Father knows Himself only by looking at the Son, and only as He sees Himself imaged in the Son, or even that He knows Himself better. He knows Himself totally, by being Himself. Infinite knowledge is an attribute of infinite spirit: there is no distinction between God's attributes and God: God *is* His knowledge as He is His love and His power.

So that God as God is infinite knowledge, infinite self-knowledge. He does not need to produce self-knowledge, He *is* self-knowledge. So that He produces the Idea not as a step on the way to fuller knowledge, or as a means to total knowledge. He produces the Idea out of the sheer fecundity of His knowing power as the total utterance of the Infinite knowledge which simply by being God He has of Himself: contemplating the idea He learns nothing He does not already know, for it proceeds from Him wholly: there is nothing in It but what in the infinite light of His all-knowledge, He has given It.

What the Idea gives Him is not new knowledge, but companionship. The Idea is a companion, a Son, not It but He. St. Paul tells us (Ephesians 3:15) that from the Father "every family in heaven and on earth is named." Studying what fatherhood and sonship means among men is a way into the depth of the relation between the Father and His Son: from that first parenthood we should not lightly exclude any element of the parenthood we know: above all we must remember that fatherhood is not exhausted with the act of begetting, having no function once the son is begotten; it is a relation which abides, is operative, while father and son abide: the love this Father and Son have for each other is not simply the love that flows from God as God, it is special to their fatherhood and sonship.

One who hears all this for the first time may have an uneasy feeling that the Son is less real, his hold upon existence less real, for being an Idea in the Father's mind. He might carry his unease further, feeling that the Second Person is only a thought after all, whereas we ourselves are not merely thoughts in God's mind, we really exist. But it is not like that. What, after all, is any one of us? God's thought mirrored in nothingness, made of nothing into something by God, but wholly dependent on God that we continue to exist. The whole of creation in a sense images God—not God Himself, but only God as limitedly and endlessly imitable. The Second Person is not imaged in nothingness but in the Infinite, not made of nothing but generated by God of His own substance. He is the Father's Thought produced and sustained in being by the divine Mind, but this does not mean, as with our thoughts, transience—thoughts born, then rejected or merely forgotten; or any form of contingency. Not transience, because the infinite Thinker possesses His Thought of Himself in the eternal, changeless, present of His being; not contingency because the Thought could no more not-be than the Thinker.

There is profound difficulty for us in this, perhaps the mystery of the Trinity is nowhere darker than here. We cannot see any obvious reconciliation between being produced, as the Son is, and being necessary, as the Son is. Yet in a way we do "see" it as an exigency of the divine being that the Father should thus know Himself, and in that same eternal act of knowing eternally generate the Idea of Himself; there is no element of contingency, of might-not-have-been, in the existence of the Son. There is origin but no contingency. God is as necessarily Son as He is Father.

2. The Holy Spirit

The production of a Second Self does not exhaust the inner richness of the divine Oneness. Our Lord tells us of a Third. There is a Spirit—ghost was the old English word for spirit— to whom He will entrust His followers when He Himself shall have ascended to the Father, one whose coming is sufficient reason for Our Lord's leaving them. "I will ask the

Father, and he will give you another Paraclete, that he may abide with you" (John 14.16). The Spirit, like the Word, is a person, He, not It. "But the Paraclete, the Holy Spirit whom the Father will send in my name, He will teach you all things" (John 14.26). And again, like the Word, the Spirit is God. Christ tells the Apostles to baptize in (or into) the name of the Father and of the Son and of the Holy Spirit: the Spirit has one same name with Father and Son, is of the same kind therefore.

As with the Second Person, so with the Third, we shall leave to later the consideration of what the phrases we have quoted may have meant to those who first heard them. Our concern here is with the realities the Church has found in them and formulated for us.

Let us pause upon the word "Spirit"—in Latin *spiritus*, in Greek *pneuma*, in Hebrew *ruah*, best rendered in English as "breath." It might be well at this point to re-read what is said about the Old Testament use of *"ruah"* in Chapter Six. Here we remind ourselves that air—air in motion, wind, breath—is the original meaning of spirit, from which by a natural analogy our remote ancestors got the word spirit as we now normally use it, spirit being invisible as air is. In our normal use, the Third Person has no claim to be called spirit that Father and Son have not equally. The word's special aptness to Him as distinct from Them lies in its literal sense, breath or breathing. In some sense He is the Breath of God as the Son is the Word: the Son is *generated,* the Spirit is *breathed forth* ("spirated," say the theologians, a beautiful word in Latin but rather lost in English).

Breathed forth by whom? By the Father and Son we say: by the Father only, say the Greeks. The difference is more than verbal but not a great deal more, not exactly accidental but perhaps so in part—the "accident" being that East and West had to safeguard the doctrine of the Trinity against different errors. The Greeks felt forced to resist anything that might make the Third Person in any way inferior to the Second: to proceed from the Second might at least sound like inferiority. In Spain particularly the Latins had to combat a teaching that made the Second Person inferior to the First: with the word *filioque*, "*and* from the Son," they emphasized the equality of Father and Son by bringing into the Nicene Creed the teaching already widely held according to which the Holy Spirit proceeded from both.

The Nicene Creed as we have it now says *qui ex Patre filioque procedit*. In the hymn we sing at Benediction we speak of the Holy Spirit as *procedenti ab utroque*—to him who proceeds from both. The process in ourselves by which we produce an Idea or Mental Word had helped us to see a little into the relation within the Blessed Trinity of the first two Persons. Our own mental processes will similarly shed a little light for us as to the breathing forth by these Two of the Third. If to any reader this line of thought is new, it may be worth his while to concentrate rather especially on the next paragraph.

An idea I conceive becomes an element in myself, an element in my mind's being and muscularity: whatever my mind does from that time forward, the new idea is operative in it. And it is not simply "I plus the new idea," but I enriched by the new idea, enriched in my very self. The new idea has its part in the production of *whatever else* comes forth from my mind. This is so even more evidently when the Idea is not something but Someone. It *could not* be simply a matter of the same Mind going on to produce another Idea to lay alongside the first. How could the Father have excluded the Son from the "breathing" which produced the Holy Spirit?

We have considered the question what *could* the Father know which, in the very knowing, would produce an Idea that is itself God: and we have seen the answer. A like question arises now. What could Father and Son breathe forth which in the very breathing would produce another self that is God? St. Augustine's answer is that only their love could be adequate for that—they breathe forth their love of each other and of the Godhead which is theirs. The Church has not defined this, but her theologians have almost to a man said, "Of course." Let us examine what is being said.

As we have already seen, there is one huge difference between God's Idea of Himself, and any idea you and I may form of ourselves. His is Someone, ours is only something. Between me and my idea of myself, therefore, there can be no mutuality, no interflow: I can know it, it cannot know me; in an eccentric moment I might admire its beauty, it cannot admire mine; I can even love it, it cannot return my love. But with an Idea which is Someone, and an infinite Someone, there is infinite dialogue, an infinite interflow.

Father and Son love each other, with infinite intensity. It is St. Augustine's theory that this love is what they unite in breathing forth, and that a Third divine Person is thereby produced. Just as the Father utters His self-knowledge in the Son, so Father and Son utter Their mutual love in the Holy Spirit.

Precision is necessary here at whatever risk of wearying: Father and Son do not love each other in the Holy Spirit, any more than the Father knows Himself in the Son. Love like knowledge is a divine attribute, and does not need to be produced: God *is* love. The Father knows Himself simply by being God; Father and Son love each other simply by being God. But just as the Father produces the Son as the utterance of His self-knowledge, so Father and Son produce the Holy Spirit as the utterance of their mutual love. Love is not less productive than knowledge.

Precision is needed also in the realization of what we are now doing. We are *not* proving that the Being breathed forth must be a person, must be God. We know by revelation that there *is* a Third, who is Someone, who is God. We are trying to see how this fact fits with loving.

The love of Father and Son is infinite; its expression is not less. Infinite love does not express its total reality finitely—it can no more produce an inadequate expression than infinite knowledge can produce an inadequate Idea. We realize that we are only stammering here, yet even in the stammering something is being said: so we stammer on.

In the Holy Spirit Father and Son utter Their love, each for the other, as one stream of loving. Each gives Himself wholly to the outpouring of His love, holding nothing back —indeed in this context "holding back" is meaningless. If They give Themselves at all, it can only be totally—They possess nothing but Their totality! And just as each can give totally, each can receive totally, as no created being can. The uttered love of Father and Son is infinite with Their own infinity; no perfection that They have is lacking to it. It is idle to pretend that we could have seen for ourselves that this breathed-forth loving would produce one who is a Person, one who is God. But when we learn that it has done so, we can at least glimpse a perfect aptness.

The utterance of love within the lover is not as easy for us to put into words as the utterance within the knower of the act of knowing. For this latter we have Idea, Mental Word. But for love what *is* there? In what does love utter itself best? It must be something proceeding immediately from the organism, proceeding so immediately from it that it remains within it. Our Lord's term is Spirit, Breath. The Fathers have found a variety of terms.

The Holy Spirit is, for instance, the "sigh" of Father and Son; the term is not perhaps wholly satisfying, for transience seems of the very essence of a sigh; one can, perhaps, conceive (though not, of course, imagine) eternal ecstasy uttered in an eternal sigh: yet again one associates a certain discouragement with a sigh, a song is better, a song in the heart. Another term the Fathers like is "kiss"; but it is not easy to think of a kiss as a person; and while, in the world the Fathers knew, the kiss was a universal way of expressing love, it is not so in the vaster world which the explorers were to open up in the centuries to follow. St. Augustine uses the word "donum," gift, which suggests what the Holy Ghost does, or is, to us, but not so readily what He is to Father and Son. We find the word "vinculum" used, as though the Third Person were a bond linking the First and Second, but we must not forget the bond that already exists between Thinker and Thought.

Obviously Our Lord's word "breath" is best—otherwise he would not have chosen it. It is not difficult for the mind to see a connection between love and breathing together (which may well have been what caused the Fathers to use the word "kiss"), and it has another connotation, namely life—when we stop breathing, we die: Our Lord breathed on the Apostles when he said: "Receive the Holy Spirit." This is the emphasis

of the Nicene Creed—"the Holy Spirit, the Lord and life-
giver" (both words were inserted at the next Ecumenical
Council after Nicaea to affirm the equality of the Third Person with the Second). By "lifegiver" the Creed means, of
course, that He gives life *to us:* but lifegiving would not thus
be attributed especially to Him, unless life were in some way
especially His, within the Blessed Trinity. The Creed was
drawn up before St. Augustine's superb intuition that just as
the Second Person proceeds by the way of knowledge, so the
Third Person proceeds by the way of love, which is spirit's
other supreme activity. But the link between life and love was
not hard to see: love is a total self-giving, a giving of life,
therefore, and in their depths, love and life are interchangeable.

Sigh, song, kiss, breath: the Holy Spirit is the expression by
Father and Son of their love. If we want to find something in
human experience as an analogy, perhaps it lies in the whole
complexus of being in love, what we might call the state of
lovingness—but in God this lovingness is Someone, not something, as with us. The lovingness is distinct from the Lovers
who breathe it forth, but it is not separable from them, it has
its existence within them, a further richness in infinite Oneness. Its effects may radiate, but the center from which the
radiation comes remains within the being of the Lovers, produced by it, sustained by it, inseparable from it; but filling it
wholly, so that there is no element in it not caught up into
that lovingness, nothing left for any other outpouring of love
to utter, but only to echo. Every other act of love, at whatever level of creation, echoes this first one. And at the Last
Supper we hear Christ Our Lord speak of a love to be given
to men which not only echoes it, but is it—"that the love
with which thou hast loved me may be in them" (John 27.26).

Thus the Holy Spirit receives as his own the whole divine being. The First Council of Constantinople (381) applies the "consubstantial" which belongs to the Son to the Third Person as well—it declares him to be of the same substance as Father and Son. Why, then, is he not also called Son? Whenever we are dealing with any question about the inner life of God to which God himself has not revealed the answer, we must walk modestly. We can never too often remind ourselves that we have not established the doctrine of the Three divine Persons by a series of logical deductions from spirit and its dialectic as we know it. We have received it from God; and, God encouraging, upon the meaning of what is revealed we have gained further light by meditating on created spirit, using our own spirit as the one most conveniently to hand.

All the same, upon our precise question as to why the Third Person was never called Son, even by those who avoided the difficulty of double paternity by having him proceed from the Father only, the theologians have produced a most suggestive answer. It is true that Son and Holy Spirit each possess the same divine nature, each having received it. But the way of knowledge, by which the Second Person receives it, tends of itself to the production of likeness—the whole value of a thought lies in its likeness to the object; so that it is naturally to be spoken of as generation—it was not to justify the doctrine of the Trinity that the pagan Greeks had related verbs for "knowing" and "being born." What knowing produces—in the solitary instance where it produces a Person—is naturally called Son. But the Third Person proceeds by the way of love, and it is not the natural tendency of love to produce a likeness to the object loved. It breathes a sigh, a song, a kiss, or more generally produces a state of lovingness, and none of these is in any sense an image of the object loved. It is only because those who breathe forth the Third Person are infinite that the being they produce is like in kind to themselves.

3. One God

But we must look still closer, answer a deeper difficulty and find another gleam of light. The Son is produced by knowing, the Holy Ghost by loving. But there is no distinction between God's attributes and God Himself. God's knowing *is* God, God's loving *is* God. His knowing and loving, therefore, are indistinguishable from Himself, and therefore from each other. How, if two processes are indistinguishable, can their product be distinct?

It is imagination which creates the difficulty, or perhaps the related mental indolence which makes us almost automatically feel that what we are accustomed to is the norm of all things. With ourselves, knowing and loving are activities, distinct from the self which knows and loves (since we can suspend either as we cannot suspend our own being), and distinct from each other. Even when we have followed the logical demonstration that they are not distinct from Himself, not less than Himself, but Himself, we have a feeling that they are somehow diminished thereby, not really knowing and loving at all. Something similar happens in us when we first learn that our soul, being spiritual, has no parts: it seems that the soul must be so tied up in one tight bundle that it can never do anything at all. It is only as the mind continues to work on the concept that it sees that the soul is more powerful by having its whole self and all its powers concentrated in one single act of being.

So with God's attributes. We begin with the feeling that if they are all indistinguishable from Him and identical with one another, they are not themselves at all, indeed that a God so "concentrated" barely exists—as though His attributes were all inside Him, struggling to get out and be themselves but eternally doomed to frustration. This, of course, is quite wild. Knowledge and love are not less themselves for being infinite. God really is all-knowing and can produce whatever knowing produces. God really is all-loving and can produce whatever loving produces. The way of it must still be dark to us, but only from want of anything in our experience to give it the comfort of the familiar. And at least there is one further faint gleam of light in it: it is not so surprising that Knowledge which is itself Someone should produce an idea which is Someone, Love which is Someone should breathe itself forth in a Breath that is Someone.

So we have three Persons, three Selves, three Someones, but not three Gods. We are as monotheist as any Jew or Mohammedan. We cannot *see* this, but once we know what the Word through His Church is telling us we can get a certain small aid from looking at ourselves. A man with an idea in his head and love in his heart is one being, not three. Even if the idea grew to the point where it could itself know and love it would still be within him, existing by his thinking it, having no possibility of separate existence. He would still be one man. So with God. The Word is true Person and True God, a second Person but not a second God. And so with the love which is the Holy Spirit, existing *within* in the same way, existing *by* in the same way, in the same impossibility of separate existence, a third Person but not a third God.

TWELVE

The Trinity
in the New Testament (1)

In the last chapter is the doctrine of the Trinity as the Church gives it to us, that is, as the Word in his Mystical Body gives it to us. What has that same Word given us in Scripture?

The relation between the New Testament and the Teaching Church is discussed in Chapter Two (4). That section provides the context within which, or the background against which, this present chapter is to be read. It is worth a second look. Here I simply summarize. The New Testament writers assumed a body of teaching already known to their readers. They did not ordinarily set out to state a doctrine in its fullness, but to shed light upon elements in it—either because there was error about them in one place or another; or because the writer himself found some one truth especially alive in him at the moment of writing. There is no reason-in-advance why any given fact or facet of doctrine should be mentioned in any given book; or why the whole of every doctrine should be found—a piece here, a piece there—in the New Testament as a whole.

Take an obvious example: of the Evangelists John has most to say of the Trinity. But he is clearly concerned with deepening the understanding of a doctrine known to his readers. Thus he nowhere says what it *means* that God should have a Son, what fatherhood (of a son who could be made flesh) can possibly mean in a pure spirit. From his teaching about the Word, as we have seen, we get light upon this; but he does not actually work out the connection for us. He gives us great shafts of light into the life of God and man. But his Gospel would make very little sense, save as written for people who had already been told about the Father and the Son and the Holy Spirit. What had they been told? There is no record.

No part of the New Testament was written save to be read in the light of truths already known. To treat it as if it were independent, autonomous, self-sufficient, is to treat it as it was not written. The most we can expect for any doctrine is that such parts of it as do emerge in Scripture should be in harmony with what the Church teaches. To offer, or demand, Scriptural proof of the whole of any doctrine shows an ignorance, an innocence almost, of how Scripture came to be written.

1. Two Persons

Duality within the Godhead appears earlier than Trinity. We look at it first. There is a second reality, called Son, called Word. Is this a distinct Someone, is this really God?

People whose Scripture reading is not recent or frequent assume that John, or whoever wrote the Fourth Gospel, created the Second Person. But we find in Matthew and Luke a statement from the lips of Christ himself which is as startling as anything in John, more startling perhaps because we come on it unprepared. We have already glanced at it. We must now look at it more lengthily. "All things have been delivered to me by my Father; and no one knows who the Son is except the Father, and no one knows who the Father is except the Son, and one to whom the Son chooses to reveal him" (Luke 10.22, Matt. 11.27).

"*All* has been delivered"—it *could* mean the totality of the divine Being, or it could mean the whole of the created universe, angels and men and things. For the moment we may leave the question undiscussed: at the very least what is given by Father to Son is immense, incomparable. Indeed, in the excitement of what follows, one hardly notices that opening phrase. Christ is asserting a mutuality in knowing between the Son and the Father—rather like the balance of "No one comes to the Father but by me" (John 14.6) and "No one can come to me unless the Father who sent me draws him" (John 6.44). It is knowing at a level which is only theirs. So Christ says: and Dr. Dodd comments (*The Fourth Gospel*, pp. 160 and 163) that there are very few passages in the Old Testament where it is categorically asserted that man knows God: "I cannot discover a place where a prophet expressly says that he knows God." This mutuality in knowing is balanced elsewhere in the Gospels by an equality in *un*-knownness: "He came into the world and the world knew him not" (John 1.10): this is said of the Word. "The world has not known thee" (John 17.25)—this is said of the Father by that same Word.

One has to allow for the possibility of seeing, in any given passage of Scripture, what one already holds. But I, for one, can never read the passage we are now discussing without an overwhelming sense that the speaker is assuming equality between the Father's knowing and his own, there is no faintest hint of inferiority, none of the air of one saying something incredible, something that would need to be explained away: it could not flow more naturally. And for a believer in the Trinity, there is a kind of delight in noting that the action in which equality is assumed is precisely that knowing by which the Son proceeds from the Father: in the light of Catholic doctrine, we feel this is how Christ would naturally have spoken.

We come now to the Prologue of John's Gospel. "In the beginning was the Word, and the Word was with God, and the Word was God. All things were made by him, and without him nothing was made." More has been written on this one verse, probably, than on most single books of the Bible. On the face of it, at least, it seems to be saying what we have already seen to be the Catholic doctrine—that God utters a Word, a Word which abides within Him, so that it is an utterance made eternally to Himself, and that this Word, Idea, Utterance, is God, as He is.

But to balance that plain meaning is the plain fact that what it seems to assert is all but beyond comprehension, dark to a point where the light of the human mind cannot reach it. A text which seems to be saying something so hard to accept, or even to see meaning in, is bound to be subject to the closest scrutiny.

Thus we find one of the earliest geniuses of Christianity, Origen, commenting on the absence of the definite article before "God" in the phrase "The Word was God." In Greek it would be normal to have *ho theos*. Origen argued from this that this second Someone was not quite God, an inferior or subordinate God, not God in the fullness of the term. The grammatical point is for grammarians. One has heard it said that the article was not required in the nominative after the verb "to be"; again, that had John wanted to convey the lesser meaning, there was to hand the word *theios*. The profounder answer lies in the nature of God: it was all very well for the pagans to have demigods; but with the God of the Old Testament there could be no question of degrees, no almost-God. What was not God was less than God, and the gulf between was measureless.

But had John, perhaps, strayed too far from the Old Testament, under the influence of Greek philosophy? The word he uses for Word, namely *logos*, had a long history. It was five or six hundred years since Heraclitus first gave it significance in the philosophy of the cosmos (scholars are not agreed that he did!); it had come to new prestige in the teaching of the Stoics. Our own man in the street, if he be literate, thinks that John got it from Plato. But it is not one of Plato's words. It came into neo-Platonism—six hundred years after Plato and two hundred years after John—with Plotinus (who was a fellow-pupil with Origen of Ammonius Saccas in Alexandria): he equated the Logos with Plato's world of ideas.

John's considerably older contemporary, Philo, a Jew of Alexandria, had made a magnificent effort to bring the *Logos,* along with a great deal of other Greek philosophy, into harmony with the Old Testament. Precisely because of this, there is a tendency to assume that John's logos is Philo's with Christian additions and adaptations. But it is not. Philo's is still in essence the logos of the Stoics, the thought of God of which the created universe was the expression (Philo in fact, well before Plotinus, made the plural *logoi* mean very much what Plato's "ideas" meant). As it existed in the mind of God, the Greek logos was simply God, thinking, knowing: as expressed in, built into, the universe, it bore something of the same relation to God that a work of art bears to the mind of the artist. But John's was Jesus of Nazareth.

Augustine was to say later of neo-Platonism, which had held him for a while and never perhaps wholly lost its hold, that it could have brought him to "the Word was God" but by no possibility to "the Word was made flesh." And this might have been said of Philo too, not simply because flesh was a degradation, but because his logos was not Someone, but only something.

One might read a vast amount of discussion of "the Johannine logos" without realizing that John barely mentions the word (except, of course, in its ordinary sense of "something said"). We might get the impression that John was wholly logos-minded, logos-soaked, perhaps converted to the logos in some Patmos vision, as totally possessed by it as Paul by his experience on the Damascus road. In fact, John mentions it only twice (or three times, if he was the author of the Apocalypse); and he gives no indication of why he uses it at all: he never discusses the concept or draws anything from it. From Word he passes within a few verses to Son, and Son it remains for the rest of the Gospel. In the perspective of his Gospel as a whole, one wonders if he might not just as well have said "In the beginning was the Son, and the Son was with God, and the Son was God."

Logos is John's special word only in the sense that no other

New Testament writer uses it of Christ[1] at all. In the opening of his First Epistle, John has: "Our message concerns that
Word, who is Life; what he was from the first, what we have
heard about him, what our own eyes have seen of him; what
it was that met our gaze and the touch of our hands." In the
Apocalypse (written, if not by John, at least by someone
close to his thought) we find the vision of the Rider on the
white horse: "He went clad in a garment deep dyed with
blood, and the name by which he is called is the Word of
God . . . from his mouth came a two-edged sword, ready
to smite the nations . . . and this title is written on his cloak,
over his thigh, the King of kings, and the Lord of lords"
(19.13).

Why did John use the word if he was going to make no
use of it, so to speak? We have already spoken of the use
Christians have made of it from John's day to our own: we
should have been hard put to it to give any meaning to God's
having a Son, if we had not been able to think of the divine
Mind conceiving a Word, in which the whole of the divine
reality was uttered. Was John throwing light on the question
how God could have a Son?

At least we have the fact we have already noted, that Word
gives place almost instantly to Son. He tells us that he and

[1] The opening of Romans 12 has always bothered me—"Present
your bodies as a living sacrifice . . . your reasonable service." The
last two words are of a moderation not common in Paul. What he
wrote was *logiken latreian*. For *latreia* the dictionary gives "service"
and tells us the word was used for the worship of the gods; Christians
use it for the adoration due to God only. But "reasonable worship"
sounds even less Pauline. I felt how pleasant it would be if we could
take *logiken* here as the adjective not from *logos* but from *Logos*—
if only we could! RSV and the *Bible de Jérusalem* translate logiken
(unusually) as "spiritual."

the others saw, in the Word made flesh, "the glory as of the only-begotten of the Father." We may note here that "only-begotten" is not a strict translation of the Greek word, which is not *monogennetos* but *monogenes*. John uses the same word when he speaks of God so loving the world that he sent his only-begotten Son. But if *monogenes* does not—or did not at that time—actually mean *monogennetos*, it comes to the same thing: for it means "alone of his kind," so that the *monogenes* of a Father would be an only son. And neither John nor any other of the New Testament writers leave any doubt of the uniqueness of this particular sonship.

One other phrase in the Prologue must be noted—"All things were made by him, and without him nothing was made." We have already discussed this. For the moment it might be worth while to re-read Proverbs 8.22–6, Wisdom 7.26, and Ecclesiasticus 1.1. Here we find the Wisdom of God personified, and spoken of as being at work with God in the creation of the world. Further, God's Wisdom and God's Word are interchangeable: "I am that word," says Wisdom, "that was uttered by the mouth of the Most High, the primal birth before ever creation began" (Eccles. 24.3). So after all it may have been Greeks that put the word "Word" in John's mind—the Hellenistic Jews, not Greek by race but formed in Greek philosophy, who wrote the Wisdom literature of the Old Testament, which Philo also had read. (It has been suggested that both John and Philo chose Word rather than Wisdom because Logos was masculine whereas Sophia was feminine.)

We have lingered upon the Prologue to St. John's Gospel, and there are other sections of the Gospel, notably in the fifth chapter, which develop the equality of Son and Father.

Yet it would be hard to find anything in John which cannot
be matched in Acts and the rest of the New Testament. The
Prologue itself is echoed by—or more probably echoes—the
opening of the Epistle to the Hebrews. "In many and various
ways God spoke of old to our fathers by the prophets; but in
these last days he has spoken to us by a Son, whom he ap-
pointed the heir of all things, through whom also he created
the world. He reflects the glory of God and bears the very
stamp of his nature, upholding the universe by his word of
power." It is not hard to see a resemblance between the
Word, which Christian theology interprets as the fullness of
God's own reality, and a Son who "bears the very stamp of
God's nature." This last phrase is translated by Monsignor
Knox as "the full expression of his being." The Jerusalem
Bible has "*effigie de sa substance.*" The literal translation of
the Greek phrase thus so variously rendered is "the character
of his hypostasis."

Paul's writings are filled with Father and Son. Where John
chose "word," Paul thinks in terms of "wisdom" (1 Cor.
1.24). Where we ourselves find Idea as a word to express the
relation of Son to Father, Paul thinks in terms of Image. "He
is the image of the invisible God, the first-born of all creation"
(Col. 1.25): for this last phrase Monsignor Knox has the
splendid rendering "His is that first birth which precedes
every act of creation." Paul continues—"in him all things
were created, in heaven and on earth, visible and invisible,
whether thrones or dominions or principalities or authorities
[these four words represent angels, about whom the Colossians were tempted to error]—all things were created through
him and for him. He is before all things, and in him all things
hold together." Paul had certainly read Psalm 32—"By the

word of the Lord the heavens were made, and all their host by the breath of his mouth."

To balance John's "We saw his glory, the glory as of the only Son from the Father" and the phrase of Hebrews, "He reflects the glory of God," Paul gives us "the glory of God in the face of Christ" (2 Cor. 4.6). "Glory" *must* have been in the Deposit of Faith.

There is no hint in Paul of the Son as a secondary God ruling the created universe while the Father stays remote and inaccessible to men. St. John had quoted Our Lord himself as saying "My Father is working still, and I am working" (5.17). And Paul quite naturally speaks of the action of both Father and Son in relation to the bringing into being, and the holding in being, of creation. On the Areopagus he speaks of God in a line of Epimenides of Cnossos—"In him we live and move and have our being." He says the same thing to the Corinthians, but with an added statement about the Son—"There is one God, the Father, *from* whom are all things and *for* whom we exist, and one Lord, Jesus Christ, *through* whom are all things and *through* whom we exist" (1 Cor. 8.6).

We shall see a little later that Christ's Lordship means no diminution of deity, for Kyrios, Lord, is the Septuagint translation of the Old Testament Yahweh. St. Paul tells the Colossians, "In Christ the whole fullness of deity dwells bodily" (2.9). And there is a text in the Epistle to the Romans which may be interpreted variously according to the punctuation the interpreter supposes. Monsignor Knox translates it "Christ, who rules as God over all things, blessed forever, Amen" (Rom. 9.5). The Revised Standard Version ends a sentence with "Christ" and makes "God who is over all be blessed for ever" a separate sentence. The Jerusalem Bible gives the same meaning as Knox; and the Scripture scholar Oscar Cullmann regards the verse as directly calling Christ God.

It is no wild exaggeration to say that whatever John affirms about the Son as a second Person within the Godhead can be paralleled by the other New Testament writers. For myself, and I think for most people who have studied the Catholic doctrine of the Trinity, it seems clear beyond a question that Paul and John are seeing the same divine reality, and responding, each in his own highly personal way. What is special to John is the amount of this common doctrine which he places in the mouth of Christ himself. As to the reason of this, we can only speculate. After all, no one can be absolutely certain who the writer was. Until very recently, it was not questioned that he was the beloved disciple. Then came the suggestion that John the Presbyter, named by Papias as the author, was a different John, of whom nothing else was known. Scholars now seem to be drawing to something approaching a consensus—the Gospel is Johannine, perhaps by John the Apostle himself, if not, then by one of the group formed by him.

In either event, we are brought face to face with Our Lord's Mother. Following Christ's instruction from the Cross, John took Mary to his own: she would be his mother, he her son. The Gospel is his, whether written by him or by one of his disciples; the years of companionship with Christ's mother would surely have poured into it. A number of times I have seen this dismissed as neither theology nor history. It is true that theology does not require it, nor does history give any evidence in support of it. But it seems to me that common sense fairly shouts it.

There is another possible explanation. At the Last Supper,

John had heard Our Lord's promise that when the Holy Spirit came, he would teach them all things, and bring to their remembrance all that Christ had said to them (John 14.26). It can hardly mean only that they would re-hear their Master's words gramaphonically—linked up with "teach" it surely means insight into his mind as he spoke them. Nor does it seem that this would be a sudden flash of illumination in which all Christ's teaching would appear on the screen of their mind, with all its profundities clearly drawn out and arranged in order to their gaze. It is more likely to have been a gradual progress into the depths of Christ's teachings, as we find him saying a little later: "When the Spirit of truth comes, he will guide you into all truth" (John 16.13). The guidance may have come sooner or later, more luminously to some than to others; but in its light John may very well have come to see all that he puts into Christ's mouth as having been fully contained in brief utterances whose richness neither he nor any of the others glimpsed when they heard them uttered, whose richness even his Gospel did not exhaust, nor has his Church exhausted them yet.

2. Three Persons

There is no greater difference between the monotheistic Old Testament and monotheistic New Testament than the frequency with which in the New God is spoken of in three terms. The word Trinity is not Scriptural. In its Greek form *Trias* we meet it first round about the year 180 in Theophilus of Antioch. Soon afterwards Tertullian, in his *De Pudicitia*, gives us *Trinitas*. But, whatever their meaning, the use of three terms in speaking of God is already standard practice in the New Testament. Karl Rahner counts forty-four occasions in which the One God is spoken of as Three.

The phrase "Father, Son and Holy Spirit" appears once only: towards the end of his time on earth, Our Lord is quoted by Matthew as instructing the Apostles to baptize "into the Name of the Father and of the Son and of the Holy Spirit." For the rest, the terminology varies. The First Person is called Father, or simply God; the Second is Son or Lord or Lamb; but the Third is always Spirit. Before we come to examine the Three, let us pause upon this Third. Is he a distinct Someone as the Son, the kyrios, is? Is he equal to each, as truly God as the Father is and the Son is?

The Greek word is *pneuma*. The first peculiarity that strikes us is that although the word is neuter, the pronoun used is He, not It. And he is always in action, doing something. He is shown at the very origin of Christ: it is by his power that the Virgin conceives. "The Holy Spirit will come upon you and the power of the Most High will overshadow you; therefore the Child to be born will be called holy, the Son of God" (Luke 1.35). This linking of the Holy Spirit with power we find again and again in St. Paul's Epistles. At the baptism in Jordan, he descends upon Christ in the form of a dove, and "immediately drove him out into the wilderness" (Mark 1.12). When the temptations were over "Jesus returned in the power of the Spirit into Galilee" (Luke 4.14). By him Our Lord says that he cast out demons (Matt. 12.28). On the return of the seventy-two disciples, Christ "rejoiced in the Holy Spirit" (Luke 10.21). And so throughout Our Lord's earthly life, the dynamism of the Spirit is in him and with him.

In the idea of the Spirit of God working upon men, there is

nothing that would surprise any of Our Lord's hearers: as Old Testament readers they would take it in their stride. The Spirit of God was simply God himself in his actions upon men. But there begins to appear a distinction which they would have found puzzling, and indeed frightening. When the Pharisees accused Christ of casting out demons by Beelzebul, the prince of demons, Our Lord answers them with showing how fantastic the accusation was in itself: then he goes on "Every sin and blasphemy will be forgiven man, but the blasphemy against the Spirit will not be forgiven. And whoever says a word against the Son of Man will be forgiven; but whoever speaks against the Holy Spirit will not be forgiven, either in this world or in the world to come" (Matt. 12.31, 32).

The more one looks at these words, the more one realizes how startling they must have sounded, and in two ways particularly. To speak against the Son of Man is called blasphemy; startling enough since blasphemy is a direct insult to God. But the statement that *any* sin and blasphemy—that is, any assault upon the majesty of God, any refusal of obedience to God—is forgivable, but blasphemy against the Spirit is not, startles us more. Clearly Our Lord must be referring to something in the nature of the sin. It is not that the Spirit is greater than the Son, greater than the Father; there must be a special kind of malice in sinning against the Holy Spirit. We cannot pretend to know just what was in the mind of Christ: but we can hardly help reminding ourselves of the Catholic belief that the Holy Spirit is produced by the love of Father and Son, *is* love hypostatized: and that an ultimate refusal of love is the only thing that makes forgiveness impossible.

Are we entitled to see the Spirit as distinct from the Father,

distinct as we have already seen that the Son is? Upon this
question Our Lord casts light. "From God I proceeded"
(John 8.42), he says of himself; and he speaks of "the Spirit
of Truth, who proceeds from the Father" (John 15.26).
Again of himself he says: "I have spoken the truth which I
have heard from God" (John 8). And of the Holy Spirit he
says: "What things soever he shall hear, he shall speak"
(John 6.13). But there is a difference. After the last phrase
quoted, Our Lord goes on "Because he shall receive of mine
and shall show it to you": with the Nature the Second Person
received from the First goes the truth which he proclaims:
and it would seem from the words just used that the Third
Person also has received that Nature, and the truth which
belongs in it, from the Son and not from the Father only.

This is clearer still in the Sendings. Our Lord speaks of
himself as sent by his Father (John 8.38), but both Father and
Son are spoken of as sending the Holy Spirit. "I will ask the
Father, and he will send another Paraclete" (John 14.16). "I
will send the Paraclete to you" (John 16.7). So the Father,
from whom Son and Holy Spirit proceed and who himself
proceeds from no other, sends Son and Holy Spirit to men
and is not himself sent. And again the Son is sent by the
Father, and sends the Holy Spirit. The Holy Spirit sends no
divine Person, he sends only men. But, as we have seen, one
of the men he sends is the God-man.

The sending of the Paraclete does also, in its own way,
underline what we may call a parallel between himself and the
Son. At the Last Supper Our Lord speaks of his own approaching departure from this earth. The Apostles are desolate. And what does he say for their comfort? "It is to your
advantage that I go away, for if I do not go away, the Coun-

sellor will not come to you; but if I go, I will send him to you" (John 16.7). The word here translated Counsellor is the word we know better as Paraclete. The trouble is that the exact Greek word used by John is not found in Greek. There are two words from which his word might be derived. In his First Epistle, it seems to mean Advocate; here perhaps it might mean Comforter.

If so, it could not have been much comfort to the Apostles. They were losing the presence of a person they knew and loved: his place was to be taken by One of whom they could have had no clear idea. What could he do for them greater than Christ could? Was he even a person? They had the same difficulty about this Third Someone that men have had ever since—he was not made flesh, he did not live as man among us. If only he too had had an Incarnation!

At least it seems clear from what Christ says that the Paraclete is a Person as Christ is, distinct from the Father as Christ is, not simply a special power of God: a divine Person was not to yield place to, be succeeded by, a divine attribute. And succeeded by the Spirit Christ was. One has heard the Acts of the Apostles called the Gospel of the Holy Spirit; and the whole book is as much the Spirit's as the Gospels are Christ's.

Why must Christ go if the Spirit was to come? Why was it so urgent that the Spirit *should* come—so urgent that it was gain for men to lose the immediate presence of Christ? These questions we shall discuss when we come to treat of the operations of the Blessed Trinity upon the created order, ourselves included. Here our concern is with the Trinity in itself —"even the depths of God, which the Spirit searches" (1 Cor. 2.10). We are dwelling upon this "replacement" because it shows that the Spirit is Someone, a Person, distinct from

Father and Son. Is he God? We know from the Church that
he is. Is anything said in the New Testament that makes this
clear?

It is not easy to single out any one text which could mean
only that. Yet Christ's going that the Spirit might come suggests that he was not less than Christ; and if we believe in
Christ's divinity, then we can hardly find some lower level of
being for the Spirit. Indeed that no lower level is seen as his
by the first Christians seems the only explanation of the forty
times recurrent Triad. Men may still differ about the meaning
of the second term and the third, but that there are three
terms is not in question—the divine Oneness demands to be
expressed as triplicity. The Spirit is always there; and if he is
not divine, as the First Person and the Second are, his invariable presence is meaningless, almost embarrassing, as of one
who does not belong but cannot be left out.

As we have already noted, the Church's chosen phrase—
Father, Son and Holy Spirit—occurs only once in Scripture;
but Matthew places it on the lips of Christ himself. The
Eleven were on a mountain in Galilee. "And Jesus came and
said to them, 'All authority in heaven and on earth has been
given to me. Go therefore and make disciples of all nations,
baptizing them in the name of the Father and of the Son and
of the Holy Spirit.' " (Matt. 28.18–19) The use of the word
"name" in the singular is decisive as to what the phrase is saying. When Scripture uses Name solemnly, as we have noted,
it is never a mere label to distinguish one being from another:
the name utters a person's profoundest reality. The Spirit
could not have one name with Father and Son unless he has
the nature that the name expresses which is theirs.

Because this arrangement of words is without parallel in the

New Testament, there are those who think that Christ did not actually use it, but only said "baptizing them"; and that the Evangelist, writing forty years after, inserted the baptismal formula by then in use. The suggestion is not impossible, of course; punctuation then was not as precise as we have made it. Yet it does not seem necessary. Christ had already spoken often enough of each of the three Persons: there is nothing unthinkable, or even improbable, in his bringing them together, so close to the end of his time upon earth, to indicate the fullness of the divine reality with which baptism is to bring men into new and redemptive relation.

There is a great profit in reading all the triad texts. Some are clearer than others. One of the most splendid could easily be overlooked—I mean we might not notice its relevance to our quest. It is the opening verse of the last chapter of Scripture's last book. "Then he showed me the river of the water of life, bright as crystal, flowing from the throne of God and of the Lamb." Only if we remember Our Lord's reference to "rivers of living water" (John 7.39), and the Evangelist's comment "This he said about the Spirit," do we realize that there is a Third Person involved here. The few texts I shall quote from St. Paul have not this difficulty.

St. Paul speaks of himself as "a minister of Christ Jesus to the Gentiles in the priestly service of the gospel of God, so that the offering of the Gentiles may be acceptable, sanctified by the Holy Spirit" (Rom. 15.16). At the beginning of the same Epistle, he speaks of serving God "in the gospel of his Son."

"Because you are sons, God has sent the Spirit of his Son into your hearts, crying 'Abba! Father!' " (Gal. 4.6).

"There are varieties of gifts, but the same Spirit; and there are varieties of service, but the same Lord; and there are varieties of working, but it is the same God who inspires them all in every one" (1 Cor. 12.4–6).

"There is one body and one Spirit, just as you were called to the one hope that belongs to your call; one Lord, one Faith, one baptism; one God and Father of us all, who is above all, and through all, and in all."

In none of these texts or in any others is Paul *teaching* the doctrine of the Trinity; he is assuming it, applying it, or crying out in it—as when he ends his Second Epistle to the Corinthians—"The grace of the Lord Jesus Christ and the love of God and the fellowship of the Holy Spirit be with you all."

THIRTEEN

The Trinity
in the New Testament (2)

Why do not all readers find the Blessed Trinity in the New Testament? Why, in particular, do scholars who have given their whole lives to the study of these books not find the doctrine there? The reasons are of two sorts: objective—the content of the document under study; and subjective—the content and habits of the mind men bring to the making of the study.

1. The Mind We Bring to Scripture

We shall consider the mind first: it has a special value for ourselves: watching great scholars at work, we are enabled to put ourselves on guard. We do not suspect ourselves of reading our own religion or philosophy into Scripture until we watch someone else reading his. The discovery can be very cleansing.

There is no conscious dishonesty, no dishonesty at all. But once the scholar has an axe to grind, he is tempted to something very close to what we may call, mildly, tendentiousness. We suddenly realize that the disinterested scholar, whom we have been following with admiration and great profit, has become an advocate. A scholar in any field can be in love with his own discovery, and lovers can act strangely. Scripture scholars are not immune. Unconsciously, they will accept without inquiry texts that go their way, but texts that go against are subjected to the most rigid scrutiny; a single text is sufficient if it says what they want said; if not it is written off as "unsupported," or "peculiar to this evangelist." They will treat a writer's silence as of immense significance if what some other writer has said on the same matter does not harmonize with their thesis; they will say, for instance, that a given writer "carefully avoids" mentioning something or other, or is "not interested" in it, or displays a "reverent reticence" about it—when all they actually know is that he does not mention it. And it is all too easy to glide from demonstrating that a given interpretation is possible to assuming that it is true.

Dominating all is the practically universal tendency to use logic as a weapon, not as a building-tool. We know that our own views are not built by logic only, all sorts of value-elements enter which are not susceptible of proof—life, we tell ourselves, is larger than logic. But if a view differs from ours, with what relentless logic we dissect it. These are human weaknesses, and we too are human. Once one is aware of them, they can be kept in reasonable check.

What matters even more is the effect that the whole cast of

our mind has upon our judgment of what we are reading. If the apparent meaning of Scripture strikes the reader as wholly impossible, then he automatically looks for another meaning: there *must* be another meaning, no man in his senses could possibly have meant *that!* When men were told for the first time that the sun does not go round the earth, they met the statement with a guffaw—after all, they have *seen* the sun going round the earth. And it is a matter of common experience that a high degree of sophistication in the scientific field can be accompanied by sheer primitivism in the spiritual: and vice versa, of course.

In studying Scripture, there are two attitudes to mystery either of which may get in the way of understanding, or even hearing, what the writer is saying. We may call them mysteriophobia and mysteriophilia. The former is not usually stated, but can be powerful for rejection. So great a scholar as Dr. Bultmann has so total a certainty that the supernatural is not real that on whole areas of Scripture his judgment does not function, his assertions are sheerly reflex. And the mysteriophobe is supported in his dismissal of mystery by the happy assertions of those who will swallow anything, for whom no better evidence is required for any belief than its impossibility.

Very common today is the mind which rejects mystery, the supernatural, the preternatural, in relation to the finite—angels, for instance, or the Virgin Birth—while surrounding the Infinite with mystery which it cannot bear that any ray of light should pierce. This, whether in the mixed state I have just described or complete in itself with no such distinction of finite and infinite, is what I have called mysteriophilia. We have already had a good look at it. Here it is worth while to

remind ourselves that there is a state of mind for which the
Ultimate is the Unknowable. The Absolute can be intoxicating: I remember the fury of a man at hearing the word Infinite used as a substitute—the concept of Infinity, he said,
was a degradation of the Absolute! Short of this extreme, we
find men rigidly set against any suggestion that the Absolute
does anything or knows anything, who see it as if it were a
further area lying beyond or beneath the Trinity itself.

Whether one of these, or any one of half a dozen others, is
the cast of mind—whether a particular doctrine is either in
possession, or not specially thought about, or an object of special aversion—the reading of Scripture cannot but be profoundly affected.

For one who believes in the Trinity, certain texts leap out
of the page. For one who does not, they lie embedded. To
one who reflects that maternity does not consist solely in
conceiving the child and bearing it, but is a relation which
abides and grows deeper, every mention of Christ's Mother
can be precious: but in his book *The Fourth Gospel* Dr. Dodd
does not discuss either her part at Cana or Christ's giving her
as mother to the Beloved Disciple on Calvary. On the other
hand, one who sees Christ as continuing to live and work in
the world through his Body the Church gets deep satisfaction
from Dr. Dodd's treatment of the Vine and the Branches,
whereas Dr. Cullmann can write a whole book on *The Christology of the New Testament* with only passing mention of
the Mystical Body.

And so it is with any other view strongly held, or not
regarded, or simply rejected. What is a fundamental text for
one reader is merely peripheral for another, at worst a difficulty to be reconciled or a problem to be solved, leaving un-

affected the main corpus of texts that support his view. We have already noted what Marcion made of the words uttered by the voice from heaven, when Our Lord stood with Moses and Elias on the Mount of Transfiguration—"This is my beloved Son in whom I am well pleased. Hear ye him." Marcion held as primary that the Old Testament was wholly to be cast aside: therefore he interpreted the words "Hear ye him" as meaning "Listen to Christ, not to Moses and Elias." We may take this as a kind of parable or symbol of a normal tendency against which we must all be on the watch.

Lying midway between the reasons I have called Subjective and Objective lies a special temptation to which the scholar is more exposed than the rest of us—document-mindedness. It takes two forms.

The first is a refusal of non-documentary evidence, especially any suggestion tentatively offered by common sense. We have already noted the reaction of some scholars to the notion that the years John spent as son to Our Lord's mother might have done something to account for special elements, or emphases, in the way the doctrines of Trinity and Incarnation emerge in the Fourth Gospel. Common sense suggests that Our Lord's mother and his beloved disciple had better topics of conversation than the doings of the people next door: they must have talked of things they knew better than any other people in the world. But there is no document that says they did, and only a document will do. Indeed, for many, "the historical Jesus" means "the Jesus of the documents"—that is, of the words actually written. Thus, the documents show Our Lord as man, and men love their mothers: but as it is not written that he loved his, we are not allowed to say that "the historical Jesus" did.

The second form of document-mindedness is an exaggeration of the sufficiency of the document, a tendency to ignore the shortness of the period it covers or the slightness of the information it gives, a tendency to build upon the fragmentary as though it were at once inclusive and conclusive.

To take an example: St. Paul has left us some dozen Letters written over a space of perhaps fourteen years, covering less than half of his life as a Christian, containing things he did and things he said in roughly the same period. As a publisher observing and working with writers for forty years, I marvel at the certainty with which scholars can reconstruct the whole mind of Paul and the stages in the development of his understanding of the revelation of Christ—rather like an anthropologist reconstructing Pithecanthropus from a couple of bones.

Apparently this can be done with bones, but it cannot be done with books. One has to take into account the people for whom different letters were written and the problems that had to be met: something may have happened to bring one particular element before the writer's mind: and there is always his own temperament, which moves on no known law. Paul emphasizes one aspect of truth in one letter: he might have written another letter the same day with quite different aspects emphasized.

I remember an experience of my own which may be used—like the Marcion interpretation mentioned above—as a warning to others. In 1 Corinthians (written, they think, in 57 A.D.) Paul wrote that it was better to marry than to burn (7.9)—no thinner compliment has ever been paid to marriage. In the Letter to the Ephesians (written five or six years later) he compares marriage with the union of Christ and his

Church. I not only assumed that there was a development of his mind in the years between, but I provided myself with a reason to account for the development—his growing intimacy with that splendid husband and wife, Aquila and Priscilla. I had forgotten that a few chapters on (10.3), in that very same Letter to the Corinthians, Paul compares marriage to the union of Christ and his Church! There still remains the problem, that Paul appears to be saying that if a man and woman cannot control their carnal lusts, they had better become a symbol of the union of Christ and his Church: but my explanation was oversimplified.[1] And I have met explanations of other passages equally oversimplified by men who tower over me in scholarship.

2. Problems of Terminology

We turn now to the objective reason why some do, while some do not, find the Trinity plainly contained in the New Testament—I mean the writings themselves. From Thessalonians to John's Gospel they are spread over, say, forty years. The mind of the Apostles was not static over all that period. Two elements were at work. Our Lord had said that those who live by the Commandments shall know of the doctrine, and living is a day by day matter. And he had said that the Spirit of Truth would lead them into all truth, and this too would be a continuing process, truth not bursting on them in one blaze, but themselves guided into it.

Of just how these two influences worked upon the Apostles,

[1] Still in the later Epistle marriage *is* treated more warmly and humanly: so that Ephesians 5 may have been Paul's tribute to Aquila and Priscilla.

to say nothing of the body of believers, we have no record. Paul's doctrine, as the *Bible de Jérusalem* reminds us, followed a line of development towards "a plenitude which finds its complete utterance in the Epistle to the Ephesians" (p. 1483). Yet it could not have been as peculiar to himself as we are apt to think, or he could not have taken for granted that Churches so far apart would receive it. We naturally—but not of necessity correctly—attribute a particular teaching to the writer in whom we first meet it. Yet one of Paul's most splendid things —Philippians 2.6–8—is increasingly seen as a quotation from the Church's liturgy; so is the Maranatha of 1 Corinthians 16.22, and the Trinitarian ending of 2 Corinthians.

Similarly, the difference between John and the other Evangelists is never discussed without mention of the thirty-year gap (generally assumed but not actually established) between their writing and his. But this is too often seen only as accounting for a development of his own personal thinking; we must remember that thirty years was half the Church's lifetime, and there may have been a "Johannine" development in the Church as a whole. Anyhow there was a development of understanding within the apostolic body. From the first they were guarded against teaching error and there would be an increase in richness and profundity of understanding.

But there was something else. There was the question of terminology—in what words could all this newness be expressed?

I do not mean only that there were realities to be expressed which the Greeks had never known and for which their language had no words: existent words had to be chosen out and given a new depth of meaning—thus *charis*, and the Latin word *gratia*, were made to carry the richness of Sanctifying

Grace. I mean the general impossibility of stating anything at all in words to which only one meaning can ever be attached; and there was the special impossibility arising from the inadequacy of human language to the mystery of God, to which no human words are or ever will be wholly adequate.

Supposing that the Apostles knew that Father and Son and Holy Spirit are one God, the fact remained that the Father alone is Origin, that he alone possesses the divinity unreceived. There was the almost immeasurably difficult problem of so stating the doctrine that the equality would stand clear, yet this special reality of the Father not be obscured; the related problem of how to keep clear the divinity of each without seeming to deny the Oneness of God, which might lead pagan converts, especially, to feel that there were three gods; and the problem of problems—how to show men the light that had been shown the Apostles, while preserving their awareness of the mightier darkness surrounding the precious circle of light.

We cannot feel that for any of these problems the precisely adequate terminology has yet been found, nineteen hundred years after. We have certain key words chosen out by the Church and continually clarified, and we have a series of definitions. Both terms and definitions are light-bearing, yet a mass of explanation has to accompany them: they will not yield much light unless there are teachers authorized to convey them to us. We have no reason to expect at the very beginning something men will not have obtained at the end of man's time upon earth—namely a precision of statement, inclusive of all the truth to be conveyed, exclusive of all possibility of misunderstanding.

With terminology not yet standardized, different Apostles

would tend to meet this complexus of problems differently. St. Paul's preferred terms for the Three are God, Lord and Spirit: yet he will speak of the first two individually as Father and Son, he calls Christ Son of God as readily as he calls him Lord, and is quite capable of using Son instead of Lord in the Triad (Gal. 4.6).

What was in his mind when he called the First Person God and the Second Lord, Kyrios? What was the force of Kyrios? To begin with, it is a common noun in Greek, meaning Master, a courtesy term likely to be used of anyone having authority—as we find it used of Christ in the Gospel by those who were not his disciples. But it has a religious use as well. When, a century before Christ, the Jews translated the Old Testament into Greek, they translated the divine Name, *Yahweh*, as *Kyrios*, Lord, which was what the pagans would have used for one of their own gods. To a Greek-speaking Jew, *Kyrios* was the God of the Old Testament. It seems that, in the century before Christ and the century after, the rabbis used the word Adonai, Lord, for God.

In the Acts of the Apostles, by Dr. Arendzen's count, *Kyrios* is used 110 times, one third of them in speaking of God, one third of Christ. Half a dozen times in the Apocalypse, we have "the Lord God" *kyrios ho theos*, to remind us of Peter's "the Lord our God" (Acts 2.39). In the episode of Ananias and Sapphira (Acts 5.3–9), we find Peter, in describing one single sin, moving with all naturalness from God to Lord to Spirit—Ananias "lied to the Holy Spirit," "lied to God," and agreed with his wife "to tempt the Spirit of the Lord." And we have Paul in successive verses (2 Cor. 6.16–18) giving us "as God said," "says the Lord," "says the Lord Almighty."

Paul never, save when quoting, uses "Lord" of any but Christ. John, save when quoting, never uses it at all, either in Gospel or Epistles. But clearly it could carry divinity with it, could be used freely of the Second Person without any implications that he was not divine. It would hardly have been used as a regular name for the Son by Jews who did not think him God.

Why was St. Paul moved to use it as he did (260 times, by the count in the *Catholic Commentary*)? One can only speculate, of course. For a man of his lucidity, it was good to have a word which would indicate distinction between the First Person and the Second, while leaving the Second also divine. And this particular word had special associations with his last days as an enemy of the Christians and his first meeting with Christ. He was there at the stoning of Stephen (Acts 7), "consenting to his death": he had heard Stephen cry out "Lord Jesus, receive my spirit," and again "Lord, do not hold this sin against them." It does not seem likely that he knew how close these words were to words uttered by Christ on the Cross. But even the fire-and-slaughter-breathing Saul could not have failed to find them enormously impressive. And not long after, on the road to Damascus, he answered the voice which said to him, "Saul, Saul, why do you persecute me?" with the words "Who are you, Lord?"

There is another problem of terminology, how to speak of One who is both God and man—the only-begotten Son of God, the only-conceived son of Mary: as God uncreated, as man created: yet one Person, one "I." In his godhead he *is* Lord, but in his humanity he is *made* Lord—"God *has made* both Lord and Messias this Jesus whom you have crucified" (Acts 2.35). Lordship means authority—absolute authority in

God, but true authority in men to whom God gives it for the furtherance of work he wants done. Christ had both: for as man he was given by God supreme authority—when he earned it by "obedience unto death." Read carefully Hebrews 5.7–10 and Philippians 2.5–11.

We begin with Hebrews. There we meet the only virtue we are told Christ "learned." Following a description of the Agony in the Garden the writer says: "Whereas, indeed, he was the Son of God, he learned obedience by the things he suffered: and being consummated, he *became* the source of eternal salvation to all that obey him." "Consummated" is a mysterious word. We remember Our Lord's "It is consummated" on the Cross (John 19.30). Immediately before, we have the same Greek verb twice—"Jesus knowing that all things were *consummated*, that the Scripture might be *consummated*." It contains the idea of completion, applied by Our Lord to Scripture and to the work of Redemption: in Hebrews it is applied to Our Lord himself.

And it was by obedience that he achieved it. We must be obedient to him if he is to save us: there is here the same linking of Lordship and saving-power as in the phrase of Peter we have just quoted—"God *made him* both Lord and Messias." We have it again—and again from Peter—in Acts 5.31: "God *has exalted* him to be prince and saviour." In his divinity Christ could not be exalted, but only as man. And this, as the Philippians passage tells, only because he humbled himself, emptied himself, chose *not* to have from the beginning that glory in the humanity he had made his own to which as God the Son's it was entitled. It must *grow* to the consummation, the perfection, which befitted the divine Person whose humanity it was. "He humbled himself, becoming obedient unto death, even to the death of the cross. For which cause God also has *exalted* him, and has given him a name that is above all names: that in the name of Jesus every knee should bow of those that are in heaven, on earth, and under the earth. . . ." This last phrase—"every knee should bow . . ." is another kind of reminder of the problem of speaking of One who is both God and man. For, here applied to the One who obeyed, it is a quotation of Isaiah 14.23, where it applies to God.

This interchangeability of reference to Christ-as-God and Christ-as-man is not readily reducible to a fixed system. The man Christ was born at a given moment of time, but the Person, the one who in Christ's humanity said "I"—is eternal. It is not always easy to know with certainty whether a reference is to the Son-in-his-eternity, or to the Son-made-flesh; and things are said of the Christ of our earth which could be true only of the divine Person he was. Of the Son-in-his-eternity, Paul speaks as the Image of God, where John says Word; but as Son-made-flesh Christ is *in* the image and likeness of God—as all men are, though only he wholly. A question can arise whether in a given text the uncreated image is meant or the created—an example is "being in the form of God" in Philippians 2.6. When the question does arise, the reader will tend to settle it according to the theological or philosophical views he already holds.

Like the word Image, the word Lord can leave a question. When Peter says in his first sermon that God has made Christ "Lord" it is clearly of the manhood he is speaking. So also when Christ himself says, "You call me Teacher and Lord; and you are right, for so I am" (John 13.13), he is quoting words used of him by the Apostles, and they were hardly

ready yet for a matter-of-course assertion that he was Yahweh. But in the triads "Lord" can mean only the divinity.

For the high point of what I have called "interchangeability" we may take John 3.13—"No one has ascended into
heaven but he who descended from heaven, the Son of Man
who dwells in heaven." Msgr. Knox translates slightly differently—"there is one who descended . . ."—but the strangeness remains. And this is so whether we take the words as said
by Our Lord or as a comment inserted by the Evangelist. The
Christ who ascended into heaven is the Son-made-flesh; the
one who "descended," i.e. who was made flesh, is the Son-in-
his eternity: strictly it was not the Son of Man who descended
—the Son of Man came to be because God the Son "descended."

And of course the word "descended" has its own strangeness. The Second Person, made man, did not leave the Father:
as we have seen, such a notion is meaningless. His very existence is "in" the Father. A human nature, soul and body, was
brought into existence and related to him as my nature to me,
so that he acted in a lower nature and a lower sphere: but he
remained within the eternal oneness of the Blessed Trinity.
We shall examine this more closely when we come to talk of
the Incarnation. We merely note here that "descent" is a
figure of speech with less instant reference than many. So is
the notion of Christ's "return," implied in the descent and
ascent. In strict literalness Christ as God could not be said to
return to the heaven he had never left, nor Christ as man to
the heaven in which as man he had not dwelt. Our Lord himself speaks of "coming forth from the Father," of "going to
the Father," but not of "returning to the Father." Yet it is not
only as a compliment to Hegel that men have talked of

the return. There is a kind of naturalness in it, and we find no problem stirring in our mind as we say the Nicene Creed— "and in Jesus Christ His only-begotten Son, God of God . . . consubstantial with the Father . . . who for us men and our salvation came down from heaven."

"A kind of naturalness," I say, for those who accept the Church's doctrine on the Trinity and have been saying the Nicene Creed for sixteen hundred years. But for those who regard Scripture solely as a literature to be explored on its own terms, like any other, all these difficulties—of terminology and the rest—can issue in a vast variety of solutions. It would be naive to count upon a single solution of any one problem being acceptable to all. It may be helpful at this point to choose for consideration one of the great scholars who study the New Testament without special reference to the Catholic Church. A few years ago I should have chosen Rudolf Bultmann, but now Oscar Cullmann seems to be in possession. I hasten to say that the purpose of this all too brief study of some of his ideas is not to prove him wrong but to clarify our own position by seeing how a mind so very able can read the same Scriptures so very differently. No one should think that from this rapid sketch of some elements in his thought it is possible to form a judgment of his work. For that one must read at least *The Christology of the New Testament.*[2]

3. A Very Different Reading

"Functional theology is the only kind that exists," writes Dr. Cullmann in *The Christology* (p. 325): which means that

[2] Philadelphia, Westminster, 1959.

Scripture, New Testament as well as Old Testament, tells us nothing of God in himself but only of God as he acts upon men. The theory can best be illustrated from the Prologue to the Fourth Gospel: "In the beginning was the Word and the Word was with God and the Word was God. All things were made by him . . ." Dr. Cullmann comments: "Almost as if the writer of the Prologue of John feared further speculation, he moves immediately from *being* to the *act* of creation—all things were made by Him" (p. 248). In this theory the same principle is seen as operative throughout—Scripture does not tell of God as he is in himself but in his functioning, his action upon the universe he has created, which action includes as much showing of himself-as-functioning as he chooses to give. Dr. Cullmann seems to assert that this is all that men *can* know and even that to seek further is irreverence: though I have seen him quoted recently as saying that he is not denying the doctrine of the Trinity as a truth about the inner life of God, only saying that Scripture does not show it so.

As we have noted, the Church's teaching on the Trinity does not need to be proved from Scripture but only to be shown as in harmony with it: and if all that Scripture says of God is in fact only "functional," then with God-thus-functioning the God-in-Himself of our Trinitarian doctrine is wholly harmonious. But does the New Testament in fact limit itself to God as we experience his action?

Even in relation to St. John's Prologue, the position is not as clear as all that. It is quite true that the opening statement, which Catholics have assumed to be about God's own being, is limited to a single sentence: but what a sentence! It is without parallel in all the world's writing. It is only by a count of words that it would seem limited. Merely as it stands it is stunning. That having spoken of the Word who is God, the writer should proceed immediately to speak of the Word first as creator, then as made flesh and dwelling among us, does not seem to call for any very spectacular explanation—for first there is more to be said on Creation and Incarnation as being not so far beyond human compass, since elements of the finite are in both; and secondly these affect men more evidently. But in both the function flows from, gets its measure from, the reality of God himself already uttered in the opening words—there is production within the Infinite prior to production in the finite, men can be sons of God because in his own being God is Father.

A dozen other phrases crowd in on the mind, phrases which seem to be directly about God, with function given reality by the fact that God *is* so. "God is a spirit"—I do not mean that this or any other arrangement of words can utter the reality of God adequately, but on that reality they do give light, and in that light lies the force of the phrase that follows —"they that worship him must worship him in spirit and in truth" (John 4.24).

It is the same with "God is love" (1 John 4.8)—which continues: "By this has the love of God appeared to us, because God has sent his only-begotten Son into the world that we may live by him." It is much the same with "God is light and in him there is no darkness" (1 John 1.5)—followed by "If we walk in the light, as he is in the light, we have fellowship with one another, and the blood of Jesus his Son cleanses us from all sin."

The idea that action is not grounded in being, that what is done is not what it is because the doer is what *he* is, is a non-idea: it would mean that any being might do anything, merely as chance falls. God himself is not anarchically exempt from the universal rule at work in his creation—namely that beings act as what they are. So that revelation of function *is* revelation of being, at one remove certainly, but genuine revelation. With God-as-spirit, God-as-love and God-as-light there is the same firm grounding of what-God-does in what-God-is as we have seen with God-as-Word. And it is the same with "No one knows the Son but the Father, and no one knows the Father but the Son, and him to whom the Son shall reveal him" (Matt. 11.27; Luke 10.22)—the last few words are functional, but they are linked organically with the reality of the inter-knowledge of Father and Son within the Godhead. Dr. Cullmann says that it is "only meaningful to speak of the Son of Man in view of God's revelatory action, not in view of His being." But, once again, function is grounded in, and thus reveals, being. In Christ "the whole fullness of deity dwells bodily" (Col. 2.9)—a statement of being, surely—"and you have come to fullness of life in him." Our fullness, our completion, is possible because of his.

Linger a moment on that word "completion." Dr. Cullmann says excellently (p. 63) that the Son is "the complete disclosure of God to man": so he is, *because* he is the complete utterance of God to himself. We do not *receive* the disclosure in its completeness, but the lack is in us, not in the Reality shown us, the Reality into which we are invited to enter.

Since great scholars have read the New Testament thus functionally, clearly it *can* be read so, however much this may seem to be forcing texts—not, in the usual way of men in love with a thesis, forcing them to say more than is in them but less.

It seems to me a way of thrusting back to the God of the Old Testament, knowable only in his interventions in human affairs, but in himself unknowable: as though, with the veil of the Temple rent, the old awe still held men from entering: whereas with Christ revealing, Christ guiding, one can go deeper into the Holy of Holies than High Priest ever went, make our dwelling in regions Caiphas never knew. There is the phrase of Dr. Cullmann: "One can say of the being of the logos only what the Johannine preface says and no more." Why? Even one who believed that the words were written by that John who leaned on Our Lord's breast would not treat them as an ultimate beyond which no advance is possible. Why should one treat them so, who does not even claim to know who wrote them? And of course Dr. Cullmann does in fact go further. Upon the being of the pre-existent, pre-temporal, Word who was with God, and who was God, by whom all things are made, and who was made flesh and dwelt among us, he has much to say, along two lines—he sees him as God-in-his-self-revelation and as the Heavenly Man.

The Heavenly Man comes from a single text, 1 Corinthians 15.45. St. Paul writes: "The first Adam was made into a living soul: the last Adam was made into a life-giving spirit . . . The first man was from the earth, as man of dust: the second man is from heaven." The traditional meaning is that whereas Adam was of this world as other men are, the Person who was to be Christ already existed as God the Son in the bosom of his Father: it is simply part of the mystery of the Incarnation. But outside Scripture there was a literature concerning an Original Man, a Heavenly Man—Philo has him, and Jewish writers between the two Testaments. He was linked with the First Man (Philo sees two distinct Adams in Genesis—the

Heavenly Man of the first chapter, the Earthly Man of the second); he was linked with Daniel's Son of Man, and so with Christ.

Dr. Cullmann sees the Original Man, made in God's image, the model of what God wanted humanity to be, "the pre-existent Son of Man" (p. 196), as the Word in John's Pro-logue: "The form of God in which Jesus existed at the be-ginning means the form of the heavenly man who alone is the true image of God" (p. 36). This man was God, as the Pro-logue says—meaning that He was God "in so far as God speaks and reveals Himself" (p. 265): "Jesus the divine Heavenly Man was divine already in His pre-existence, that is He was the highest possible being in His relation with God" (p. 180).

All this I find unthinkable—not that I cannot think it true or even think it possible, but that I cannot think it at all. I simply do not know what is being said, so that my mind can-not take any hold of it. "God in so far as . . ." "Divine" mean-ing "highest possible being in His relation with God." When Dr. Cullmann says "God," what is he saying? The God of such passages as these does not seem to be the God of Jew or Christian. The same silence as to the meaning of the key word is there to leave us lightless when he speaks of "Christ's exalta-tion to equality with God" (p. 234)—"Christ becomes equal with God for the first time with his exaltation" (p. 238) but he is "not only now exalted to deity—Jesus the divine Heav-enly Man was divine already . . . Now complete equality with God is granted in the exercise of divine sovereignty" (p. 180).

There are three assumptions here—that there may be deity without equality with God; that complete equality with God may be given to one who lacks it; that there may be equality in power or glory without equality in being. These assumptions make even more urgent the need to know what the writer means by God—certainly each seems to involve a denial of God's infinity. And indeed each leaves one wondering what the writer means by man: in what sense is the Heavenly Man "man"—has he a body, for instance? And how can a being without human ancestry be called "son of man"? I am not suggesting that the writer could not answer these questions, but in the book he does not answer them. And, that being so, I cannot see how it is possible to know what he is saying. What the mental equivalents of his terms may be, I do not know.

It is no argument against any statement about God that it is not all-luminous. Mystery is the atmosphere in which Catholics live their Faith. God *must* be mysterious to creatures, we cannot know him as well as he knows himself: there must be elements whose reconciliation we cannot see: the light our eyes can respond to is immeasurably precious, but it is ringed inescapably with darkness. The darkness has its own splendor. Dr. Cullmann knows this, but he not only never says it, but never seems even to allow for it. He speaks of the Pagan Mysteries, but not of Mystery at the center of all reality: of felt darkness he says nothing. Neither does Dr. Dodd, whose book *The Fourth Gospel* is awe-inspiring in its learning. I have already quoted from his *Authority of the Bible*.

It would have been helpful to Catholics if either had told us why he regards the Catholic doctrine of the Trinity as irrelevant to the Christology of the New Testament or to the Fourth Gospel; neither mentions the doctrine even for dismissal. Yet how close they come to it, at least as regards the First Person and the Second. Dr. Dodd speaks of "the idea of Christ as word, the spoken word of God though conceived in some sort hypostatically" (p. 272). And there are moments when Dr. Cullmann has us holding our breath at the nearness of his approach!

"The author's purpose [in the Prologue] is specifically to nip in the bud the idea of a doctrine of two gods. The word which God spoke is not to be separated from God himself; it was with God. There is nothing here either for the Arian doctrine of the creation of the logos from nothing, or of Origen's doctrine of emanation . . . nor is the logos subordinate to God; he simply belongs to God. He is neither subordinate to God nor a Second being beside God . . ." (p. 265).

4. Reconstructing the Original Revelation

Writing of three of the Gnostics, Dr. Dodd says: "We may recognize Valentinus as a Christian thinker concerned to provide Christianity with a more adequate theology, as it seems to him, than the conservative teachers of the Church offered . . . Both [Ptolemy and Heraclean] find the Valentinian system in the Gospel and perhaps do so with no greater strain on the original meaning than may sometimes be detected in more orthodox commentators" (p. 100).

The effort to reconstruct from the New Testament the foundation doctrine or system which its writers are—*not* setting out (that is the difficulty)—but taking for granted and applying, can produce no definitive result. Many systems have been produced—as by Valentinus—harmonizing well enough with Scripture, with here and there, of course, a text fitting at best jaggedly—with what Dr. Dodd calls a "strain on the

original meaning." The Catholic doctrine of the Trinity har-
monizes wonderfully: did the Fourth Evangelist, for instance,
hold that doctrine? Those who do hold it find what he writes
about God really harmonious with it; if he was writing from
some different view the coincidences would be startling indeed. Yet, unless we can check by some standard distinct from
itself either the Trinitarian doctrine or any other system offered
us as what the scriptural writers held, we can be sure of nothing
but its brilliance.

Two such "checks" suggest themselves. If God guarantees
it, that is decisive; if a great number and variety of men have
prayed by it and lived by it over a long space of time, that is
very strong evidence, and might come close to being decisive.
For us who believe that Christ has promised to be with the
Church in its teaching, the doctrine of the Trinity is guaranteed decisively. Not only that: as we acquire the mental
equivalent of the Church's statement, the doctrine is a superb
construct, simply to gaze on: but more important than that is
its richness as a reality to be prayed to and lived by—through
the centuries, and now.

I have made it a matter of mild complaint that Dr. Cullmann has not given us the mental equivalent of his doctrine.
He does not give us the vital equivalent either, but that can
hardly be matter of complaint—scholarship is scholarship,
after all. But one wonders what kind of spirituality of the
Heavenly Man could be written—what hymns to match the
Veni Sancte Spiritus or the *Adoro te devote,* what sermons to
match Pope Leo the Great's or Augustine's?

FOURTEEN

The Trinity and Ourselves

1. Mental Equivalents

We are made in the image and likeness of God, and God is Trinity. Ignorance of the Trinity, then, has as a by-product ignorance of ourselves, both ignorances are widespread, the second rooted in the first. To know the formula, even to be willing to die rather than deny it, would still leave ignorance of the Trinity very much in possession, unless we proceed from the terms to the mental equivalents. Otherwise we do not know what the Church is telling us—that is, what the Word is telling us through the Church. What a critic has called "the whole toilsome discussion which dominates the early christological controversies" is the most rewarding toil I ever embarked on.

Before a doctrine so immense, it seems almost mockery to

talk of having mental equivalents for our terms. But the terms are God's, not ours, and God addressed them to our minds. We cannot always define them, but at least we can know what we are saying—to the extent at least of knowing why we use one word and reject another. The reality contained in them must exceed not only what we can draw from them but what as words they can *mean:* our being is not God's being, is called being, in fact, only by analogy, and the analogy is stained with our nothingness. But the meaning in the words *is* meaning. The Church may go on from them, but to deepen, not deny them. They are light-bearing, they will always be light-bearing, we shall never exhaust their light.

One may be tempted to feel that with such vast subjects, precision is out of place, that a kind of large vagueness would be better. But the mind's grip upon the infinite is not helped by having it feign an infinity of its own in a shapelessness which is only a parody of the infinite. Precision is not simply hair-splitting, as in our impatience we are apt to think it: in every area precision is the key to beauty—in faces, for instance, or music. To repeat an illustration I used in an earlier book: if the radio is trying to pick up a symphony concert on long wave, only if the tuning is precise to near-perfection do we get anything that we can bear to listen to.

We have made some first steps in the understanding of the doctrine of the Trinity. We must try to bring together what we have learnt and contemplate in its totality God's revelation of himself—infinite Spirit triply hypostatized, Father uttering his self-knowledge in a Son, Father and Son uttering their mutual love as a Breath in which the whole of their Being is breathed. We must remind ourselves—and one reminder is not enough, the reminding must be practically continuous—

that space does not enter into this Reality, which *is* real, all the same, and only the more real for being spaceless.

Return for a moment to our earlier consideration of a finite mind in action, Einstein's, for instance. It is like some monster machine, producing ideas which have revolutionized the world. Yet it is not itself in space. Its ideas, which have brought the conquest of outer space within our grasp if they do not blow our earth into outer space first, are themselves not in space. We may think of such a mind as a machine, but a machine with no parts, possessing its existence and generating its ideas in the one single simple spaceless reality which it is. We must not think of the ideas shooting out of the mind like fireworks, or growing out of it to adorn its outer surface, or pinned on to it for all to see; we must not see the mind bulging or glowing with them. Imagination produces no picture that will help. The mind must be conceived as simply itself, energizing as ideas, becoming its ideas while remaining itself. So it is with Einstein's mind. So it is with anybody's mind. And with that we turn again to the Infinite Mind, an infinite spiritual energy, infinitely fecund.

The Church has stated the doctrine as three Persons in one Nature. As a formula it is a masterpiece, one of the most memorable products of the grace-aided intellect: it is not in Scripture, but Scripture is in it. Yet to the theologically untrained, it is not very inspiring, and rather cryptic than informative. Armies have never rushed into battle shouting it, the average Christian is not much in the habit of gazing rapt at it. It requires some philosophical training to know what the Church is saying when she uses the words "Person" and "Nature." Quite a lot of Christians would hardly notice the difference if they met the formula as Three Natures in one

Person. In actual fact, attaching no meaning to either of these nouns, many tend to drop them out of their own thinking, and so are left with three-in-one—any three will do, we almost feel, a triangle, for instance, or a shamrock.

There is no stranger chapter in the history of spirituality than that which tells of all the figures of speech used as substitutes for the quite easily statable, though never wholly fathomable, truth, that in one divine Nature there are three divine Persons. A glance at any one of these figures will make the strangeness apparent: for us of the English-speaking world, the shamrock will do. Not only does the shamrock leaf with its three lobes shed no light at all upon the Trinity, it does nothing else for the soul either. To accept as the supreme truth of revelation that God is structured like a shamrock takes one no further. There is nothing one can do with it. The sole object of using it was to prevent the mind being bothered by the mystery, an object which could have been better achieved by not mentioning the mystery at all.

What lies behind this desire to escape at all costs into images is the belief that the doctrine is too difficult, combined with the feeling that it is, if not actually repellent, at least unattractive. In fact, it is not really difficult: as with all mysteries, it is difficult to know *how it can be,* but not to know *what is being said;* and once the formula is unwrapped, the reality is immensely attractive.

We of the Catholic Evidence Guild made both these discoveries on the street corner. Through no choice of our own, but with much fear and trembling and impelled solely by the crowd's need, we began to teach the doctrine of the Trinity: and our audiences not only grasped what we were saying, but were drawn by it as they were drawn by no other truth we taught them. I have said that we were impelled to this by their need—the discovery of the need was for us at the street corner practically a revelation in its own right. It was the discovery that in not giving them the Trinity, we had not been giving them God: for God is Trinity. A God scaled down to our own presumed capacity for understanding is a poor substitute for the God of the Christian Revelation. We must try to make *him* our own.

The Processions are a beginning. Once we have grasped what the Church is saying about generation and spiration, not only are the grosser analogies dead, but the finer-seeming along with them. The equilateral triangle is a perfect example of these. As an analogy making it easier for the mind to cope with the doctrine of three Persons in one Nature, the triangle has one overwhelming drawback, namely that there is no such thing. The triangle, a plane figure bounded by three straight lines, does not exist in the real order; for, even apart from the question whether the curvature of space allows for the possibility of a plane surface, lines have length only, no breadth; and one dimension will not take hold upon space. The triangle does not even exist in the mind, for the mind, being a spirit, has no surface upon which it might rest its three sides: all that exists in the mind is the idea of a triangle, and a very useful mental gadget it is. But what is gained by comparing the Trinity of the self-existent Being to a being which not only does not exist but cannot exist?

For seeing purposes, the Processions go further than such comparisons as these can take us; anything clearer is illusion; indeed, if we will take the trouble to master what the Church is saying, no analogy even *seems* clearer. But observe that in stating the doctrine of Son and Holy Spirit produced within the divine nature by knowledge and love, we are not simply substituting the human soul for shamrock or triangle as an analogy for the Trinity. The object of these other analogies is to make the doctrine easier to accept; but the mystery of one Nature totally possessed by three Persons is not made any easier by reminding people that after all the human soul has existence and two faculties. The soul with its faculties is a starting point for our journey into the doctrine, not something brought in at the end as evidence that the Trinity is not so impossible after all. And we can use the soul as a starting point precisely because it is made, as nothing else in our world is, in God's image; it is a spirit with the powers of knowing and loving; by studying it one can see a little how knowing and loving function, and can catch a glimpse therefore of how —in the infinite spirit—knowing and loving can produce Son and Holy Ghost.

The Church's progress in understanding has been expressed, not exactly in Greek terms, but within the general structure of Greek philosophical thinking by men whose minds had been trained in Greek philosophy. She might have used, she may yet use, other philosophical structures. But this is what she did use. The concepts of Person and Nature are a good example of her use of the Greek mind to produce terms which it had not arrived at. Indeed, one has seen it stated that Christ could not have "thought" them, not only because they do not belong to the Old Testament but also because they were not yet formulated by philosophers.

But in fact their reality and the distinction between them is pre-philosophical—very much as singular and plural, numbers and counting, are pre-mathematical. The world did not have to wait millions of years for some subtle thinker—Greek perhaps—to notice that cats are not snakes, and that men are different from both. There is something all cats have, a different something all snakes have, a different something all men have—a difference of structure, a difference in what they can do, in what they can experience, in what can be done to or with them. Call it what you like, we call it nature—that by which a thing is the kind of thing it is, and does the things it does. If the light is bad and we hear something moving, we say: "What's that?" We are asking about the thing's nature, is it cat or rat or burglar? The word doesn't matter, different people may use different words, but the fact is unmistakable.

At the same pre-philosophical level, men were aware that while all cats are cats, one cat is not another. Each has a self of its own, each is itself. So with men. I am not you. I am aware of other I's (I call them You, He, She, They) who have the same nature as I, who do and suffer and experience similarly. Not precisely similarly, of course. One man differs from another not only in who he is but in what he is. Nonetheless the difference between one individual and another of the same nature is of a different sort from the difference between men and cats. You and I share a nature different from the nature that all cats share. But each self, man or cat, has the same relation to its nature. When a cat yowls, it is not felinity that yowls, not some universal cat or essence of cat, it is that cat. Yet the felinity makes the yowling possible; a snake, equally annoyed, could not yowl: it is not in its nature to yowl, it can only hiss. The nature settles what the being can do; but the individual being, the self, does it. When the being is rational, we call the self a person.

None of this can be dismissed as metaphysical. Men could not conduct the simplest affairs of life without these distinctions: even the higher animals operate according to them, in embryo at least. They were not drawn out in their present form, nor did philosophy proceed to analyze them further, because until the revelation of Trinity and Incarnation they were not needed. As to the statement we occasionally meet that Christ could not have used the concept "nature" in his thinking, the reply is obvious: he may have had a better concept which we have not reached yet, but the reality he must have expressed to himself somehow. He found himself acting and speaking on two levels, using the pronoun "I" on two levels. If he never asked, "What, then, am I?" he must have been a person of singular obtuseness.

As to the words: "nature," which means literally what we are born to be, what a thing by origin is, strikes me as a good word, "person" less so. *Persona* means, as does the Greek word *prosopon*, the mask worn by an actor—one has seen the suggestion that it came not from that but by the formation of a noun from the words *per se:* but this seems too good to be true. From actor's mask, both the Latin word and the Greek word came to be used for "person." We have in English a somewhat similar interchange between the stage and real life in the verb "to act," which can mean either real action or the feigned action of the theatre. A vast amount of misunderstanding could have been avoided if only Greek or Latin had had the word "self." However, "person" it is. The next movement of the mind must be towards understanding, analyzing, organizing, "placing" our knowledge of that concept.

The things of our experience are either complete in themselves or have their existence in some other thing. If this book were a treatise on Philosophy, we should have to do a great deal of distinguishing and defining at this point. In our present context, a few examples will make clear what the distinction is that I have in mind. A jewel exists in itself; its lustre exists in it. These lesser beings which only exist as energizings of some other are called accidents. Those which are complete in themselves are substances. Between the two come beings which have accidents of their own but still are not complete in themselves—like a rose-leaf, which has color and shape but can exist only as part of the rose-tree, or the human nose, which has a rich variety of accidents, but belongs in the face: which in turn belongs in the human body: which in turn belongs in the compound of spirit and matter which constitutes the human person.

A being complete in itself, one which cannot be compounded with some other as part of a real oneness (the word for this latter attribute is "incommunicable"), philosophers call in Latin a suppositum, or in Greek a hypostasis. We use the word "substance" and the word "nature" of such a being: the difference here is simply one of emphasis, "nature" being used as a statement of what the thing is, more especially as a source of what the thing does, while "substance" is used to express the completeness of the thing in itself. When a suppositum is rational, we have a person—in the famous definition of Boethius, "a complete individual substance of a rational nature." So a person is a rational suppositum, a rational hypostasis.

There are thus two essential elements of a person. One is *subsistence,* which means that he is the bearer of a nature complete in itself, so that he is wholly himself, he is the whole of himself, he is not part of some other being; the other is *rationality,* one effect of which is that he is conscious of himself as himself, distinct from every other person. One compact and useful definition of person is "the center of attribution in a rational nature"—whatever is done or experienced or suffered in a rational nature is done or experienced or suffered by the person, by the one who says "I" (to reduce the definition to its uttermost simplicity). When we come to talk of the Incarnation, we shall have to try for further precision, especially as to where, in a given rational being, nature ends and person begins. But what we have seen so far will help us with Father, Son and Holy Spirit.

One occasionally meets the opinion that, while the Triad is a certainty, we cannot answer the question "Three What?" In this view we say Persons only to avoid saying nothing, that *Tres Nescio Quid*—three I don't know whats—would be more accurate. But in the sense we have defined, each Person of the Trinity *is* a person. Each is in complete possession of a nature, and that nature is rational (or supra-rational perhaps).

The Father possesses the nature completely, he is not part of any other reality; so with the Son, so with the Holy Spirit.

The Son does not add to the Father's personality and thus complete it, but simply expresses its completeness; equally the Son is complete in himself, not completed by the Father but produced in his completeness; and so with the Holy Spirit.

Each knows himself to be himself—not, of course, to the exclusion of the others: since each is essentially related to the others, in being aware of himself, each is aware of the relationship. Each is infinitely in action, knows infinitely, loves infinitely (and of that action of each we are the beneficiaries, as we shall see in Volume Two).

To return to our definitions, there is one Nature, one Substance; but three Persons, subsistences, (supra-) rational hypostases. Each possesses a nature, but it is one identical nature possessed in its completeness by each with no shadow of inequality. Each subsists, but by virtue of one single substance. So that though each is God, they are not three gods but one, because that by which they are God is one. Though each is absolute, they are not three absolutes but one, because that by which they are absolute is one. Though each *is*, they are not three beings but one, because that by which they *are* is one.

Different theologians have approached the relation of Nature and Persons in God differently. They are all seeking to utter the same realities—three Persons each of whom is God, yet only one God; but the emphasis will vary according to the point from which they start—from "God is a spirit," for instance, or from "God is one," or (like St. Bonaventure) from "God is love." The West has mainly followed Augustine, beginning with the one infinite Nature of God and showing Father, Son and Holy Spirit as its (eternally complete) unfolding. The East, while affirming the oneness in Nature, begins its thinking with the distinction of the persons.

I have used the word "begins." In fact, of course, East and West know that the divine Nature and the three divine Persons exist, co-exist eternally, that there was no stretch of eternity, or even instant of eternity, in which the Nature existed and the Persons were yet to be. Such phrases would be meaningless with regard to eternity, nor would they represent any reality in God. But in the effort to enter into mental possession of the divine Reality, one has to begin somewhere. Athanasius and Basil, Gregory Nazianzen and Gregory of Nyssa start from the Father as the source, with Son and Holy Spirit proceeding. Augustine gives a priority, not of succession but of origin, to the divine Nature—seen as God, but necessarily subsisting in the three Persons. In the one approach the "Father" in the Lord's Prayer will be the First Person of the Trinity; in the second "Father" can be (and with Aquinas is) all three Persons.

It is the same doctrine, but approached differently. Each way is true, though neither is (nor could any human way be) wholly adequate. And each is liable to a deformation—the Greek way can turn into what is in effect an acceptance of three Gods, Augustine's into treatment of the three Persons as no more than modes or aspects of the one God. Modern Catholic theologians try to use the richness of each, with perhaps a tendency towards beginning with the approach of the Greek fathers.

We have just reminded ourselves that the three Persons are co-eternal. The Father did not have to wait till he was mature enough to beget a Son, or lonely enough to want one. He eternally *is* in the fullness of life and power, and in that fullness, he eternally produces the Idea, the Son. He never is, save as Father. Father is *what* he is. He possesses the divine nature as his own, not received from any other: he possesses it as his own, but not for himself alone: he possesses it to communicate it. Similarly Father and Son have no need to wait till their love might grow to the point where it could produce a third Person. Their love exists eternally in its fullness: the Holy Spirit is as inevitable as Father and Son.

There is no difference in eternity or necessity; there is no inequality in being. In a paean of humility St. Paul cries, "What have I that I have not received?" The Son could have asked the same question: for there is nothing in him that he has not received from his Father. But he could have asked, as

St. Paul could not, *"What has my Father* that I have not received?" We hear him say: "All things whatsoever that the Father has are mine" (John 16.15). And so with the Holy Spirit: everything *received* indeed, but *everything* received. Son and Holy Spirit have the same knowing-power and the same loving-power as the Father—not simply equal knowledge and love, but the identical knowledge and love. The Son does not produce another Idea, but then the knowledge which is his has already flowered as Idea. The Spirit does not produce a Spirit of his own, because there is no Person with whom he stands in a relation like that from which he himself is breathed forth. There is one identical divine Nature, totally possessed by each with no shadow of inequality.

There is one further step for us to go, before the darkness becomes impenetrable. Father, Son and Holy Spirit are distinct from each other, but no one of them is distinct from the divine Nature. If any one of them were, then there would be composition within the Godhead, something would be brought in that is not God. If the divine Nature were distinct from all three, then we should have a Quaternity, not a Trinity. It is necessary for us, constituted as we are, to distinguish in our mind the Persons from the Nature, to think of each Person as "possessing" the Nature; but we must not let the word deceive us into thinking that the reality is easier to cope with than it is. Possession here means the very perfection of possession, namely identity. Each one *is* the divine Nature: who he is and what he is are one single reality, one single meaning: in the living fact what he is *means* who he is.

This is darker, as I warned. But the darkness is not yet total. Each one possesses the divine Nature but in his own way, each one *is* it in his own way; and his own way, for each, arises from the Processions. The Father is the divine Nature as un-received; the Son is the divine Nature as received by way of generation; the Holy Spirit is the divine Nature as received by spiration. Thus the Second and Third Persons are each identical with the Nature, but each has his own way of being identical with it, which is not each other's and not the First Person's. As St. Anselm phrases it, there is no other distinction among them, no other distinction within the Godhead, save that "opposition of relation" by which each subsists.

It is easy for us to interpret this as practically no distinction at all, or merely a philosophical distinction corresponding with no reality, a distinction represented quite adequately by the numbers first, second and third, as it might be a top copy with two carbons. But we know that the three Persons are not only distinct, but infinitely distinct. Because we have no experience of a person who *is* his nature, we have not even a beginning of a clue as to what the living fact can be of Three, each of whom is one same nature in his own way. We can easily slip into thinking of Father, Son and Holy Spirit as something like identical triplets, whom one cannot tell apart. We cannot tell the Persons of the Trinity apart, because they never could be apart: but in their inseparability they are infinitely distinct all the same. And so, if we come to heaven, we shall see them.

That it would be wrong, in the light of the doctrine, to speak of three gods emerges from the Processions within the one Godhead. We can come to it from another angle—by considering what we mean when we speak of three men. Three men are three human persons, distinct from one another: so far the parallel with three divine Persons holds. But the three human persons are not only distinct, they are separate. All three have human nature, but each has his own "allotment" of human nature, his own body and soul which is not the body and soul of any other. A cannot know with B's intellect or love with C's will. Whereas in God, the three Persons are distinct but not separate or separable, for each has the one same divine Nature to know with and love with, not his own individual allotment of it (this sort of crudity in speaking of the infinite can be justified only if one return from it to the Infinite with added clearness of vision). In men there is separateness of one person from another because human nature is multiplied; but in God the divine Nature is not multiplied by three, the one same Nature is triply possessed. We cannot see what this is in its own reality, this living by Three of an infinite fullness of life "within" one another: the Latins began by calling it *circuminsessio*, which is a mutual indwelling, and came to call it *circumincessio*, an infinite movement, an infinite interflow: the Greeks call it *perichoresis*, as though they saw the movement as a dance.

Whether a created spiritual nature could be possessed by more than one person is for the philosophers to argue about, with no probability that it will be settled here below, at any rate to the satisfaction of all philosophers. But that the uncreated Nature can, we know upon the word of God. It is pleasant to remind ourselves that Our Lord knew what philosophical problems he was leaving to us, pleasant to observe that he *has* left them to us. But along with the problems, he has left us the certainty. There are Three. Each is God. There is but one God. Trinity is the other face of the Infinite Oneness, the face Oneness shows to God, the face that in heaven God will show to us.

2. Vital Equivalents

All this philosophical exploration of person and nature may seem intolerably cold-blooded, or as I said a moment ago, crude. The Church's thinkers have undertaken it solely to bring light into our mental possession and ultimately into our vital possession of Father, Son and Holy Spirit. The analysis is not the object of our contemplation, it is a means by which we may contemplate with new clarity, intimacy, excitement, joy. And for this purpose it is effective, especially for those who have already been living in the acceptance of the revelation before beginning this exploration in depth.

You cannot learn the theory of music in one lesson; it is worth many a year of study, with joy not only at the end but in the very learning. It is like that with the Trinity too. I suppose that most people who have made an effort to grasp what God is telling us about his innermost self have had an experience not unlike mine. I spent twenty years or so with acceptance and no curiosity. The first time I heard a really competent lecture on the Trinity, I made nothing very much of it. A year later I heard a second lecture, and this time I think I grasped all that the lecturer actually said, I was lost in admiration at the intellectual perfection of the doctrine's structure, and from that time on I could have told anyone else the doctrine as I had heard it. But in no sense was it alive in my mind; it was simply an intellectual possession, something I could visit when I felt like it, enjoy visiting, then put away again into the back of my mind. It was a year or two later that another series of lectures came my way, and the doctrine was at last alive for me. For most people something like this happens, first an intellectual response, then a vital response, the doctrine at last possessing the mind: and a time can come when the possession is so full that if the mind lost the Trinity nothing would seem wholly real, without the Trinity the mind could see only desolation.

It is worth our while to analyze both states, beginning with the strangeness of the first, the acceptance without personal commitment. It is at the Last Supper that John places Our Lord's gathering together of the hints he had been giving of a plurality within the one God. The Evangelist may have brought forward things said by Our Lord after his Resurrection: certainly we can see a fitness in dwelling on the deathless life he lives within the Godhead, just before he died as man. To return to an earlier phrase, there is a certain thrill in hearing him lay his divine life open to us just before we see him laying his human life down for us. This consideration emphasizes the incredibility of any believer's asking what difference it makes to us whether God be three Persons or one, what do we gain by knowing? God-made-man pours out to men his innermost life secret, and there are those who give the effect of answering "All this is very interesting, no doubt, but it is only about *You:* what difference does it make to *me?*"

If what God shows us of his own inner life were less fascinating than it becomes as we grow into it—or it into us—it would still be a great thing that he *wants* to show it to us. There could be no surer evidence of his love, no clearer evidence of its quality. One might give to the limit, give one's life even, out of sympathy or pity or sense of duty. But the desire to be known by another can be born only of love, and lifts the other to a kind of equality—at least it treats any inferiority there may be as irrelevant.

With Robert Farren we smile at those foolish ones

Learned in minutiae
Witless of the Trinity

and it is only with an effort that we come to realize that we have been witless of the Trinity ourselves for a good part of our lives; and that the fundamental reason for our not meeting God's desire to be known with a desire to know is that we do not quite see what there is in the doctrine, religiously, for us. Earlier, we asked, What does the Father gain by having a Son? and the answer was simple: Someone to love, of course. The whole truth about God makes possible a new depth of love of God.

So we come to the second state, the mind possessing the doctrine and possessed by it. As we live with the doctrine, the light begins to grow: it is with no swimming head that we realize that there are still depths in God deeper than we can see: there is something even steadying in darkness when we know why we cannot see. But does it leave our heart cold?

As we have seen, there is joy for us in knowing that God loves us, but we cannot pretend that we are adequate objects of infinite love, an intensity of love which we can neither comprehend nor return save meagrely. But in Son and Holy Spirit infinite love is infinitely accepted and infinitely returned. There is an excitement in the realization that just as the infinite loving energy produces an infinite Person, so also the infinite knowing energy is not eternally unproductive, the womb of the Infinite not eternally barren.

Let us pause upon this matter of the divine paternity. By grace we are adopted sons of God, so that God is our Father —by adoption. But just as adoptive sonship is not the fullness of sonship, adoptive fatherhood is not the fullness of father-

hood either. Unless God had a son of his own, he is not truly
father: we could hardly escape the feeling that men know a
real fatherhood and God only an adoptive; we should find it
hard to say with our whole heart, "I bow my knees to the
Father of Our Lord Jesus Christ, from whom all paternity in
heaven and earth is named." How could all paternity be
named after a God who had no son of his own?

Knowing that he has, we can see how much more we image
God than we first knew, how much more of ourselves reflects a
reality within the Godhead. There for our gaze we have the
perfection of fatherhood. We have the perfection of filiality
too. With this as clue, we find a new poignancy in the intense
devotion of Christ Our Lord to his heavenly Father: a new
literalness in the distinction he made, "My Father and your
Father," but with it a new realization of the sonship which
incorporation with Christ brings to ourselves.

But little of this comes at a first hearing. The effort must
be made to bring every element of our being into a living relation—an illumining, nourishing relation—not with the doctrine, but through the doctrine with the reality it utters. Unless we make the effort, we are in peril of remaining as
lightless and unnourished by it as the Catholic I heard respond
to a talk on the Trinity with the remark "Christ is enough for
me. What I want is a person, not a doctrine."

God did not adopt us as sons in order to hold us at arm's
length, we have not accepted the adoption in order to hold
our Father at arm's length. To know the God of Abraham,
Isaac and Jacob was a vast stride forward, comparable with
the astronomical discovery of Copernicus and Galileo. But
with the Trinity—to continue the analogy—we are in the
universe of Einstein—it is tragic that that master of relativity

did not know of the subsistent relations in God. To be without the knowledge of Father, Son and Holy Spirit is to see God as a dark cloud in which we sense a luminousness which somehow does not reach us, a personality to which we have no clue.

Without the knowledge of the Trinity what indeed can we say about God, or even think about God? About what he can do *for us*, what he demands *of us*, there is a vast amount to say: but about God himself—the One who does so much, demands so much—what is there to say? And what understanding can we have of the actions and the demands if we have no understanding of the One from whom they come? What of God's own life, his own living activity? Not knowing the Trinity we find genuine communication all but impossible.

So we return to fatherhood. Once or twice already we have noted that the meaning of fatherhood is not exhausted by generation: it involves a continuing relation with the son generated: a continuing paternal-filial love that is theirs only: having a son is not a single episode, of no further meaning to a father.

In relation to God, we cannot pursue this line of thought far, but we must not ignore it because what I have called theometry can find no place for it. It is Our Lord who gives us the word Father. And St. John, using the Father's sending his Son as a proof of his love for the world (John 3.16), like St. Paul, telling us that in his love for man God spared not his own Son (Rom. 8.32), puts it beyond doubt that within the Godhead the Father has no less care for his Son than good fathers have here upon earth! We are far indeed from the solitary God, companionless in infinity, whom men have always feared.

We are far indeed from a certain rigidity in which Catholic devotion in our area of the Church seems to have taken refuge. I am not suggesting that our religious life should be corybantic, but we may have moved too far in a safer direction, excluding exuberance too timorously. I remember the shock the American poet Vachel Lindsay gave me with his poem on the entry into heaven of General Booth, founder of the Salvation Army:

> Banjos rattled and the tambourines
> Jing-jing-jingled in the hands of Queens.

That may not be to everybody's taste as a picture of life in heaven: but the theological diagram, which is the opposite extreme, can hardly be to anybody's taste. Certainly there is a richness of life within the Godhead: our inability to conceive it is no excuse for a failure to make any allowance for it at all. We have already noted that the Greeks speak of the innermost life of the Blessed Trinity as *perichoresis*, daring to bring in the notion of dance.

The Trinity is the God who is at the very root of our being, living his own life *in us*, Father generating Son, Father and Son producing Holy Spirit—generation and production not simply actions which happened in the distant reaches of eternity, but happening in eternity's ceaseless Now. The infinite energy of the Trinitarian life is within us at every instant. That is one reason why ignorance of the Trinity carries with it ignorance of ourselves.

A second reason is that the Trinity is the original of which we are the image and likeness. Our knowing and loving image

God's. Not only that. Man cannot be properly saved as an individual, he is a social being linked organically with others, community is of his essence. Now we know that there is community within God's very being, so that by that too we are in his image. Nor do we image God statically, so to speak, each element in ourselves representing something in him: we are not just pictures of God flashed on the screen of nothingness. We image his powers too, and so properly image him in action: we must be his living image, that is the image of him living.

Does this first fact about men, that they are made in God's image, ever manifest itself in their actions or reactions? Not often, perhaps; at least not often unmistakably. But it may be the explanation of the effect that the doctrine of the Trinity, provided it is stated with fair lucidity, has on our chance crowds at the street-corner meetings of the Catholic Evidence Guild. It draws a response drawn by no other doctrine. My own explanation is that this is a familiar human reaction—but in reverse. One has had the experience of coming suddenly upon a photograph of oneself—there is a moment of blankness, then recognition: the original recognizes the image. In this solitary instance of the Trinity we have the reverse—the image stirred by, drawn towards, the Original.

As one goes on letting the mind live with the doctrine, new realizations constantly emerge to answer the question, What gain is there in it for us? When we come in Volume Two, *God and the Human Race*, to consider our relation to the Persons of the Trinity as Creator, Redeemer and Sanctifier there will be more of these realizations. But even if no such things emerged for our obvious and statable profit, it still remains that our principal reason for accepting the doctrine and clinging to it is that it is true, and it is true about God.

Intellect is one of the great twin powers of the soul. In so far as it remains unnourished, our personality lacks full development. The food of the intellect is truth, and the Trinity is the supreme truth about the Supreme Being. Merely because it is truth, there would be a defect of human dignity in ignoring it. Thinking that there is only one Person in God is incomparably worse than thinking that the earth is flat. People would find the latter piece of ignorance intolerable, quite apart from any practical difference that the earth's sphericality makes to us—it would be shameful not to know. But ignorance about the Supreme Being is a more abject poverty than ignorance about any of the lesser beings he has created of nothing. Of these greater truths, as of all truths, the rule remains that it is sufficient reason of acceptance that they are true. If there were no other profit, that would be sufficient.

Index